T0375182

MINDLESS
BODY,
ENDLESS
SOUL 2

MINDLESS
BODY,
ENDLESS
SOUL 2

Amar J. Singh, MD,DFAPA

MINDLESS BODY, ENDLESS SOUL 2

iUniverse books may be ordered through booksellers or by contacting:

iUniverse
1663 Liberty Drive
Bloomington, IN 47403
www.iuniverse.com
1-800-Authors (1-800-288-4677)

ISBN: 978-1-5320-4110-5 (sc)
ISBN: 978-1-5320-4112-9 (hc)
ISBN: 978-1-5320-4111-2 (e)

Library of Congress Control Number: 2018903671

Print information available on the last page.

iUniverse rev. date: 04/03/2018

DEDICATED TO MY MOTHER WHO DIED WHEN
I WAS 5 AND A HALF YEARS

CONTENTS

PREFACE AND INTRODUCTION

This book was inspired by the great wise people of the world who have hunted for the soul, from ancient humans to philosophers, neuroscientists, religious sages, atheists, and common people. This journey has been arduous and difficult to get a handle on. Everyone has the desire to find the answer to this myth or reality including me. Mystics tried their best to explain it through their experience and imaginations, lacking scientific tools, which fortunately we have now. Humans had a long, evolutionary transformation, which they followed regularly with the development of the brain (especially the frontal lobe).As philosophies evolved, so did religions. Science took a leap but remained unable to explain the nature of the soul. Descartes did try to explain it in scientific terms with the knowledge he had at the time, but he fell short of explaining the true nature of the soul. I was highly moved by Dr. Penfield, who, during his experiments mapping the functions of various parts of the brain to connect them with various functions of the body explained that there is something higher than the function of the neurons of the brain. He called it higher neuronal "functions." Neuroscientists were and are still trying to understand how the brain combines all the actions, thoughts, and results. We have billions of neurons acting at the same time. They concluded that because of the connections between various parts of the brain, we are able to coordinate all these function in fractions of seconds. John Dylan has postulated that a decision is made seven seconds before an action is taken. To this question, my exclusive view is that it is the magnetic soul that acts as an additional mechanism to coordinate multiple tasks and decisions made in the fraction of a second. Neuroscientists call it combining theory, which is fully explained in this book. I learned about the action potential of the neurons. Physiologists found that there is an electric current that controls all bodily functions. When I learned that all electric currents produce electromagnetic fields, it gave me insight to carry on this scientific research. My own conclusion was that it is the electromagnetic field that controls not only bodily functions but our behaviors, emotions, feelings, thoughts, and actions. In order to pay my respects to those who dedicated their lives in search of the soul, I decided to name this magnetic energy "soul." Readers and researchers have an open-ended wish to call this form of energy of the brain whatever they wish to, but I am going to stick to the soul. My gratitude goes to Richard Swinburne, who, without any hesitation, stood by his belief in the existence of the human soul. He argues that there really are mental events and states that are different from brain processes and observable public behaviors, and they really do make a difference to the organism's public behaviors. We can only make sense of the continuity of this conscious life by supposing that there are two parts to a person. The body is the ordinary material object, and the brain is an essential part of it and is connected to the soul. This book explains in depth the statement of Richard Swinburne, who predicted that someday, we will have a scientific answer to the burning question of soul in his YouTube interview. This book is not a text but a simplified version of neurology and neuroscience. I have made a sincere effort to simplify the neurology part of the chapter, but names of the parts are unchangeable, so I could not be helpful to my readers in that. If you feel the need to learn and understand neuroscience to integrate the scientific concept of the soul, then please feel free to read the chapter. If not, you can skip that chapter. Putting it all together will allow you to make full sense and achieve understanding of the concept of the soul. Our thoughts and feeling do not exist in thin air or a vacuum.

There is an appropriate energy and existence somewhere, which was ignored and taken over by mystics, who used their imagination and wisdom to explain human actions and thinking. Human brain science is a fast-moving field with new inventions and tools to acquire knowledge of how the brain works. These laboratory studies educate us and give us information about how the human body and brain work. Based on such scientific studies, I have made an effort to explain the anatomy and physiology of the soul. The brain is the ultimate organ. It sits in the dark box of our skull, and by it, we navigate through this world throughout our entire life. Though we humans have tried to search for our soul, now, in these modern scientific times, we do not have to search because it resides within us and in all living creatures. Countless philosophers, religious sages, and neuroscientists have dedicated their lives to understanding the mechanisms by which we think and have emotions, desires, beliefs, wisdom, and spirituality. We operate as an automatic machine day in and day out. Though we have many questions remaining, I am sure as our knowledge about neuroscience grows, we will be able to find more answers to our questions, especially in the chapter of neuroscientific investigations to support my hypotheses of the magnetic soul.

The goal of writing this book is not only to elucidate current scientific explanations of how our brain works in day-to-day life events but also to create an interest in neuroscience, psychiatry, and psychology, so researchers conduct further studies in this field of science and probe further to seek answers for our lives. They may someday find answers for the mental illnesses and behavioral problems we face in this world. Our consciousness, thoughts, and feelings have a neurological basis. They all are based on the principle of energy use, so I have made an effort to explain to every human being so he or she can understand how humans function and how they can apply their knowledge to gain wisdom and spirituality and live a healthy and happy life. Sharon Beagle, in her book Train Your Mind and Change Your Brain, writes that one of the questions raised by his holiness Dalai Lama was particularly provocative: can the mind change the brain? He had raised this question with scientists many times over the years; he usually received a dismissive answer. After all, one of the cardinal assumptions of neuroscience is that our mental process stems from brain activity: the brain creates and shapes the mind, not the other way around. But the data reported suggests there may be a two-way street of causality, with symptomatic mental activity resulting in the very structure of the brain. I concur with this scientific fact. In this book, you will find that many neuroscientists have produced studies with scientific data that meditation can cause neurogenesis and neuroplasticity throughout our entire life regardless of our age. Neurogenesis occurs in the dentate nucleus of the brain. How we train our brain to achieve that goal has been answered by Jon Kabata-Zinn, PhD, in his book Full Catastrophe Living. He has cited many studies to prove the neuroanatomical changes in our brain. His program is the mindfulness-based reduction program of stressful reduction (MBSR) clinic at the University of Massachusetts

Medical Center. For enthusiasts, I strongly recommend the book and the program at the clinic. My theory enhances the concept based on energy generated by our nervous system and the rest of the body. There is an enormous amount of electric current generated in our body and brain; all the functions of our brain and body are based on this electric current, which generates an electromagnetic field. I call this electromagnetic field the soul. Our soul interacts with our neurons, and this form of energy generates thoughts, consciousness, emotions, feelings, love, and all aspects of our behaviors and actions through a two-way mechanism. Our soul and neurons have a symbiotic relationship. One cannot survive without the other. Both work together to promote wisdom, spirituality, beliefs, and the way of life we choose to live. I have explained all in this book.

Physiologists and neuroscientists have studied action potential and mechanisms of electrical activity and conduction to and from the brain in various parts of the body extensively. As a matter of fact, some neuroscientists (Penfield) have suggested that physicists may have learned how to produce and distribute electricity from human physiology. The evolutionary physiologists have studied genetic makeup, the structure of the human cells, and functioning of the cells, but seldom have these scientists given any account of important aspects and characteristics of humans, like feelings, desires, hope, beliefs, and emotions. Orthodox neuroscience has basically abandoned the centuries-old concept of the soul and focused on the mind. There are many explanations of the mind in philosophy. I do not believe or buy the concept of the mind. Is it energy or a composite of energies? Does it exist in imagination or in a vacuum. Is the mind a material, or is it a functional unit of the brain? In either case, what exactly is it—air, metal, or cell bodies? Is it attached to something? Is it the sum total description of the functioning of the brain or body or both? Is it a mystery invented by mystics? Is it a physical property of living beings? Then why don't neuroscientists, neurophysiologists, or some other kind of scientists explain it? I propose you read the "Structure of the Soul" chapter in this book to replace the concept of the unknown mind. The new science will start explaining the body-soul interaction so we are able to understand and investigate the mechanisms involved in human and animal behavior. My view of the soul is clear; every living creature has a soul, including trees and shrubs.

Love is a higher neuronal function. Our love is felt and initiated in our soul in a magnetic form of energy. A mother's love has additional mechanisms; it is not only nine months of pregnancy, where the fetus gets all the nutrition, neurotransmitters, hormones, and various chemicals through the placenta and umbilical cord. Besides rearing and protecting the baby, mothers love their babies. There is an unconditional truth of a mother's love. The truth is that all the mitochondria in the fetus come from the mother's egg. After fertilization, the tail of the sperm, which has small percentage of mitochondria, is shed, and fetus has all the mitochondria in each cell of the body. Mitochondria are the soul of the cell and provide oxygen and nutrition to each cell of our body regardless of the sex of the fetus. My hypothesis is that we all have soul energy from our mother's cells in the cells of our body; therefore, love for our mothers and the love of our mothers is unconditional and everlasting in our lives. Without mitochondria, a cell cannot survive. I have explained in a later chapter that the soul is the seat of our love for our mothers and vice versa.

The anatomy and physiology of consciousness and unconsciousness is very well defined in this book; as we understand very well that neurons and synapses grow at a fast pace in young children. At or around age twenty-five, there is a pruning of our dendrites and synapses. This process of neurogenesis and neuroplasticity continues throughout our entire lives as our learning process continues. My hypothesis is that some of our neurons, dendrites, and synapses die forever, and memory of our experiences disappears forever because there is no magnetic energy generated. This file disappears from the soul's cloud computing system. Some of the neurons, dendrites, and synapses remain dormant and still store the memory and experiences of our lives. They produce some magnetic energy, and at times, these dormant connections become an unconscious part of our lives, which could be stimulated during sleep, hypnosis, and therapy sessions by analysts or professional psychiatrists and therapists. At times, even a symbolic representation of past experiences that remain dormant can be stimulated, and such thoughts or events can become activated and become conscious events or thoughts. Dreams could be explained on such anatomical and physiological bases. Activation of such neurons and synapses produces bizarre and sometimes real events of our life in our dreams. Neurons, dendrites, and synapses that remain active and continue to form new connections become the conscious parts of our lives. This process continues throughout our entire lives, and our brain becomes the site of our consciousness. The brain never stops producing electromagnetic energy even while we are asleep. This is how our magnetic soul keeps storing memories and experiences. For example, if you get bitten by a snake in your dream, you will feel the same pain and fear as if you were awake. This pain goes away when we wake up from our dream. In a nutshell, the neurons, dendrites, and synapses that remain activated give rise to our consciousness, and those neurons, dendrites, and synapses that remain dormant give rise to unconsciousness. Wisdom is an evolutionary process; though our brain is the primary organ for storing the knowledge and experience gained in our lifetimes, higher neuronal mechanisms are the function by which our wisdom is demonstrated. It is the magnetic energy of our soul that hosts our wisdom and makes it available to us on demand when needed. It starts with Amar's six A's, which are the primary ingredients to attain wisdom:

1. Accumulation of information
2. Assimilation and processing of information
3. Association of information
4. Authorization of the information to be dispersed
5. Availability
6. Addition

All of these are explained in the chapter "Wisdom and the Soul." The frontal lobe and all sensory apparatuses are involved in attaining a state of wisdom. Spirituality is the final stage of wisdom. To attain this state in one's life, each step of wisdom has to be attained. Meditation and yoga practice are major factors in reaching such a state of mind, which is the goal of those humans who wish to have such a blessing.

CHAPTER 1

SELF, STRESS AND THE SOUL

The concept of self existed way before anyone wrote about it. I would argue self existed in a certain shape, form, or belief since humans developed cognitive functioning. It existed whether we human beings recognized it or not, just like the magnetic soul existed once living beings came into existence by the evolutionary process. The belief system, once evolved, added strength to the existence of self. Thousands of years ago, the Bhagavad Gita recognized the self. Anthropologists have recognized the carvings of humans and animals from a hundred and fifty thousand years ago in caves, which tells me the tale. I assume they reflected some aspects of a developed belief system and rituals that were performed by shamans, who would heal other group members sixty-five thousand years ago. This gives me the feeling of existence and reorganization of the self by humans, even accepting the existence of other lives within their group system. The reorganization and invention of God explain the existence of the self and the existence of the force of God. Without self, God would not have existed. God is an English word, but shamans had their own names and ways of recognizing their own godly forces. In a nutshell, I would say that self existed just like gravity existed way before Newton stumbled on it.

The magnetic soul existed at the inception of life, before I stumbled upon it. None of this is an invention; it is all explorations and explanations of the self. A book written by Somali Bhatt Marwaha, PhD, has quoted

Singh (1997), talking about the great guru and practical wise man of his time, who was the first guru of Sikhism. It is a fairly modern religion of the world, not very well known to the average Westerner. According to his teachings, the moral self in man is I in a person, a person that is conscious of both the behavior of the self and behavior of others. The whole approach of the Sikh teachings is the evolution of a strong moral self. Gurus make it clear how, from the smallest speck of life, humankind has evolved after millions of years and myriads of births. The human has a sense of discrimination and awareness of his own thinking and the capacity to deliberate his or her thinking. In addition, humans make judgments and choices to distinguish between right and wrong. The gurus in Sikhism state unambiguously that a social or civilized life is not possible unless people develops their internal and moral life, which alone can make for a social life. The evolution of the real self in humans required them to face the realities of life in a disciplined manner in day-to-day actions. Uncontrolled desires, undisciplined indulgences in sensual pleasures, and egocentric behavior result in impulsive living and the destruction of an integrated personality. The basic requirement of the real self should be an object of examination of the self itself. It looks at the self as it looks at an object. It judges its own actions dispassionately and objectively and makes suitable amends. The moral conscience is developed not only by implanting prohibitions against doing wrong but by developing love for goodness, honesty, and sincerity. There should be an internal urge to act righteously and truthfully. This is what the positive conscience is. If such a conscience is developed, the evil is avoided automatically and without repression. It makes possible deliberations and a mature positive conscience. It coordinates and regulates our behavior, and what is right and best comes out spontaneously. The urge and the will unite to form the moral self. What we are to do and what we want to do coincide. Then there is no internal conflict between the internal self and the conscience. We should not be forced to conform to the moral code by fear of punishment for doing the wrong but should imbibe the love for righteousness. This is positive thinking.

Freedom lies only in the spontaneous functioning of the total integrated personality. Guru Nank emphasized the social self. The primary responsibility of a Sikh is acceptance of equality between men and women in both religious and social aspects. A good argument made by Guru Nank for not downgrading women is that without women "there would be none." The second responsibility is maintaining equality between man and a man, which eliminated the caste system altogether in India. The serving of parsad and food (langer) to all from the same kitchen in the same gathering ensures that the high castes consume food received from the hands of outcasts and outcasts from the hands of high castes. This system is highly evolved in India and in the rest of the world to offer food to millions of people every day. The third social responsibility that Guru Nank emphasized is the importance of work to sustain life. The fourth social responsibility is to share wealth with others in order to eliminate poverty. The fifth social responsibility is to eradicate injustice, oppression, greed, and hypocrisy from society, as it prevailed in the North Indian society created by Muslim rulers during ther period of reform.

Those of you who have read the Bhagavad Gita and Upanishads and understand them well will attest to the fact that the teacher Sri Krishna's task was to arouse Arjuna from his despair and set him on the way to self-realization. As described in the Bhagavad Gita, Arjuna was a man of action, renowned for his bravery, nobility, and skill in the arts of war. During his crisis of war, he was able to ask questions of life and death, like does he have a soul? Does it survive death? Is there a deeper reality around the world beyond what we perceive? And what effect does it have in our day-to-day life. Sri Krishna reminded Arjuna of his immortal nature, his real self. The atman (soul) never dies and is eternal. Arjuna asked Sri Krishna to be his guru. Krishna is a symbol of "atma" (soul), and Arjuna is a symbol of the deepest "self" (3, 84). Krishna teaches Arjuna that the only way to realize the truth of life and death is to look beyond the dualities of life, like pleasure and pain, success and failure, and even heat and cold. Detachment from these and identification with the atman (soul), the immortal self, will raise you above the dualities of life. Krishna taught Arjuna that if he can establish himself in yoga, in unshakable mental calmness, composure, and evenness of temper (equanimity), especially in a difficult situation, he would have profound peace. One who has attained these will be more effective in the realm of action. His or her judgments will be better, and his or her vision will be clear if he or she is not emotionally entangled in the outcome of what he or she does. This is spiritual wisdom—direct experiential knowledge of the immortal self.

Arjuna wanted to know how this wisdom affects the life of each individual. Krishna replied, "Those who establish such wisdom (sthita-prajna) live in continuous unbroken awareness, that they are not the perishable body but the atman (soul). They see the same self in everyone,

3

because atman (soul) is universally present in all. Such individuals do not identify with personal desires. Desires are on the surface, and self is in the core of it."

The self-realized man or woman is not motivated by personal desires and the desires of karma. The word karma refers to any gratification of the ego or the sense of entanglement, which draws us away from the core of our being the self. Krishna reminded Arjuna that those established in self-realization control their senses instead of letting their senses control them. If senses are not controlled, then emotions will follow to whatever they want, which leads to spiritual destruction. When you keep thinking about senses, they become an object of attachment. Attachment breeds desires and the lust for possession that burns to anger, which clouds the judgment; you can no longer learn from past mistakes. Lost in the power to choose between what is wise and what is unwise, your life is an utter waste. As one abandons worn-out clothes and acquires new ones, so when the body is worn out, a new one is acquired by the self, who lives within. The self cannot be pierced by weapons or burned by fire. Water cannot wet it, nor can wind dry it. It is everlasting and infinite, standing on the motionless foundation of eternity. The self is unmanifested, beyond all thoughts, beyond all changes. Krishna advises Arjuna that the glory of self is beheld by few, and few describe it. A few listen about it but many without understanding it. The self of all beings living with the body is eternal and cannot be harmed. Therefore, do not grieve.

This was a question that intrigued Krishna. The question Arjuna asked Krishna is "Tell me of those who live established in wisdom, ever aware of self. How do they talk? How do they sit? How do they move?"

Krishna's answer was simple and clear. They live in wisdom that sees themselves in all and all in those who have renounced every selfish desire and sense of craving fermenting the heart. Neither agitated by grief nor hankering after pleasure, they have lived free from lust, fear, and anger. The senses are higher than the body; the mind is higher than the senses, and the intellect is above and higher than the mind. Atman (soul) is higher than intellect, thus atman (soul) controls the ego. It is the ultimate force of humans and living creatures, which liberates them from all evils (atman the soul).

Here is a description of self in the Bhagavad Gita:

> There shines not the sun,
> Neither the moon nor stars

The self is the light by all
He shining, everything shines after him.

Son asked the father, "Father, what is self?"

Father explained to him about self. "It is a part of your soul. How your soul perceives you and your body as a whole and how your soul perceives the self of others is the self. You cannot see soul or self."

Son replied, "Dad, I do not understand this entirely. Can you explain it to me in simple terms?"

"All right. Bring me five glasses of water and a teaspoonful of sugar," asked the father.

Son brought all these, and Father asked the son, "What is in the spoon?"

Son said, "Sugar, Dad."

"Okay, you can see the five glasses of water and sugar?"

"Yes, Dad," replied the son.

Father said, "Put the sugar in five glasses of water." And then Father asked the son, "Can you see the sugar?"

The son said, "No, Dad."

"Okay, taste each one of the glasses and tell me what you taste."

The son sipped from all five glasses of water one by one and replied, "Dad, they all are sweet."

The father said, "Good. I am glad to know they are all sweet."

The son replied, "Yes, Dad."

Father said, "Son, this is the self you tasted. You cannot see it but can taste it, feel it, and enjoy it. This is the self, Son."

The son said, "Thanks, Dad. I got it and understand it."

Father said, "Son, the body does not perceive the self. It is soul and self that perceive the body and the bodies of other selves.

The son asked the father, "If we have the soul and the self, then why do we have different names?"

Father said, "Each one of us has the soul, the self, and a body. We all have different individual souls, selves, and bodies. Names are given to identify each one of us. If everybody is John, then how can we identify each soul and body? Names give us a sense of identification since each one of us has an individual soul and self.

Son said, "Thank you, Dad, but I did not understand what happens to the soul, self, and body after death?"

"Son, once the body dies, it is disintegrated and blends with the earth. But our self and soul blends with the vast cosmic energy of the universe, called the super soul and super selves. The soul blends with the magnetic energy of the universe and carries self along with it but remains everlasting. Self, which had a name, exists with us, like you know your grandfather's and grandmother's names. They exist as long as we can remember them. Their names remain in the archives of the courthouse as the owner of a house or landowners once before. Their name represents their selves though their bodies are gone. The soul remains part of the universal super soul's cosmic magnetic force.

"Dad, I do not understand. Can you explain it to me in simple terms?"

"Son, it is just like our rivers, which travel from north to south and east to west. Finally, they join the vast ocean and become part of it. In the same way, we pass the journey of life and finally reach the destination like rivers do. The journey of rivers represents the journey of our life. Rivers have seen storms, harsh flooding, tranquil calm waters, beautiful sunshine, and nights of glorious moon and stars. They constantly flow and reach their destination. They give life to others (creatures, fish, plants, trees, and grains we eat.). They are dynamic, not static. In the same way, our soul, self, and body have seen good and bad, right and wrong. There will be ups and downs until we reach the final destination."

"I got it, but we cannot see the soul and the self after death?"

"Son, can you see the water of a river when it joins the ocean? Does that mean the water of the river disappears and does not exist? It blends with the ocean, still providing life to sea creatures and rain to our earth for the existence of living creatures. In the same way, our soul and self continues existing in union with the cosmic magnetic super soul. That is why we are unable to see them when we die."

"Dad, it sounds too philosophical, but I am confused about the whole concept. Can you simplify?"

"Well, self is an English word. It has its own names in different cultures, languages, and different religions. Their meaning in the end is the same. According to www.Dictionary.com, self is a person or thing referred to with respect individually, like one's own self. It refers to a person's nature, character, and so on and personal interest. In philosophy, it is the ego, that which knows, remembers, desires, suffers, and so on. The uniting principle is a soul, underlying all subjective experience. Sometimes, we use myself, himself, herself, themselves, and ourselves. Karen Horney, MD, used the term self-analysis in her book (280). Self in medicine is the total, essential, or particular of a person, the individual one's consciousness of his or her own being or identity, the ego. There is no concrete definition of self because we are all different selves, like billions of stars have their own shape, form, structure, and properties. In the same way, we billions of people in the world have our own shape, size, form, and wiring of the brain and belief system. I wish, Son, there was something called the 'collective self,' or as C. G. Jung called it, the 'collective unconscious' (281). In this class of ideas, people find it strange but soon come to possess and use it as a familiar concept. The unconscious is a part of self, which we call the unconscious self and conscious self. According to Jung, there is a superficial layer of unconsciousness that is personal, and he called it the 'personal unconscious.' The deeper layer is genetic and inborn. He called it the 'collective unconscious.' Self is a reference by a subject to the same subject, like me. When we refer to others, we call the other self or selves. Many disciplines, like philosophy, psychology, psychiatry, neurology, neuroscience, and religion have their own definitions. The anatomical site for self is claimed to be in the insula, which is part of the brain below the neocortical surface of the brain. In addition to that, mirror neurons fire electrical impulses while the self is performing a task and when it is watching someone else (other) executing the same task.

"A very well-known scientist studying evolution mentioned the self eloquently. Mark B. Adams said, 'I am not only alive but aware of being alive, but each of us is aware of being a self; aware of his identity through considerable period of time, and through breaks in his self-awareness due to periods of sleep, or to periods of unconsciousness; and each of us is aware of his moral responsibilities for his actions this self-identity is no doubt closely related to the self-identity of our body, which changes greatly during its lifetime. It changes constantly its constituents and material particles. This is the identity of us and the identity of our bodies. We should always be clear that the numerical identity is not strictly a logical identity."(282)

"Yes, Dad, that makes a lot of sense to realize, accept, and understand that every living creature has a birth and death certificate written before they are even born. It is written in our genes, and thereafter, the environment and our genes together give rise to the self and soul and define our destiny. If so, how does the self develop in between birth and death?"

"It is an amazing question you have asked me. You will have to wait for a few years and have to grow on your own to understand how the entire process takes place. In the meantime, I will keep exploring and learning about myself too. My view is the self is born when the first breath of life is taken. The feeling of the sensation of (air) oxygen stimulates the brain and the rest of the body. An incipient self is born along with the soul, which already existed in the womb of the mother. The first cry of the baby, the first hunger pain, the first thirst, the first slap on the back of the baby, the first sound, and the first vision of the surroundings and face of the nurse (or whoever helped with the delivery), the first smell, the first taste, the first sense of touch, the first look of the surroundings around me gave birth to self Karl R. Popper writes in his book, The Self and the Brain, on page 100,(203) 'We are not born selves, but that we have to learn that we are selves.We can know quite a bit about ourselves. Knowledge is not always based on observations. Knowledge is based on actions and thoughts about problem solving. Observation does play a role, but this role is that of posing problems to us and helping us to try to weed out our conjectures. How do we obtain self-knowledge? It is by becoming selves and developing theories about ourselves. We become aware of others, like our parents. It is a well-known fact that babies fixate on a schematic representation of a face for a long period of time. It may be genetic instinct that we are born with. Karl further suggested that a consciousness of self begins to develop through the medium of other persons. Just as we learn to see ourselves in a mirror, a child learns to know his or her environment, but people are the most important objects within the environment. Learning about his or her own body, the child learns in time that he or she is a person him- or herself. This process later depends upon language. But even before the child learns the language, he or she learns to be called by his or her name. The smile of a child already contains the primitive prelinguistic characteristic expressed by gestures. As memory develops, there are experiences of the past and present and expectations of the future. I call this the incipient stage of the self and soul. I concur with Karl, but I differ in one sense—that we are born as selves and we learn to become a mature self through the process of our neurological and physical growth. If we look at the neuroplasticity of our brain, it is clear that both genetics and the development of neurons and dendrites and their connections develop the sense of self. As mentioned earlier, my view is all five senses help us to develop the sense of self."

"Who knows, Dad, what is truth and what is a lie or falsehood?"

"Son, you have obviously grown to ask me this question. It is the self and soul who know the truth and what are lies or falsehoods. You have your own secrets and beliefs. You live with others who assume or may not assume you told the truth or lied or falsified. You have deep secrets of your own. Your body does not know whether you lied or told the truth. Ask yourself who knows it better than you? You can deny all you can when confronted by others, but you know better than others, and as we grow, our senses and soul are equipped to accept or not the truth and lies. It is all a neurobiological mechanism, not merely philosophical jargon or merely a figment of our imagination or merely the belief system that we adopt and develop to protect ourselves and souls from suffering from our own doings of telling the truth or falsifying. Our self knows much more than anyone else knows. I hope I answered your question. As you grow, Son, you will learn more and explore more. You will have more question than I could answer, because we will continue evolving and questions will erupt. So will answers. Our senses stimulate the neurogenesis and neuroplasticity, which is the biological hallmark of our development of the self and soul. Due to our protracted childhood, the brain continually pares back its connections after growing at a rapid speed. A child, under normal circumstances, has the highest curiosity for exploring the environment and others. I presume this must be very stressful when we restrain a toddler who is getting into everything, like the hot stove and insects on the floor. Our neurons, axons, and dendrites pare back and shape ourselves to the demands of a particular environment. This is a smart strategy of the brain to match the environment for the adaptability and shaping of the self. Does it mean that we have to deal with the cards dealt to us from the deck of cards of our life? Let us look at a child born in the family of Mr. Bill Gates and a child born to a family in rural Bangladesh, India, China, or anywhere else. Will all of them have the same sense of self? I am of the view that no, each one of them has to deal with a set of cards dealt to them. Hence, they will have a different view of self. I call it heterogeneous selves. The self is a universal truth and belongs to all. In that case, we call it a homogenous self. Since we all are differently wired in our brain and have different environments, the self is heterogeneous. That is why we are all different with different experiences and different environments, which dictate the evolution of different selves. Let us look at children born in different religions, sects, or cultural settings. Researchers have shown that the self evolves constantly because of the complexities of cultures, religions, and societies. Some children are born into terroristic societies, where war has riddled the country with guns and bombs, and they have no chance to see the beauty of life. There is no difference between day and night. Life is perishable at any time, and fight or flight is the norm of the day. Hatred toward the aggressor or a killer develops strong hatred genes for years of war, for example in the Middle East. Their selves and souls are full of anger and revenge. Right or wrong, it is what it is.

That is how terrorist souls and selves develop into full-blown terrorists. Life and death mean nothing to them. For them, birth and death are integrated into revenge. A recent article, published by Murad Moosa Khan, about suicide terrorism in Pakistan may be motivated by a range of factors, including culture, revenge, retaliation religious beliefs (desire for a higher place in paradise), social glorification, foreign occupation, and political financial gains. Young men are usually recruited by organizations' authorities. They range in age from 15.5 to midteens. Fifty-two percent came from low socioeconomic status ($3 per day), 30 percent were school dropouts, 65 percent grew up in homes where supervising figures were absent, 37 percent had five to six siblings, and 29.5 percent had eight to nine siblings. According to Peracha et al., militants had abducted 58.5 percent of the boys and 41.5 percent had volunteered for militancy. More than 65 percent of them had attended madrassahs. The World Health Organization estimated that in 2012, in Pakistan, there were 13,377 suicides. The risk factors include male gender, youth, single marital status, poverty, unemployment, lack of education, low socioeconomic class, a breakdown in social networks and families, life events, and depression (402).

That is why we see terrorists attacking all over the world without any remorse or guilt. As a matter of fact, the unification of birth and death becomes an accomplishment of the self by killing innocent people. They even brag about it and experience feelings of accomplishment, which are claimed by other selves. Showing the killing of innocent people on TV, Internet, and in daily papers (news) gives them a sense of gratification and accomplishment of their planned goal. That is how suicidal bombers can not care about blowing themselves up and killing all those who are around them at that time. They are not simply suicidal bombers; they are suicidal-homicidal bombers, because their goal is not simply to blow themselves up. Their goal is to blow up as many as other selves as they can.

Some authors have described the concept of the self as a dynamic, responsive process that structures neuronal pathways (dendrites, axons, neurons, connections) developing as a learning process, according to past and present environments, including material, social, and spiritual aspects.

There is a great deal of difference between a suicidal self and a suicidal-homicidal self. In individuals who are suicidal, the accomplishment and existence of others is acknowledged. Their survival of self is well recognized and respected, thus there must be cognitive thinking and remorse and guilt if anyone else is killed or hurt. In individual who are suicidal, the frontal lobe of cognition is not dominated by belief in the self and soul. The limbic system is disintegrated by a lack of neurotransmitters, like serotonin, adrenaline, noradrenalin, and others. My hypothesis is that dopamine levels may have a sudden surge, creating a micropsychotic episode where reality is distorted and unification of birth and death lead to them believing the nonexistence of life to be justified. They then take action to end their lives. Freud would say they still have a "superego," while in suicidal-homicidal individuals, aspartate and dopamine activate the agitated state of the brain. In that event, the sense of self and the sense of others is dissolved and disintegrated. An instant micropsychotic episode takes place, and reality does not exist. Their belief system takes over their self and soul. It does not matter who is who and who exists or vanishes. At that moment, there is no start of self or end of self. The unification of birth and death takes place, meaning the life between birth and death does not exist. The hippocampus is dominated by the neurotransmitters, as mentioned. Aggression is perceived to be the norm of life and reality. It has a lot to do with cultural belief and religious beliefs. Though each self is an individual self and soul, the collective belief empowers the cultural belief, which leads to collective selves and common beliefs shared by all. This leads to collective actions. The suicidal-homicidal terrorists, right before their action of pushing the button of a bomb, go through a phase of intense storms in their brain, body, and soul. There is a surge of adrenergic, dopaminergic, and other neurotransmitters, which shuts down the mechanism of reality. There is an intense fight-or-flight state. In the case of a vest fastened to their bodies, flight is impossible. The self is dissolved and shattered. There is chaos and confusion, and I presume a state of psychosis for a brief time. All the mirror neurons of passion are shut down because of an enormous amount of corticosteroid hormone. There is an elation and a state of euphoria. Their brain is just like a tornado that strikes in a fraction of a second with confusion at its peak. The self cannot reason present, past, and future. All the cognitive processes of self are paralyzed. All the sensations, like vision, hearing, smell, and taste are shut down. Only the sensation of touch remains intact to push the button to blast the bomb. Impulsivity and belief in immortality take over all the brain mechanisms. In such a heightened state of mind, fear does not exist. Emotions, feelings, and thoughts collapse, and the desire to perform a set of goals is predominant. There is darkness. Nothing exists around. Some of them may have hallucinations and may have delusions of omnipotence. Others disappear for a fraction of a second. The self is dissolved because of the union of birth and death. Morality and altruism never even erupt. They remain buried in the dark shadow of their lives. Faith and belief in performing the act are dominant. There is a distortion of perceptions. There is a paralysis of the will to change. There is a heightened sense of euphoria and of elation. Their motor system remains intact. That is how they can move their hands or any other part of the body to push the bottom of the bomb attached to their bodies. With such enormous physiological and psychological changes, the self, soul, and image of the body disappear. Thus the final act of pushing the button takes place, resulting in their bodies being shattered and others' too. Some die, and some get injured. This ends the story of life and other lives. These are my views due to my experience in psychiatry. I have no studies or experiments to prove this. I presume there is an enormous amount of electrical energy surging, which leads to an enormous surge of the magnetic field (soul) to the point that all the essential physiological mechanisms are shut down—just like an electric transformer, which when confronted with a high electric surge blows and burns out. The electricity to the area is shut down and a state of blackout prevails in that area.

There is sorrow, grief, anger, and darkness left behind for the loved ones who lost their precious souls. This is what one destructive self can do to other innocent selves and souls. This happens sometimes when there is a peaceful march against ruling authorities and sometimes in the devastation and destruction of countries like Kashmir in India and the Middle East with ISIL. An old example would be the Jihad versus Crusaders.

I was born in Kashmir, and our basic upbringing was in the form of collective selves, where we helped each other and went to temple (Gurudwara Sikh Temple) as frequently as we could. We recited Gurbani (versus from the Sikh holy book) every evening and at night as a family with my father and sisters and brothers, which led to a cohesive learning of self. We were free to interact with each other and share and care about the norms of culture, which cultivated traits of a moral self. When I immigrated to the United States, I learned that culture is more goal oriented for individualism. The whole cultural concept is to beat other individuals to advance one's own being. Kanagawa (283) has explained in the studies done about Eastern and Western cultures the rise of the self. The conclusions were that in Western culture, self is usually seen as an abstract private individual, and they separate themselves from the rest of the group, whereas in Eastern cultures the self might be presented as open and flexible. For example, Japanese culture focuses heavily on self-criticism and trying to improve to become better individuals. They rely on negative feedback and aspects of themselves so that they can advance and help the entire culture and society. The goal is to maintain harmony and balance within the society. The main issues with the self are the self as fact or fiction, the self as knower versus the self as known, the self as structure (static) versus the self as a process (dynamic), and the self as one or many.

William James described and clarified this by distinguishing between these concepts. According to him, the self is known as me, the empirical ego, and as knower. Constituent parts of me are "the material me," "the social me," and "the spiritual me." Personal identity and unity are properties of the empirical self (421). Dawkins proposed the concept of the "genetic self." By that, he meant that our genetic system is the universal system of all lives on the planet. Life is just bytes and bytes and bytes of digital information. Genes are pure information that can be encoded, recoded, and decoded. Genes not only make copies of themselves, which they pass on down the generations, they actually spend their times in bodies and they influence the shape and behavior of the successive bodies in which they find themselves. Bodies are important too. The true utility function of life is DNA survival. This utility function seldom turns out to be the greatest good for a large number. The utility function betrays its origin in an uncoordinated scramble for selfish gains. Genes maximize their selfish welfare at their level by programming unselfish cooperation or even self-sacrifice by the organism at its level. They cooperate specifically in the enterprise of building individual bodies. This is the meaning of selfish genes. In this sense, there nonlinguistic, biochemical senses of self at the genetic level, where each cell organizes itself toward the primary goal of life—survival (422). I concur with Stuss and Brown who created the concept of a "neural self." According to their hypothesis, the psychological construct of self is related to brain functioning. The key processes are awareness (of self), monitoring of the self's conditioning, and integrating experiences across time into the self (423). Damasio stressed that the

13

biological forerunner for the sense of self is found in the ensemble of the brain devices that continuously and unconsciously maintain the body-state within the narrow range and relative stability required for survival. He postulated five facts about the consciousness and self.

1. Some processes of consciousness can be related to the operation of specific brain regions and systems.
2. Consciousness and wakefulness, as well as consciousness and low-level attention can be separated.
3. Consciousness and emotions are not separable; when consciousness is impaired, so is emotion.
4. Core consciousness provides the organism with a sense of self about one moment now and about one place. Some neurological diseases reveal a lack of consciousness and concept of self.
5. Language, reason, memory, attention, and working memory are not required by core consciousness.

Our sense of self is a state of the organism, due to the results of cells, tissues, organs, and systems, operating in a certain manner and interacting in a certain way within certain parameters. Damasio distinguished between three interdependent selves based on the level of our conscious awareness: protoself, core self, and autobiographical self.

The proto-self is an interconnected and temporarily coherent collection of neural patterns, which represent the state of the organism, moment by moment, at multiple levels of the brain. We are not conscious protoself. The sense of self is the first answer to a question the organism never posed. To whom do the ongoing mental patterns now unfolding belong? The answer is they belong to the organism as represented by the protoself. The simplest form in which the wordless knowledge emerges mentally is the feeling of knowing. It is the feeling that accompanies the making of any kind of image—visual, auditory, tactile, and visceral—within our living organism. The apparent self emerges as a feeling of feeling. It does not occur in one place only; it emerges dynamically and continuously out of multifarious interacting signals that span a varied order of the nervous system. It is a reference point at each point. Damasio hypothesizes that the core consciousness depends on various parts of the brain structures. Some of them include the reticular nuclei, the hypothalamus, the basal forebrain, and the somatosensory and cingulate cortices. The evidence for this rests in patients with brain stem damage, resulting in coma or a persistent vegetative state (423). It creates numerous questions in my brain:

a) Where do these feeling come from?
b) If the brain is active all the time, what keeps it active?
c) Who feels the sense of self?
d) Is there a form of energy prevailing beyond the neurons, which keeps it running twenty-four/seven?
e) If the brain is deprived of sensory nerve supply, then how does it feel sensations?
f) What is the role of sensory apparatuses, like vision, hearing, smelling, pain, and so on and so forth?

There could be numerous questions raised about this hypotheses. My experience and view about this have been explained. I will still mention the neuroscience of self. All the information is sent to the various parts of the brain designated for their functions in the form of electric current energy, which stimulates our neurons in the brain. When stimulated, they activate electric current for sharing information, which results in the generation of a magnetic field. This magnetic field may be lost over time but stores a wealth of information. This is a form of energy stored, like in cloud computation, which interacts with our neurons, at times at will and at times automatically. This form of interaction of energy shapes us, depending on our genetic makeup and the stored experiences of our lives. I am in a medical school, knowing that I will be a doctor. So I know other students will become doctors too. I am aware of my professors and teachers. My core self and autobiographic self start shaping and evolving with time and constant magnetic energy stored and generated whenever needed. I know my strengths, weaknesses, and limitations, which are registered in the magnetic soul of my brain. This is the ultimate description of myself. As experiences and learning continue, there are archives of digital information stored like in the cloud computation of modern computer servers. Though cloud computation is a storage facility far away, we can access to that stored information with the click of a button. This storage needs an electric current and electromagnetic energy, without which we cannot store or retrieve information. In the same way, we humans and other living creatures have cloud computation mechanisms around our bodies and souls. To explain in the form of modern science, our magnetic soul acts as a server that stores archives of our life experiences, emotions, and actions and the formation of our individual personality. Anything wrong with the hardware or software of our brain will lead to malfunctioning of behavior or other functions of life in general.

The answer to (a) is that our sensory system sends all the information, both internally from our body and externally from our environment through transduction of the stimulus. It is finally the brain in the dark box of the head that figures out what to make of it by talking to each other and consulting the magnetic soul to produce the response as needed. If needed, cloud computation of the soul integrates responses and sends information to neurons to perform their job and functions assigned to them.

The answer to (b) is that nothing is possible without energy. Every aspect of our lifetime functioning is based on the consumption of energy. Every action and reaction consumes energy. We need nutrition for the energy; otherwise, our cells and neurons will die. Our neurons and other cells produce electric energy, which is transduced to magnetic energy of the soul. This supplies constant energy to our neurons with designated functions to perform. Thus, there is a constant supply of electric energy to the neurons of the brain, regardless of whether we are awake or asleep. That is how we trigger our thoughts or have dreams while we are asleep, as written in earlier chapters. This form of our energy keeps the brain active at all times.

For (c), the sense of self is the sum total energy stored in our magnetic soul. The sense of self works with our wisdom, beliefs, perceptions, and spirituality, which are also stored in the form of energy in our magnetic soul.

For (d), as mentioned, it is the interaction of the magnetic energy of the soul that can induce neurogenesis and neuroplasticity of the neurons, the synapses, and the connections of our dendrites.

In answer to (e), since the brain does not have a nerve supply, it is the magnetic soul that feels emotions and the inner feelings of our body and the organs of the body. Excessive energy may produce mania, and low magnetic energy may produce depression and other emotional issues.

For (f), our sensory apparatuses are the source of feeding information to our brain, from both inside and outside. This information is a form of transduced (changed) electric current constantly stimulating our neurons, which generate the magnetic energy of the soul and store information constantly, like in cloud computation, for information to be available to our brain on demand.

As per Karen Horney, MD (2), the self has three separate concepts of self.

- The actual self—the sum total of a person's experience
- The real self—the harmonious, healthy person
- The idealized self—the neurotic expectations or glorified image that a person feels he or she should be.

A person's pride system alienates him or her from the real self by overemphasizing prestige, intellect, power, strength, appearance, sexual power, and other qualities that can lead to self-effacement and self-hatred. She also established the concepts of basic anxiety and basic trust. The therapeutic process aims for self-realization by exploring the distorting influences that prevent personality from growing. For more depth of information, I recommend her book Self-Analysis.

Self-individuation is frequently used in various theories. In humans, who have highly centralized nervous systems, individuation represents one of the best ways of establishing an instinct for defense and survival, and it seems fundamental for the evolution of a self. As we humans grow from childhood to teenage life, there is extensive registration of experiences from our parents, teachers, friends, and other existing souls in the environment. We gain and lose billions of dendrites and synaptic connections and replace old ones, which are not as important as the new ones, due to which our self keeps emerging as we grow. No matter how many theories there are, my view sticks to the fact that the identity and integrity of the self have a physical basis. It is centered in the brain and becomes part of our magnetic soul.

It is well documented and well understood in the field of neuroscience that after childhood, just before puberty, there is a second period of overproduction of neurons in the brain, especially in the prefrontal cortex. Coupled with this, there is overproduction of sexual hormones like estrogen, progesterone, testosterone, growth hormone, and many more neurotransmitters. It is a time of enormous change, not by choice but by the nature of genetic makeup. After full development, growth of neurons, and connection of dendrites, there is a pruning process of thinning dendrites. David Eagleman (35) states that almost 1 percent of dendrites and synapses are lost per year. The dorsolateral prefrontal cortex is important for controlling impulses. It fully matures in the early twenties. Eagleman cites that well before neuroscientists found out about these changes, car insurance companies noticed them. They accordingly charge more for teen drivers. The justice system treats juveniles differently from the adults. He adds that the area of the brain called the medial prefrontal cortex (mpfc) (284) is involved in thinking and thought processes. This region becomes active when you think about yourself, especially the emotional significance of a situation including yourself. At this stage, self-evaluation begins. In adults, the brain has grown and is accustomed to the notion of self. It is more rational and less impulsive in normal adults. At this stage of adolescence, thinking about the self becomes important. Self-evaluation is a higher priority. Who am I? Besides social awkwardness and emotional hypersensitivity, the teen brain is still in the process of development and is prone to risk-taking. Risky behavior is more thrilling to them. The teen brain has increased responses to rewards and pleasure-seeking behaviors (in the nucleus accumbens). Teens are less able to control their emotions. David Eagleman writes in his book on page 16,

> How we see as a teenager is the consequence of a changing brain that's right on schedule. These changes lead us to be more self conscious, more risk taking and more prone to peer motivated behavior. For frustrated parents the world over, there is an important message who we are as a teenager is not simply the result of choice or attitude; it is the product of a period of intense and inevitable neural change.

Well, every teenager is not the same. Some are unlucky and get stuck at this phase of development of self and soul for the rest of their lives. We use the term in psychiatry fixated which refer to someone stuck at an earlier stage of self. I really can attest to this phase of life. In high school, my older brother was very pushy, and his main question was about my school performance. There were mock exams conducted by him, and if I did well, I got a smile. If I did not do well, I got a good dose of lecturing and a basketful of harsh words and criticism. To be honest, I felt as if there was a heavy load on my shoulders. I felt like a bull plowing the fields, like a bicycle rider dragging a cart full of a heavy load, like a boat with an anchor attached to it. I was trying hard but could not move at the pace I would have liked.

One afternoon, when I was around fifteen years and in the ninth grade, I came home and all of sudden, something happened. I remember this vividly because it was one of the most memorable days of my entire life. Everything looked bright. I felt lighter; there was no weight on my shoulders. I was free to move. There was joy, happiness, and a feeling of delightedness. Everything looked real and hopeful, joyful. It seemed there was bright light all around me. There was a bright light in the dark shadow of my life. I relaxed a little bit after school and looked at my bag full of books. Something told me, "These are my books. I have to read them and finish reading them. I have to complete my homework. It is all for me, my future. It does not belong to my older brother or anyone else, like teachers or friends. It is my property, my responsibility, my vision of the future." There was a sudden overwhelming love and interest in my studies. My interest was heightened. Thereafter, I was on the road to success. I was number one in the class with feelings of joy. Before that day, I was number one or number two in the class but felt burdened and pressured. What was that? I did not understand then, but given the knowledge I have now, I can reflect. That was the day of my self-actualization. That was the day of my self-integration with my soul, the removal of the weight that I carried on my shoulders. I was feeling pushed and pressured to perform well for my own good. Was it biological neuronal growth or depression and hormonal change? I assume it was all of the above. Thereafter, I confronted my brother and asked him not to push me or question my intelligence. He understood and gave me my space. But he still would examine me until he felt I was ready and I had grown and realized my responsibilities.

I assume all teenagers go through this phase of biological, psychological, and hormonal change, some earlier and some later. My two boys attained some responsibilities around nineteen and twenty. What happens to those who do not attain self-actualization or do not have an acceptance of themselves by their souls? There is little or no integration of the exterior and interior self. The growth of axons and dendrites is minimal, or there is no pruning of dendrites, so the old ones can die down and new ones appear with new experiences and positive reinforcement to enhance the self. I would think they get fixated on an earlier stage of life. Some have trouble with the law or drugs or have a lack of accomplishments in life. I would suggest to my reader go back and remember the day or days you felt the sudden sense of responsibility. I call it the day of transformation of my life. This was the Fourth of July of my life, when I got the freedom of myself to become the master of myself. Thanks to my frontal lobe, neuroplasticity, and the neurogenesis of the rest of the brain, I perceived the weight was lifted from my shoulders. My grades in school were better and better every day, every week, every month, and every year. My self-esteem was appropriate and consistent with my accomplishments, which enhanced and excelled me. I was able to understand how important self-esteem is. It constantly stokes the self to enhancement. Self-esteem is a measure of one's sense of self-worth based on perceived success and achievements, as well as perceptions of how much one is valued by peers, family members, teachers, and society in general (285).

My uncle once saw me walking with a female student and told my father about it. My father replied, "My son is number one in his class. He has the right to enjoy the social aspects of his life too. He has to grow and be himself. Someday, he has to be a father and has to learn how to understand to live with a female partner." My father told me this one day when I finished tenth grade with the highest marks anyone ever had in the school. My father's joy knew no bounds, and he felt confident about me. That is an integral part of the enhancement of self-esteem. The most important aspects of self-esteem are one's perception of positive physical appearances and high value to peers and family. Secondary features of self-esteem relate to academic achievements in this modern competitive world. Even talent and athletic abilities are essential aspects of self-esteem. I was not an athlete but a very good debater, which was one of the best talents I had. Self-esteem at this age is mediated to a significant degree by positive feedback from one's peer group, family members, teachers, and members of one's close circle. Everyone is not going to accept everything you do and everything you have. It is important for the soul and self to recognize that there are a lot of jealous people around too. They will criticize and tend to belittle you, especially in your peer group. It is up to your own self to adapt and select the peer group you want to be around.

I hardly knew anything about drugs. In this era, drugs are common, which can lead to violence. It is our soul and self that decides which of the peer group we want to associate with. You want to be part of a gang, then you will be. You want to be around a peer group who uses drugs, then you will be. You want to be around dedicated intellectual people with goals in their lives to achieve, then you will be. Your self-esteem will depend on which peer group you belong to. I understand that some adolescents seek out a peer group that offers acceptance regardless of negative unacceptable behavior. Some also seek peer groups with positive behaviors that are acceptable by the norms of the social and cultural beliefs.

During my time, the adolescent experience was different in its own way. My needs, desires, and emotions were basic and the same as those of teenagers today. But with the advancements in technology, there is a vast difference in the development of self. I had never heard of the Internet, never heard of tablets and smartphones. I never knew what Google was and what Facebook would be. Current adolescents have access to massive amounts of information—beyond one's imagination. It has a massive effect on their development of self. I had to grow with what was available and make the best of it. Old concepts and old philosophies about the self and soul are obsolete now. No wonder I can buy a used book from Amazon for 1 to 99 cents. Artificial intelligence and current technology are advancing at the fastest pace in the history of humankind. Texting and the speed of communication are the fastest right now and will get faster. The more knowledge you have available, the more you need to process, which changes the entire old concept of self, soul, and thinking. Take an adolescents now and compared to those of my time. They think faster and move faster. Google has all the answers. It is good, but the dark side of this is that you use fewer parts of the brain. It could be possible that new parts of the brain may evolve and take over the current functioning parts of our brain. We may have to write new books of neuroscience and neurophysiology. There will be more research on the magnetic soul. The new generation can understand and apply electronic gadgets faster than ever I will or can imagine myself doing. This new evolution will continue evolving our neuroplasticity and neurogenesis. There will be new sets of neurotransmitters controlling the functioning of our neurophysiologic processes. As parents, we had a different set of social issues to deal with. These adolescents will grow up and be parents and will have different sets of social issues to deal with, different than ours. In the traditional psychiatric field, we categorize adolescents in phases as follows:

Early Adolescents	12 to 14 years
Middle Adolescents	14 to 16 years
Late Adolescents	17 to 19 years

These are the stages during which the foundation of self is laid for the high-rise building of our life. This foundation will dictate the strength and weakness of the high-rise building, the so-called journey of our lives. It will determine how our self will be shaped and how weak or strong we will be to weather the storms of our lives—not to ignore the successes, failures, and pleasantries of ourselves with which we will be confronted.

The current concept of normality in adolescent development refers to the degree of psychological adaptation that is achieved while navigating the hurdles and meeting the milestones characteristic of this period of growth. According to Kaplan and Shaddock's Synopsis of Psychiatry (31, 1099), 75 percent of youth and adolescents have a successful adaptation, and 20 percent of the adolescent population has maladjustments, like self-loathing, conduct disturbances, substance and drug abuse, affective disorders (depression, bipolar disorders), and other psychiatric disorders we shall discuss as we continue. This is the stormy phase of self and soul, when emotional illness starts erupting in those who have a genetic predisposition to depression, bipolar disorder, schizophrenia, and other emotional disorders, which we will discuss as we march forward. Physical development and sexual development start at a faster pace to the point where transition from childhood to the adolescent stage becomes chaotic, confused, and difficult to understand. In females, menarche starts, in some earlier and in some later. With our food full of hormones (in chicken, beef, and GMOs), the menarche is reported to be earlier than before. Breasts grow faster than before. This is a responsible stage in females. Menarche (menstrual cycle) means a female can produce an egg and get pregnant. What a drastic, fearful, and turbulent emotional experience. I truthfully cannot explain how she would feel about herself and how her soul would respond to it since I was a boy and cannot relate to such an experience. Some of my female readers may reflect back and understand and explain it better. Teenagers are well informed about sexuality in school and also by parents, and now by TV and the almighty Internet. With a few clicks, you get it all. Female adolescents have no choice but to grow up faster than male adolescents, because if they are pregnant, they are left with responsibilities. Teen pregnancy is common and varies from country to country and culture to culture.

According to the statistical studies in Kaplan and Shaddock's synopsis, on page 1104, in the United States each year, 750,000 to 850,000 teenage girls younger than the age of nineteen become pregnant. Of this number,

432,000 give birth and the rest of them (418,000) obtain an abortion. If this happens each year, how much has this happened in the last ten years and how much will happen in the next ten years? Please you do the math. The good news is that the pregnancy rate has dropped by 19 percent from 1991. Now, how does it affect the mother and the child? It creates serious health risks and socioeconomic turmoil for the child and the parents or caregivers. This must be a shattering event to the self and the soul. Some of the young women accept it, and some are left with emotional scars to the self and soul. Children born to teenage mothers have a greater chance of dying before the age of five years. Those who survive are more likely to perform poorly in school and in social settings. There is an increased risk of premature birth. These babies have organs that are not fully developed, resulting in bleeding in the brain, respiratory distress syndrome, and intestinal problems. Teenagers are less likely to seek prenatal care. Moreover, they are more likely to smoke, drink, and use drugs. Only one-third of the teenage mothers obtain a high school diploma, and 1.5 percent have a college degree by the age of thirty. Few teenage mothers marry the father of the child, and they are not able to provide care for themselves, let alone the child and mother. Some children are placed in foster care. The teen divorce rate is very high, and most end up on welfare.

Nearly four out of ten teen pregnancies end in abortion. The abortion rate in European countries is far lower than in the United States, according to the Centers for Disease Control and Prevention. Abortion is about 30 per 1,000 there for mothers aged 15 to 19. In Holland, where contraceptives are freely available in schools, the teenage pregnancy rate is the lowest in the world.

After writing this, I am appalled to learn what happens to their selves and souls. I presume the self-esteem, self-worth, and sense of self and sense of others is shattered and fixated to an earlier stage of self. In some, there is no enhancement of the self and soul, which could lead to behavioral problems, like conduct problems, oppositional-defiant disorder, running away from home, engaging in prostitution, and antisocial behavior. Attention deficit disorder in female teenagers can further cause early promiscuity and pregnancy because of impulsive behavior. Emotional disorders, like depression, anxiety, and a mental retardation are common in children born to teenage mothers. They are more prone to suicide and even homicide.

Vehicular accidents are the number one cause of death in teens, and homicide and suicide are second and third. I am of the opinion this has an enormous effect on the development of the brain. There are neurons, dendrites, and connections developed that can cause altered, antisocial behavior. Neurons and dendrites develop accordingly in whatever environment and culture you grew up and remains the same in adulthood. What kind of self and soul will they have? I presume they will have a guiltless, remorseless self. Therefore, there is no value attached to the existence of other selves, and they put themselves in danger without caring about their own value. I could say that is a selfless, soulless society. That is why I believe in the biological and genetic aspect of the self and other selves. We become where we grow. We do not grow what we become.

This is the age of self when seeds are sown for drug and alcohol abuse, violence, bullying, cyberbullying, and gangs. The use of weapons becomes the norm for some. Each year, ten American children younger than age eighteen years old are killed with weapons. Many more are wounded, sometimes fatally. An estimated 160,000 students miss school each day due to fear of attack or intimidation from peers. There are 2,000 different youth gangs in America, and 200,000 teens are members of the gangs. About 7 percent of teachers reported they have been threatened in school. We have the examples of Columbine High School of Littleton, Colorado, on April 20, 1999. On March 21, 2005, a sixteen-year-old boy went on a shooting rampage at Red Lake High School in Minnesota. Teenagers constitute a large portion of those engaged in prostitution and are at high risk for AIDS and HIV. As many as 17,500 individuals are smuggled into the United States each year as "sex slaves" (31, 1103–1107).

My main reason for presenting these statistics is what happens to these enormous numbers of selves and others. What happens to the development of these selves when they grow up? Does the theory of self or selves explained by philosophers apply to societies? If we count the numbers for the last twenty years and thereafter the children they produce, the numbers must be mindboggling. I have no clue what kind of selves they will produce when they have their offspring. Can I say our social system is broken? As I have explained, all selves are not the same. In dissociative disorders, we have different dynamics of selves. In psychiatry, dissociation is defined as an unconscious defense mechanism involving the segregation of any group of mental behavioral processes from the rest of the person's psychic activity (285). In my view, there is a disruption between the magnetic (soul) energy and the neuronal response to stimuli. Either neurons do not receive the appropriate level of magnetic energy, or neurons do not generate specific and required electric currents for normal functioning of the self in the specific area of the brain, as specified. The specific function of the self is the interaction with other selves and the environment. What happens if the sender does not send the specific electric current to the receiver (neuron) or the receiver does not accept the sender's message (magnetic energy of the soul)?

Dissociate amnesia means an inability to recall important autobiographical information, usually of a traumatic or stressful nature. It is inconsistent with ordinary forgetting. Types of dissociative amnesia (localized amnesia) include selective amnesia, generalized amnesia, continuous amnesia, and systemized amnesia.

Usually some of the dissociative disorders are associated with the self. There is an altered self and lack of perception of the self. Let's look at dementia, delirium, and amnesic disorders due to medical conditions. In addition to the previous list, there are post-traumatic amnesia, seizure disorders, alcohol- and substance-related amnesia, and transient global amnesia.

Dissociative identity disorders usually have amnesia and fugue (loss of awareness of one's identity). It is a selfless state with the dissolution of self. Some neuroscientists have associated the depersonalization with migraine headaches and marijuana abuse due to the depletion of L-tryptophan, a precursor for serotonin. Some of the features of these disorders are as follows (288):

- Bodily change
- Duality of self as observer and actor
- Being cut off from others
- Being cut off from one's own emotions

There are numerous disorders of self. I will mention a few of them to help you understand what there is to us that creates such distortions of self. There may be neurological, psychosocial, or cultural factors.

In body-dysmorphic disorder, there is a preoccupation with an imagined defect in appearance, which can distress or impair important areas of functioning. Current data suggests that it is common between the ages of fifteen and thirty. Women are affected somewhat more than men. It can be associated with depression and psychotic disorders (291). There is an obsessive-compulsive behavior strongly involved. These individuals have a distortion of the body image and looks. Some patients feel they are ugly and that people are laughing at them, though they are well-to-do and beautiful. Some feel their nose is deformed and they are too fat or their eyes are too far apart. They look at themselves in the mirror and pick on their face. In younger teenagers, there is evidence that they may drop out of school. They usually visit their doctors, dermatologists, family, and friends for reassurance, which does not help. It is a deep-seated belief in their self and souls. I had a patient who was young man and worked at the shipyard. He had a fixed notion that he smelled horrible and that resulted in annoying people. He blamed everyone for staying away from him. He avoided any social contact. He would avoid dating or meeting any women. He responded well to clomipramine and cognitive-behavioral therapy, which suggested obsessive-compulsive behavior (292).

These individuals often make numerous visits to plastic surgeons to correct their deformities and enhance their looks. Surgical requests are varied—like the removal of facial folds, fixing the sagging lower part of the chin (jowls), removal of wrinkles, rhinoplasty (nose repair), and breast reduction or enlargement. Some men even request penile enhancement. If the perception of corrective surgery fails, they have anger, which results in suing the plastic surgeons who have the highest malpractice suit rates of any specialty.

Some suffer from an impulse to hoard objects that are not necessary in day-to-day needs. They usually buy needless things, which give them a sense of gratification. I had a patient who had five homes and all were full of goods he bought at auctions. His hobby was to go for auctions with his cocollector twice weekly and buy things every time, even if the need never existed. Separation from their possessions causes them enormous anxiety (293) and sense of loss. The hoarding becomes the norm for the self and soul. It creates a sense of security, though they tie up their money and may lose the value. Some biological research has shown a lower metabolism in the posterior cingulate cortex and the occipital cortex, which could explain some cognitive impairment in hoarders, such as attention and decision making (294). Some studies show a molecular gene for hoarding behavior and markers on chromosomes 4q, 5q, and 7q (295).

Behind every gesture, positive or negative, the action has a hidden meaning for the self and other selves. If I need you, I will call you many times. If I do not need you, I may not even return your phone calls or emails. I would like to mention some subjective relatedness to our self or selves.

- Self-motivated
- Self-conscious
- Self-made
- Self-aware
- Self-centered
- Self-less
- Self-assertive
- Self-sensitive
- Self-caring
- Self-absorbed
- Self-assuring
- Self-indulgent
- Self-serving
- Self-identity
- Self-creative
- Self enhancement
- Self-educated/taught
- Self-detachment
- Self-destructive

The list goes on and on. Pick any one of these that apply to you or write something that is not on the list. This creates self-awareness. Who? What? How do I interact with other selves and souls? How do other selves and souls interact with me? You will be amazed to reflect on where you stand and where you need to bring changes in yourself and other selves when you interact with them.

Then the journey of self becomes easier and easier, which leads to the path of self-actualization and self-individuation. It is the metamorphosis of the self, like a pupa that turns into a free-flying butterfly. It is an essential and integral part of the self. Like a butterfly, the self is free to taste the sweet nectar of the flowers. In the same way, at this stage of self, we are able to endeavor to take risks or avoid risk without fear or anguish. Stress is the enemy of our soul and self; let me explain by giving an example of one of my patients

Patient A was a very attractive, healthy, and happy young lady. She was twenty-five years old. She worked as a computer programmer and was a well-liked and respected employee of her firm. Her boss was very happy with her talent and work. She was a very ethical and motivated employee full of energy and enthusiasm. She had a good sense of humor. She dressed well and had a handsome boyfriend, whom she adored, and he adored her too. She was full of life and proud of her work. Her self-esteem was appropriate to her assets of self. She had a good, average life while growing up with loving parents and other two siblings. She was healthy and had plans to marry and have children of her own. Her boss noticed that she had been late to work for a few days and her productivity at work had diminished. She was quiet and slow, not well-dressed and did not care about her looks. She was slow to respond and not as enthusiastic as before. She would call in sick more often than before. Her boyfriend was unhappy due to her sloppiness at home and her having no sexual desire or desire to cook. She would come home, have a few glasses of wine, and go to sleep. He also noticed that she had frequent crying spells and was very sensitive to any compliment or criticism. Food did not taste as good as before. She loved Italian food but refrained to going to restaurants. She had lost twenty pounds in a month and a half. Her sleep was disturbed, and she would wake up in the middle of the night. She felt fatigued and as if she had a heavy load on her shoulders. This led to feelings of worthlessness and hopelessness. She had anhedonia, which means she found no pleasure in pleasurable activities. She was unable to think or concentrate at work or at home. She even had suicidal thoughts but no plan, which confused her. Why? Where are they coming from? She would call her mom and cry frequently.

One day, her supervisor called her into her office and asked her, "What is wrong with you? There are several mistakes in the data you entered."

She started crying and asked her supervisor to fire her. "No. No," replied the supervisor. "I think you are getting sick. Here, take a week off and call your doctor."

She called her doctor, a primary-care physician who knew her well as a patient. He prescribed an antidepressant and asked her to see him in two weeks. She went back with the same problem and burst into tears. Her primary-care physician called me and set an appointment. I saw her boyfriend with her written permission. I understood it was major depression without psychotic features. I learned her mother was treated for depression and her grandmother was treated in a psychiatric hospital, which gave me a clue that she had a genetic predisposition to depression. I explained the side effects of the medicine and told her it took two to three months to get back to normal life. I increased the dose to two pills of the same antidepressant and asked her to come back in one week. She felt reassured and thought that there was light at the end of the tunnel. I added a sleeping pill for two weeks until the antidepressant took its effect. Sure enough, she started gradually feeling bright and was able to eat and take care of her grooming and look attractive. We continued weekly cognitive-behavioral therapy. I had to add a third pill of antidepressant in four weeks. In a month and a half, she felt bright and energetic. She called her boss, happy and smiling.

"Wow! Congratulations! Come back as soon as you feel well."

She went back in two months. She felt like her old self and was productive. Her self-esteem started to blossom. Her bright light came back into the dark shadow of life. Her confidence emerged, and she blossomed like a budding rose in three months. Of course, her depression was more genetic than anything else. Her stress was enormous due to the fact that she was losing her mind, boyfriend, income to pay her bills, sleep, looks, self-worth, self-esteem, and much more. This tells me that stress is not only external. It is our perception of ourselves and souls that perceive the stress. If there is denial used as a defense mechanism, then we do not recognize such stressors, which is more common in men than women.

Ronald W. Pies, MD, wrote a simple explanation of depression. "Major depression is caused by a chemical imbalance in the brain. Major depression is caused by anger at others, turned inwards against oneself" (296).

This article is an example that we all should learn and explain in detail to patients and those who want to learn more. The explanation is very reassuring for the patients. But I wish things were that simple. I will give a few highlights.

The incidence and prevalence of depression in a lifetime is around 5 to 17 percent.

Women are more prone to depression than men.

The mean age is around twenty to fifty years of age, but it can happen to children and elderly individuals. In some cases, the prevalence is higher in single elderly people who have multiple illnesses and losses in life, like a spouse.

Comorbidity factors, which means there could be some other mental illness, make them more prone to depression: drugs and alcohol abuse, panic disorders, obsessive-compulsive disorder, anxiety disorder, personality disorders, and biological factors.

Norepinephrine; serotonin, which is the most studied neurotransmitter, dopamine, and many other neurotransmitters are also involved. Recent studies have been conducted to learn more about N-methyl-D-aspartate receptors (NMDA) (297) (298), acetylcholine, amino butyric acid (GABA), thyroid gland activity, prolactin, and growth hormone.

As for hormonal regulation, the pituitary gland is highly involved in various hormonal regulations. If you want to learn more, please read about the pituitary gland in the chapter on the anatomy and physiology of the primary soul (brain). After chronic stress, the brain-derived neurotrophic growth factor is decreased (BDNF). Because of a decrease in this growth factor, our neurogenesis is decreased; therefore, our neurons do not grow and may die. Thus, our dendrites do not grow and connect with each other, resulting in an inability to carry the message from one group of neurons to others in several parts of our brain (for names, go back and read the chapter mentioned earlier). During stress, there is an increased level of cortisol, which has severe deleterious effects on most parts of the brain involved in our emotions and day-to-day functions. High cortisol levels due to stress affect our immune system. Once that happens, we are more prone to infections and related diseases (31, 348–357).

After all this, there is a secondary mechanism, called secondary messengers. We call it G-protein, which regulates the utilization of energy and the formation of secondary messengers at the synaptic and cellular level. They help cellular enzymes like CAMP and CGMP. There is evidence that antidepressants and mood stabilizers act on G protein.

During my research and while developing my hypothesis, I have not come across a single mention of the electric current and the magnetic field by traditional psychiatrists and neurobiologists. I do not know why. None of the neurobiologists or psychiatrists have paid attention to basic action potential and electric current, which are fundamental mechanisms of transferring any message for any activity. Either they do not believe it or have ignored it. I will leave this for them to answer and scratch their heads.

You must have read in this book that every action, thought, and emotion utilizes electric current for normal functions of the brain, nervous system, and the rest of the body. My view after this question is what happens to the soul and self?

My hypothesis is simplified. At the synaptic level, either due to a lack

30

of neurotransmitters or whatever, there is not enough electric current generated to transfer messages from one neuron to the other billions of neurons in different parts of the brain designated for specific functions. They are all frozen. Since the electric current does not pass information for proper functions, there is not enough magnetic energy generated.

Weak electric current à Weak magnetic field (soul)

Therefore, our magnetic energy cannot give feedback to neurons to generate electric current to pass on information. This mechanism holds true in all mental disorders. In some, there is a sudden surge of electric current and a surge of the electromagnetic field, which increases the hyperactivity. The balance between the two is essential for stable functioning. We will discuss this further as we move along. That is how transcranial magnetic stimulation (TMS) came into the light to provide enough magnetic energy so there is enough electric current generated to stimulate the physiological process and start the engine of the brain (the primary soul).

The definition of stress is perceived to be different in different cultures, depending upon their own religious or other beliefs and the social norms and acceptance of those norms. A shaman healer may put himself or herself through different stressors to achieve the knowledge to heal. Buddha put himself through self-torture and stressors to attain the wisdom of life and nirvana. Stress is an English word, which means circumstances that disturb or disrupt the normal physiological and psychological functioning of a person. There are volumes and volumes of papers and books written. My goal is to stay simple and write enough to understand. I will mention Hans Selye, who described a model of stress (299). He called it "the general adaptation syndrome," which has three phases:

- The alarm reaction
- The stage of resistance, in which adaptability is ideally achieved
- The stage of exhaustion in which acquired adaptation or resistance may be lost

When your mother was pregnant, both of you had a certain amount of stress. In some cases, the response to stress is poor. On the day of delivery, you and your mother had your own sets of stressors like labor pains and your delivery through the birth canal. You may not remember, but your body went through enormous stress. Both of you coped well. There are some who cannot cope and adapt to that stress. So it has its own deleterious effects on the bodies, selves, and souls of those people. As you grew up, you had to deal with stress from school and stress from the demands of siblings, parents, and schoolmates (peer pressure). You grew up, met a girlfriend or boyfriend, and broke up. You must have gone through enormous stress after leaving home, and you had to get a job. It is a new environment and adjustment. Those who cannot adjust to and change in life events at any stage of life can develop adjustment disorder. It is an emotional response to a stressful event. In other words, it could be in any individual's life. For example, it could be due to financial problems, medical illness, or relationship problems. One could develop a depressed mood, anxiety, unwanted aggressive behavior, acute stress disorder, or even post-traumatic disorder (especially in war zones). Teenagers may develop conduct disorder. So if you look around, you will find countless causes of such stresses. I may mention a few, like pain, relationship conflicts, pressure for performance in exams, poverty, unemployment, heavy drinking or using drugs, death, marriage, childbirth, loss of a spouse, diagnosis of any illness or fatal illness like cancer, sexual abuse, rape, any trauma, and the list goes on and on. I am unable to complete it. You fill in the rest of the blanks. The prevalence rate is roughly2 to 8 percent more common in single mothers.

Again, stressors could be short-lived or for a long period of time. In psychiatry, we usually look for at least three months of any emotional disturbances after the stress is inflicted. Some have vague and unusual symptoms, like panic attacks, anxiety attacks, suicidal ideation, eating problems, sleeping disturbances, interpersonal problems, and many more, like self-mutilation. I think it will make more sense and give you a better understanding of external stressors if I present the example of one of my patients who went through immense losses in her life.

Mrs. B. was a freelance journalist. She had three children and a wonderful husband. One bright, beautiful day, many people went to the beach to relax, enjoy the sunshine, and feast together. Family and friends were getting together. Children played out at the beach. There was joy and happiness. The ocean was warm. People jumped into the water and made sand castles. Patient B. took her third child to her doctor for vaccinations. Her husband took the older two boys in the boat they owned. They went to Chesapeake Bay for fishing; there were many boats all around. Unfortunately, her husband's boat was stuck by another boat at a high speed at 4:00 p.m. Her husband and two boys were killed. Once she heard the bad news, she lost her mind. That is what she told me when

I was asked to see her in my office six months after this episode. She was seen by her psychologist for six months and went through a process of bereavement, grief, and mourning. These are the terms used for the psychological reactions of those who survive a significant loss in their lives. *Bereavement* means the state of being deprived of someone by death. We refer them as being in a state of mourning. Grief is a subjective feeling precipitated by the death of a loved one. Normal bereavement reactions are assumed to be the first response to loss; protest is followed by a long period of searching to reestablish the attachment. When it remains unfound, despair sets in, and the person recognizes that the lost person will never return. Detachment starts erupting gradually until acceptance sets in. At this stage, self-mortality is also perceived. Reality sets in and defense mechanisms, like generalization, creep in. We use a generalized attitude. "Well, we all have to die one day, including us." This is the norm of life and death. Everyone who is born has to go to the final destination of death after the journey of birth and death is completed. Memories remain intact about the lost person. Some replace the lost person by a new attachment, and some never do. Each one of them develops his or her own set of rules and norms for life. Nothing is universal; it is an individual choice. In American culture, the normal period of grief is expected to be a few weeks to return to work or school and be capable of pursuing new relationship in six months to a year. The lasting manifestation of grief in spousal loss is loneliness. It is often present for years after the death of the spouse. Prolonged grief can erupt intermittently, for example, when a living spouse sees a picture of the lost spouse; usually, these reactions become shorter and shorter.

Some bittersweet memories may last for a lifetime. I still cry at times about the death of my mother when I was five years old. Anticipatory grief is brought about by the slow dying process of a loved one. For example, a spouse or loved one develops cancer. We know death is certain. In some cases, there is a reaction of grief, which is triggered by holidays or birthdays or the day and date of the death of the loved one in the following year. Mourning is essentially done by the group of friends, relatives, family, and others on the day of burial or cremation. In some cases, there is chronic grief, which may involve bitterness and idealization of the dead person. It is common in close, ambivalent, or dependent relationships. Delayed grief could be complicated due to denial, anger, and guilt on the part of the grieving person.

Traumatic bereavement can occur in some individuals. They have recurrent, intense periods of grief with persistent yearning, pining, and longing for the deceased. They have recurrent intrusive images of death and distress, with a mixture of avoidance and preoccupation with reminders of the loss. Those who have underlying psychiatric illnesses, like depression or anxiety, are more prone to traumatic grief (300, 301).

During the process of treatment of Mrs. B, I learned she already had gone through the process of death as described. She was in a full-blown syndrome of depression without psychotic features. She was not only grieving the loss of her two children and her husband; the neurotransmitters in her brain were depleted. Her sleep was erratic and full of traumatic and intrusive dreams, which caused her a chaotic and painful life day after day. Life was full of doom and gloom. Nights were long, and days were longer. The only hope to live for her was her child. Her energy level was low, and her concentration was drastically reduced. She had lost a lot of weight, and her self-care was reduced. Crying spells were uncontrollable. Exhaustion was mounting. She had no family history of depression. Her family was very supportive, but she could not describe her pain; she felt numb. She described it as being as if her soul hurt, but her brain was numb. I went through a laundry list of depressive symptoms. She had almost all of them. Sometimes, she had suicidal thoughts, but the sight of her child was enough to avoid such thoughts. She had no such plans. I fully informed her of the mechanism of depression at the neurological level, and she felt relieved and agreed to start on antidepressants. She was well informed about depression, thanks to Google.

After three weeks, she started feeling somewhat better. Within three months, she was able to function better and felt reassured that there was a bright light in the dark shadow of her life. An occasional smile reassured me of my goal of treatment. She fully recovered from depression in six months, but the scars of her loss remained.

According to the Global Burden of Disease Study (2010), depression and anxiety rise abruptly in childhood (ages one to ten years) and peaks during adolescence and young adulthood (ages ten to twenty-nine). Depression emerges first and quickly worsens. It peaks robustly around the midtwenties. Even anxiety emerges quickly as conferred by some parents. "My child has been anxious since birth." Depression can cause cognitive, social, and psychological impairments. This disorder affects 2 to 3 percent of children and up to 8 percent of adolescents. There are extensive studies done that indicate that the basic mechanism is the same as in adults. The change in neurobiology is due to the interaction of genetic vulnerability and environmental stressors (14). Magnetic resonance imaging shows smaller frontal white matter volume. They have larger frontal gray matter compared to nondepressed adolescents. Some adolescents feel irritable and restless. They have a loss of interest in pleasurable activities (anhedonia). They either sleep less or excessively. They feel agitated; some have weight gain or weight loss, fatigue, loss of energy, and feelings of worthlessness and hopelessness. They have an inability to think or concentrate with recurrent thoughts of death. Some have severe grief due to the loss of loved ones or to abuse and neglect.

External stressors have an enormous effect on the mental health of the young ones. They miss the beautiful boat of life, like accomplishments and achievements. This is the foundation of life. If shattered, there is minimal or no enhancement of self and soul. In some cases, even the growth of the body is stunted.

The dark shadow of life becomes the norm. Their immune system is severely damaged due to cortisol and other stress-related hormones. When I was in medical school, I learned microglia are the cells of the brain that are the scavengers of the entire nervous system. They constantly survey the brain and the spinal cord, acting as sentries to detect and destroy the invaders, like bacteria, viruses, and any foreign agent. They migrate to any area damaged and remove the debris. Some call them the immune system of the brain, but recently, a stunning discovery was made. The lymphatic endothelial cells carried both fluid and immune cells from the cerebrospinal fluid (CSF) and were connected to the deep cervical lymph nodes in the mouse brain. If also true in humans, this can have an enormous effect in treatment of brain diseases like multiple sclerosis, Alzheimer's disease, and mental illnesses, like schizophrenia and depressive disorders. Until these studies were published, neuroscientists believed that the brain does not have a lymphatic drainage system, like rest of the body. Microglia cells were designated part of the lymphatic system (303). Dr. Brian Miller refers to studies done by A. Louveau and A. Aspelund (304,305). Why did I deviate from the subject and bring in new findings? It is essential to understand the latest discoveries and discuss them openly so that we can create new research and ways of thinking.

This tells us that the immune system of the body is not only affected by stress but our brain's immune system too, which explains another mechanism by which the immune system affects the brain of adolescents and adults. Dr. Brian Miller has tried to hypothesize that the immune system and immunotherapy may help in the treatment of schizophrenia and other mental disorders. New research also highlights that oxidative stress, which is also regulated via inflammation and an imbalance between antioxidant activity and free radical production, has been associated with depression (306). Depression is associated with heart disease and cancer, and all cause mortality (307). The interaction between oxidative stress pathways and immune inflammatory pathways is likely to contribute to the decline of neuroplasticity and neurogenesis and the increase of neurodegeneration and neuronal apoptosis (programmed cell death in multicellular organisms) in both depression and bipolar disorders (308). That is how antidepressants, like lithium and valproic acid, contribute to stopping and reversing these alterations (309). In conclusion, Sara Jimenez Fernandez, MD, suggested that oxidative stress plays a role in depression and that antidepressant activity may be mediated via improving oxidative stress and antioxidant function (310). In brief, it means that food products like coffee, blueberries, and other fruits with high levels of antioxidants may prevent depression. This question remains unanswered: Does depression cause antioxidant stress, or does the lack of antioxidants cause depression?

Dysthymia

I feel like mentioning the disorder dysthymia, which is not very well known by nonmedical individuals, though a lot has been written about major depression. Dysthymia is a low-grade form of depression. It is present in children and adolescents and peaks in one's twenties. It could prevail in adults and also in elderly individuals. It is a low-grade depression lasting for 2 years. The onset is sudden with origins often in childhood and adolescence. It has persistence and an intermittent course. In the general population, it is about 5 to 6 percent. It is common in women younger than age sixty-four years of age and is more common in unmarried people and those with low income. There is often remission, and individuals do not feel depressed and are able to function well in their day-to-day life and at their job or any profession they have. It could exist with other psychiatric disorders, like personality disorders and panic disorder. Those who have this chronic disorder can slip into major depression when stress is enormous and beyond their tolerance and adaptation to stress. Sometimes people are treated for chronic fatigue syndrome. Most adults have a depressed mood for two years, and in the case of adolescents, it is about one year. Some adolescents exhibit irritability. Some of symptoms could be

- Poor appetite or overeating
- Too little sleep or too much sleep
- Low energy or fatigue
- Low self-esteem
- Poor concentration
- Hopelessness or helplessness

These symptoms cause distress and impairment in social settings. These symptoms could be mild, moderate, or severe. These individuals do not meet the criteria for major depression. A trained mental health professional can diagnose this disorder. These individuals are sensitive and humorless, pessimistic and introverted, with a restricted social life. Some individuals do not seek professional help. They live in this state for decades. Individuals usually respond to treatment, like antidepressants and cognitive-behavioral therapy. I hope this is new information for some. The mechanism of such a disorder is the same as in major depression—genetic, neurobiological, and stress-related causes. The severity is less compared to that of depressive disorder. It is a chronic illness of the soul and self, besides low neurotransmitter levels. There is a low electric current produced at neuronal and synaptic levels. There is a chronic lack of magnetic energy produced, thus feedback to neurons is minimal. Some professionals have good results by treating patients with transcranial magnetic stimulus (TMS), which increases the magnetic field of the brain and increases the electrical activity at neuronal and synaptic levels to balance the chemicals in laymen's term.

What you learned from Wikipedia about stress and its effects on your self, soul, and body is very realistic and informative. I may add a few more effects on our body, self, and soul. Dysthymic disorder can have depressive symptoms. The only difference is the time period of more than two years. In addition, minor depressive disorder lasts for a short period of time and the person's mood is normal. We call it a euthymic mood. In dysthymia, there is no euthymic mood. Moreover, the symptoms of depression are less severe for short periods of time. Double depression occurs in some patients who already have dysthymia and slip into major depression. These patients have poor prognosis.

Dysthymic patients are more prone to using drugs and alcohol and even smoking. These are their coping mechanisms. Most of them are not aware of the underlying fire burning in their soul. Those who become aware of the underlying fire go to seek professional help. The rest of them remain wondering and wandering in the vast ocean of life. Some struggle with it their entire life.

I was amazed to read an article written by Mary Ann Moon in Clinical Psychiatry News (311). She described that the estimated prevalence of depression or depressive symptoms was 28.8 percent among residents and interns worldwide in a meta-analysis of fifty-four studies of the issue. Though the vast majority of participants were evaluated through self-reporting inventories that measured depressive symptoms, 17,560 participants were studied. This is an alarming number of doctors. How would it affect the health of these doctors and the care they provide to their patients? It is the existence of stress and pressure to perform their best. I can relate to that. When we were residents, thirty-six hours of work was the norm. A few of the residents got killed in car accidents while they were going home, and a few fell asleep at the steering wheel. Things are not getting better in health care in the United States. Cuts in reimbursement and long hours of work have created a devastating amount of stress.

"Thou the healer, shall not be able to heal thyself."

This is real stress, and its effects are deleterious on our self, soul, and body. This issue was brought up in JAMA Psychiatry by Dr. Guille and Mrs. Zhao (311). According to their report, physicians are at high risk for suicide compared with the general population. The prevalence is 1.41 times more in males and 2.27 times more in females when compared to the general population. According to the American Foundation for Suicide Prevention, three to four hundred physicians die by suicide each year. One doctor dies in a day by suicidal methods (313). It is a stress versus ambitious stress, which increases to achieve goals set above and beyond the capabilities of the individual physician. Each one of us has our own capabilities and abilities, strengths and weaknesses. We physicians were born as humans, not doctors. We learn to become doctors; we need not stretch ourselves beyond our capabilities. Yes, physicians live a competitive life. Chronic day-to-day stress releases cortisol more than we need, resulting in a depletion of cortisol output from our adrenal glands. Is it need, greed, or demands in a social setting that cause most of the stress among doctors? Does caring for others means you are not to care for yourself? Do we get gratification by helping others and feel guilty if we help ourselves? Is it due to drastic changes in the medical field and methods of payment by third-party payers? I am sure there are many other reasons for doctors to lead a stressful life. My view is that all of the above are true.

Kirk J. Brower, MD, wrote "Avoid Burnout with Self-Care and Wellness Strategies" (314). Recent studies have revealed that one-half of physicians report at least one symptom of burnout. Burnout is fairly common in high-stress professions, among nurses, doctors, lawyers, teachers, police officers, stockbrokers, and many more professions. Each one of them has to deal with the hand of cards dealt to them from the deck of life, destiny, and fate.

Christina Maslach and Susan Jackson describe burnout to have exhaustion, cynicism (belief that people are motivated purely by self-interest), and inefficiency (315). My experience with such individuals is that they have a minor depressive episode, which lasts for a short period of time. If given a chance to get out of the workplace or away from the stressors, these individuals regain the strength to function in the same environment. They have their cognitive functions and reality intact. Complaints about exhaustion and working long hours are frequent among burned-out doctors. They do not develop full-blown major depressive syndrome, but situations and commitments (like financial and family responsibilities) are high. Some develop a chronic period of burnout. At times, there is too much to do with too little. For example, from 2006 through 2010, we went through a recession, which caused companies to layoff of numerous employees, and the few left were burdened with excessive work. The burnout rate is high during these changes in socioeconomic times. Herbert Freudenberg and Gail North have come up with a theory about the burnout process (40). Some of their proposals for the causes and symptoms of burnout are as follows:

- Working harder than needed
- Denial of emerging problems
- Withdrawal from social activities
- Compulsion to prove oneself
- Neglect of one's needs
- Inner emptiness

- Depression
- A physical and emotional need for attention

I have two good friends who are psychiatrists. They call me periodically. All I hear are complaints about how bad they feel, how exhausted they feel. One of them said, "I have no gumption" (spirited initiative and resourcefulness).

We joke sometimes, "My serotonin level is licked from my brain."

Sometimes, they describe themselves as zombies. They appear emotionless, humorless, and fatigued. I usually advise them to cut down the load of patients and take some time off. Learn to play golf or tennis or go for a walk. Learn relaxation and leave some time for yourself in between patients rather than work like a machine.

One of them had dinner with me, and all I heard was "I don't care anymore. I want to lock the door and walk away."

He had gained weight, and his eating habits were very unhealthy. He had no desire to dress well. He dreaded every morning going to work. He stated, "I hate what I am doing, but I know there is nothing else I know. So what can I do?"

Kirk J. Brower, MD, described these psychiatrist friends of mine (314). According to him, psychiatrists have burn out due to long-standing issues including the following:

- Seeing difficult and complex patients
- Dealing with distressing transference and countertransference issues (likes, dislikes)
- Preventing suicide
- Avoiding malpractice litigation
- Coping with insurance authorization (more paperwork, less time for patients)
- Recovering from the trauma of patient suicide and malpractice issues
- Balancing work with other life activities
- Constant demand from the impatient hospitals

When on call all night, phone calls and disruption of sleep day in and day out can cause burnout fast and furious. If you do not sleep well, you drag yourself the next day. If it goes on, the depletion of sleep has deleterious effects on your cognitive decision making and can create physical problems. You can have a depletion of either serotonin or adrenaline and high levels of cortisol. There comes a stage when there is no more cortisol level to respond to the fight-or-flight mechanism. My suggestions, after years of practice, are as follows:

- Put yourself first; if you are healthy, you can spread the healthy vibes.
- Learn to say, "No, I cannot take any more patients."
- Have good nutrition and give yourself a lunch break. Do not discuss business.
- Take a break in between the scheduled patients.
- Learn to meditate for a few minutes.
- Set the time you want to go home.
- Remember that self-care is as important as your advice to your patients.
- Acknowledge your mistakes and correct them.
- Set limits for yourself and your staff.
- Be aware of your self-criticism and guilt.
- Treat yourself as a human being first and then a doctor.
- Refer patients to other colleagues.
- Just realize that if you work more than you can, you pay more taxes. So you lose half of it anyway.
- Get the fear of malpractice out of your system. That is why you have malpractice insurance. Just like health insurance when you get sick, you can use it.
- If you take care of your patients in a healthy state of mind, you make fewer mistakes.
- If you have something to give, you will love to give. If you have nothing, you have nothing to give.
- Learn something besides your work—go to the gym, walk, play tennis, play golf, do yoga, and meditate. These activities will stimulate endorphins and other chemicals, which will make you feel better.

Anxiety

Anxiety is a normal symptom of the energy of the magnetic soul. Everyone experiences bouts of anxiety from time to time when confronted with an uneasy situation or circumstance. It is a diffuse, unpleasant, vague sense of apprehension often accompanied by a hyperactivity of our autonomic nervous system. It is usually accompanied by some physiological responses of our body, self, and soul. At times, we have a mild headache, sweating, increased heart rate, tightness in the chest, some stomach discomfort (like butterflies in the stomach), restlessness, dryness in our mouth, shaking of our hands, hyperalertness, dilation of our pupils, tingling in our hands and arms, and increased frequency of going to the bathroom, among others. Sometimes, external threats or fears can cause such symptoms when we are confronted with a situation in which we feel helpless or not in control. Anxiety and fear are both alerting signals and act as a warning of an internal or external threat. In such cases, it is survival skill for us to avoid the threat. It prompts a person to take the necessary steps to prevent the threat or lessen its consequences. It is all done by interaction of the sympathetic and parasympathetic nervous systems, as discussed in detail in the chapter on the anatomy and physiology of the primary soul. As we grow, our magnetic energy (soul) experiences the anxiety-provoking events in our lives. This information is stored in the form of memory, which is triggered to differentiate serious threats from normal events of life. We develop an adaptability to restore our emotions to normal functioning without losing our cool.

Sonali Bhatt Marwaha, PhD, quoted Levenson (1994), who describes emotions as short-lived psychological and physiological phenomena that represent efficient modes of adaptation to changing environmental demands. They serve to establish our position and environment, pulling us toward certain people, objects, actions, and ideas and pushing us away from others. Emotions also serve as a repository for innate and learned influences, possessing certain invariant features along with others that show considerable variations across individuals, groups, and cultures (425). It is the wisdom energy of our soul, which differentiates the entire process. When we have exams, we are anxious, but we have learned that this shall pass. We are insulted, ridiculed, or denied of our needs and greeds. We use the wisdom of the magnetic soul to know that this is not the end of the world. Reasoning and cognitive experiences play a major role in accepting and reacting to any noxious external or internal stimuli. We are able to thwart the effects of such unwanted stimuli. Those who have mastered meditation or Yoga and have attained the wisdom of life have less or no anxiety under life's regular norms. We at times may be ashamed or given unwanted news by others, which may cause anxious movements in our lives, like being fired from a job. You may have lost money in the stock market or failed an examination. Maybe you are not invited by your friend who is having a party at his home. You may be accused of something you have not done. Life is full of such events, which you may have experienced. We all have different reactions to different situations, so healthy anxiety is part of healthy life.

Now then, what is anxiety? It is the pathological anxiety that is painful and abnormal. Stress can cause pathological anxiety in individuals whose magnetic energy (soul) is not in a balanced state with perceptions of external events and internal drives, and in individuals where the magnetic energy (soul) is not adaptive to both internal and external events of the environment. Any time the adaptability of our magnetic soul is disrupted by stressors, pathological anxiety overwhelms our self and the soul. When our magnetic soul and anxiety accept the existence of each other, anxiety fades away without inflicting any harm to our self and soul. Stress is just like a storm is to a big ship sailing on the high seas. It all depends on how much pounding a ship can take and resist to survive and sail smoothly in the calm waters. Some of us can tolerate multiple stressors, and some of us succumb to the minor turbulence of a wave.

There are many theories about anxiety, including psychoanalytic and behavioral theories in which anxiety is thought to be a conditioned response to a specific environmental stimulus. The constant threat of loss or perceived loss could induce anxiety. In this volatile world, the threat of nuclear explosion is a constant source of anxiety.

The anxiety disorders make up the most common group of psychiatric illness. In men, the twelve-month prevalence rate is 17.7 percent, and in women, it is roughly 30.5 percent (320). The neurobiological chain of reaction and its effects on our brain and autonomic nervous system are causes of anxiety disorders. Stress and genetic predisposition contribute to anxiety disorders. This raises questions. Does anxiety cause the biological changes in our body, brain, and soul? Or is it the changes in our biology and neurochemicals that cause anxiety? We have enough evidence that in generalized anxiety disorder, there is an increased metabolic rate in several

43

regions of the brain compared to the brains of healthy individuals. It is the hyperactivity of the autonomic nervous system caused by the central nervous system and three neurotransmitters well studied in neuroscience: norepinephrine, serotonin, and Y-amino-butyric acid. There are many more neurotransmitters involved in this mechanism. The noradrenergic system is located in the locus ceruleus of the pons. There are spurts of hyperactivity, and there is excessive stimulus to the rest of the brain and autonomic nervous system through the axon and dendrite connections (321). Hyperarousal of the neurons causes anxiety due to an excessive surge of the neurotransmitters. We can have panic attacks. Serotonin is controlled by the nuclei of raphe in the brain stem, which sends axons to the prefrontal cortex, nucleus accumbens, amygdale, and lateral hypothalamus. There is hyperactivity of the hypothalamic-pituitary-adrenal axis, which causes increased cortisol levels. This increases arousal vigilance, focused attention, and memory formation. Long-term stimulation causes massive damage to our immune system, resulting in infection in our bodies (322). Y-amino butyric acid is an essential neurotransmitter, which causes inhibitory effects to any excitatory stimulus. In anxiety disorder, the level of Y-amino-butyric acid is decreased, therefore causing the symptoms of anxiety (323).

CHAPTER 2

MOTIVATION AND THE SOUL

R eality asks me why we ever need to do anything at all. My answer to my reality is we spend energy every second of our life to survive. If we do not replace this energy, we will not survive. Hence, motivation is instrumental to fulfilling the goal of survival and enhancing us beyond the goal of survival. If, like coral or sea anemones, we were lucky enough to live in an environment where we were bombarded with food, we could just glue ourselves to the rock and keep our mouths open. We wouldn't have to do much, but even sea anemones have to have motivation to keep their mouths open to fulfill the desire of being fed. Motivation is the drive to do things for yourself and to fulfill responsibilities for others (family, friends, or whoever is dependent on you). Self-motivation is a key skill, and something that everybody is interested in in terms of personal development. It is a key part of emotional intelligence. Motivation drives us to achieve goals and feel more fulfilled and improves our overall quality of life and those of our family, which we all strive for. Motivation is an igniting force, which makes our engine of our body to move and take initiative. Whatever that is. It is different with different human beings. Motivation is the key to the success of big spenders to take on risks and invest for profits. It gets us to fulfill the needs, desires, and urges of life.

Great thinkers believe that motivated people are well organized and skillful at the management of life. Their self-esteem, self-worth, and confidence blossom more than those of unmotivated people. We shall see in further writing that the brain functions as a master of reducing the risk by making more and more accurate predictions about the likely results of any particular course of action on the basis of past experiences stored not only in our brain but also in the soul. It is not only our inner homeostasis that is controlled by hormones and the autonomic nervous system but also our external homeostasis. When there is rain, we tend to carry an umbrella in our hands. An animal's motivation is controlled by the environment. In droughts, animals are motivated to move toward green pastures in spite of the fact that they face dangers, like predators on the prowl. The rivers are infested by hungry crocodiles, watching for their crossing. Many lose their lives and get eaten by crocodiles, lions, and hyenas. Thus our movements are controlled by hunger, and we move toward the availability of food because of positive reinforcement of our motivation. We stay away from negative reinforcements, which are harsh and dangerous. Refugees leave everything and abandon their homelands. They are motivated to go out for the safety of their lives, like in the refugee crisis in Europe as people flee from the Middle East.

Motivation is somewhat complex in humans. We react to desirable and undesirable stimulation. Most of these are learned, recognized, and cognitively integrated mechanisms in our brain and soul. It is a form of experience. Consequently, each individual has his or her own classification of stimuli into desirable and undesirable categories; it is unique because these are the results of that individual's own personal experiences. We humans are motivated by food, money, and sexual desires. Motivation starts from the womb of the mother. After nine months of pregnancy, the mother is motivated to expel the baby, and the baby is motivated to get out into the world by separation of the placenta and hormonal mechanisms through the secretion of a massive amount of oxytocin, which causes contractions of the uterus. Even after massive labor pains, the mother's soul is motivated to hold the baby and breastfeed him or her. Motivation is a form of deep-seated magnetic energy, created by our entire body, and it remains hidden in the form of soul energy. The stimulus comes from needs, wants, goals, and even, in some cases, greed.

Motivation changes from hour to hour or from day to day. Intrinsic motivation is the desire to perform an action or task based on the expectation or perceived satisfaction of performing the action or task. Intrinsic motivation is to love, to have fun, to nurture loved ones, and even in some cases to have the thrill of a challenge. Extrinsic motivation is the desire to perform an action or task for other reasons, like to make lots of money, seek reward or power, earn good grades in school, become well-known athlete, climb Mount Everest, and travel the world. My motivation was to become a doctor, and I never missed a day in school. My motivation was to compete with classmates and achieve the highest rank in my class. Different people are motivated by different things and at different times of their lives. Warren Buffet was motivated by money and its value from childhood on. He became the richest man in the world. I don't think that he was ever motivated to play tennis or golf or take a year off and travel the world or hike the mountains or buy a yacht and take off to the sea for adventures. Ben Graham motivated him and told him to invest and hold and forget about market fluctuations. Some of us have both intrinsic and extrinsic motivation to balance our life so we can enjoy the benefits of all types of motivation. I am sure Warren Buffet has less stress from spending long hours at the workplace because of his enjoyment of his work. Many researchers have stated that people who enjoy long hours of work have less stress. In my experience of private practice in psychiatry, anxious patients and depressed patients have a lack of motivation and drive. Anxious patients have more fear of failure and rejection, while depressed patients have anhedonia (lack of enjoying pleasurable activities). Because of a lack of the soul's magnetic energy, there is minimal neuronal activity; thus, there is minimal or no magnetic stimulus of the neuronal pathway that initiates the energy of motivation. Most of them had learned and experienced motivated energy. Still, when there is no stimulus from the higher brain mechanisms, there is no motivation. I call it the lack of and impairment of a symbiotic relationship between the soul and neurons of the brain, since both feed each other. In animals, the olfactory system is the oldest and strongest. Motivation is driven by the olfactory bulb of the brain. Their sense of smell drives them to the source of food. Their motivation—the drive—tells their motor systems what to do. In addition, procreation and mating in animals is based on the sense of smell. When a mare is in heat, the stallion gets an erection of the penis by smelling the female horse's genitals and urine because of a hormone secreted by a mare. That is how it motivates a male horse to mate with a mare in heat and continue the existence of the species. In addition, a male horse will kiss the mare's body, and they will look at each other for acceptance to mate. In the wild, of course, there is a fight between males. The strong one will mate to produce strong offspring. The same holds true for humans. Females look at strength, looks, and the build of a man. Males look at beautiful, slim, sleek, firm, and well-built bodies of females to mate and produce healthy babies. These are instincts imprinted through our genes and registered in our souls.

The septal nuclei and amygdala are the parts of the brain known as pleasure centers. These regions, when stimulated by electric current, provide positive motivation. The hippocampus seems more concerned about the memory of places in the environment with the promise of food or pleasure and recognizes these places in the future as a source of motivation, as we call it olfactory motivation (151). In humans, money is possibly the most obvious motivator and most powerful of all. There is always motivation for a better job and to work harder and get a promotion. Of course, you will be motivated to get better job, if it is offered to you. It is about the limbic system, which acts as a motivational computer. These are like Yellow Pages with extensive files of information. It acts whenever the external motivation is needed. It is just like a tourist map in a busy city. It guides you to the destination you want. It guides our motor system to act and achieve the goal. For example, we need to fulfill our hunger and thirst. It varies in different people how intense the motivation is. Back in sixties, when hippies used marijuana for a long period of time, they developed what we called amotivational syndrome due to depletion of serotonin (dope heads). They seemed less concerned and lacked motivation. I think as time goes on, we will have them in plenty in Colorado or in states where marijuana is legalized.

Physiological State

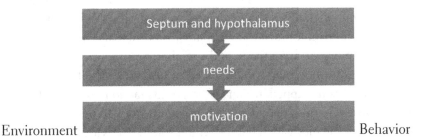

Environment

Behavior

Olfactory Stimuli, Other Stimuli, and Secondary Motivation

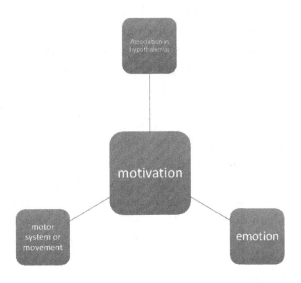

Behavior

There are brain scan studies that indicate brains of London taxi drivers have to undergo extensive spatial learning, demonstrated in an enlarged posterior hippocampus relative to matched controls (152). In addition, the hypothalamus provides information about the needs of the body based on its internal state and projects its axons and dendrites to the hippocampus via the septal nuclei. It is the center where autonomic fibers project, and its neurons monitor such physiological reactions stimulated by blood glucose concentration, temperature, and concentration of circulating hormones that decide one's state of need. It is also in the hypothalamus that primary responses, such as eating and drinking, may be triggered by electric current stimulation. The hypothalamus is thus utterly at the heart of the neural mechanism that generates motivation. "We humans have a simple mechanism to trace the mechanisms of motivation, but we live in a complex physical, man-made and social environment," writes Herbert Simon. A motivation map can be traced in human beings to describe the same mechanism mapped in a rat's actions and reactions as it looks for corn (153). The mechanism described here also connects with the frontal lobe to decide about the motivation behind which action needs to be taken. There is a constant magnetic field generated by the electrical current sending and receiving information. This magnetic field plays an important role in the completion of the act, since there is a direction and order given to neurons to complete the act, which comes from the soul.

Benjamin Libet conducted an experiment in which he used a cathode ray oscilloscope to graph the amplitude and frequency of electric signals. He also used an electroencephalogram (EEG) and electromylogram (EMG). His conclusion was that brain activity involved in the initiation of action occurred on average approximately 500 milliseconds before the trial ended with the pushing of the button. Some researchers recorded mounting brain activity related to the resultant action as many as 300 milliseconds before subjects reported the first awareness of consciousness and will to act (154, 155). Libet later concluded that there appeared to be no neural mechanism that could be viewed as directly accounting for the subjective sensory referrals backward in time. He postulated primary evoke potential (EP) serves as a "time maker." EP is a sharp, positive potential appearing in the appropriate sensory region of the brain about twenty-five milliseconds after skin stimulus. For him, this appeared to be purely mental functions with no corresponding neutral basis in the brain. The conscious mental cannot exist without the brain processes that give rise to it; however, having emerged from brain activities as a unique "property" of that physical system, the mental can exhibit phenomena not evident in the neural brain that produced it (156).

Continuing Libet's work, John Dylan Haynes wrote in the Nature Neuroscience Journal that using brain scanners, one could predict people's decisions seven seconds before the test subjects were even aware of making them. It created headlines. Some publications wrote "Brain scanners can see your decisions before you make them (157). The most recent investigation raises a question: what happens when people have to decide immediately, typically as a rapid response to an event in our environment? What happens when we focus on more interesting decisions that we make in a more natural, self-paced manner?

I. After understanding Libet's and Haynes's work, it is quite obvious that there is an energy force beyond the neurons of the brain. I absolutely agree with that. My view is clear. It is the magnetic energy created by a constant electrochemical mechanism, on the basis of which our brain and entire body function in day-to-day life. I will stick to my notion this electromagnetic energy is the soul. You can call it whatever you want. That is how motivation works. It is the soul's magnetic energy that motivates the neurons of the brain by binding all the centers of the brain to work in harmony to produce the results needed by the living being.

Edward Tolman illustrated this concept in his many experiments on rats to study motivation. He concluded that organisms may flexibly perform any of the several actions to go to the goal. He argued that reinforcers are not necessary for learning but are important for motivating instrumental behavior. He called it latent learning. Organisms that have had experience receiving a small reward may show positive contrast when they suddenly are reinforced with a large reward. Your promotion at a job or pay raise may motivate you to enhance your career. When there is a negative contrast, switching a big reward to a lesser reward, motivation becomes weaker. When you are demoted or your pay is reduced, then your motivation is weakened. In some humans, if a motivational state is going to influence an instrumental action, the individual needs first to learn how the actions reinforced will influence the motivational state. This is the process of learning about the effects the enforcer has on the motivational state, which is called incentive learning. The main idea is that an individual will perform an instrumental action when he or she knows that it produces an outcome that is desirable in the current motivational state. For example, a person who uses drugs will need to learn that drugs make him or her feel better in the withdrawal stage; therefore, withdrawal will motivate drug-seeking behavior. An anxious or depressed patient may not be motivated to take beneficial medication until he or she actually has taken the medication and felt less anxious or less depressed; thus their motivation to continue the treatment is reinforced.

During my research, I found volumes and volumes written about motivation. There are millions of motivators and others looking to be motivated. Motivators are motivated by the fees they collect and books they write. Friends motivate friends. Let's go play golf. Let me write that book or read a book. Young males and females go to bars to meet each other, which is a motivation by itself. I may highlight some of the skills involved in self-motivation as described in the article "Skills the Young Need" (157).

- Setting high but realistic goals
- Taking the right level of risk
- Singing constant feedback to work out how to improve
- Being committed to place and organizational goals and going the extra mile to achieve them
- Actively seeking other opportunities and seizing them when they occur
- Keeping motivated
- Learning and acquiring knowledge
- Keeping the company of enthusiastic people
- Keeping positive
- Doing it
- Knowing one's strengths and weaknesses
- Getting help when needed

Emotions are the mother of motivation. Positive or negative motivation is an integral part of our emotions. Without emotions, the motherly love of motivations is weak and may wither away. For example, in some individuals with personality disorders and depression, motivation may stop and fade away. Emotions have to nurture our motivation to take action. Western thinking claims that motivation comes from emotions. If you read my life history, you will see that the only way for me to survive was to be motivated and use my motivation to excel in my life. When you have no choice left in your life, motivation is the only option left for you to succeed. In such cases, cognitive skills and motivation are brothers and sisters, holding your hands to take you to the peak of your desires and wishes to be fulfilled. These people do not pay attention to emotions. They cry and laugh; they get angry, fearful, frustrated, sad, anxious, rejected or dejected, insulted, hopeful or hopeless, and painful or painless. They pay attention to the cognitive teacher and listen to that. They take the motivation to extremes. They are involved with motivation, not with a girlfriend or boyfriend. They follow the path guided by their soul and instinct. They do not look back but forward. Today is their goal, tomorrow being the result of today to be followed. Yesterday is dead and gone. They do not brood about yesterday, because emotions mean nothing to them. Though motivation needs reinforcement of the stimulus, for me, the stimulus was created by my cognitive skills and attention, thus helping me hold on to my motivation. My stimulus was an achievement for the day to use that for tomorrow. Those who rely on positive reinforcement, if they don't get it, their motivation starts fading away and all they are left with is an empty shell with a vacuum inside. They suffer from (AMS) amotivational syndrome, like hippies of the sixties movement of marijuana abuse. They were called dope heads. Their soul energy was deprived of the strength to ride the train of motivation. I am sure people without motivation suffer and pay the price in the future.

CHAPTER 3

EMOTIONS AND THE SOUL

O ur emotions are just like the ocean, which occupies three-fourths of the earth. Our emotions are vast, like the ocean of our lives. I assume it controls three-fourths of the journey of our life. Rest is controlled by the structural self. Our emotions are like vast commotions of the ocean from the beauty of the shores to the calmness of the ocean and beautiful blue waters. From cliffs, you may not see the end, but you have an awesome feeling of such beauty. This ocean gives life to beautiful creatures and an awesome cool breeze and rain to Mother Nature. Without it, life is impossible. It can create toxic gases and absorb toxic chemicals created by humans. Having lived in Virginia Beach my entire life provoked the thought of the ocean and emotions. Lying on the sand of a beautiful beach with sun rays hitting my body made me sweat and gave me all the vitamin D I needed. Whenever I felt like I needed to cool my heated body, I stepped down the dune and set my feet in the water. I gradually waded up to my knees. It felt very pleasant until I was up to my waist and up to my neck, looking around at beautiful children, young and old, males and females, splashing in the water, laughing and screaming with joy. Those who knew how to swim, I saw them swimming far away from me, surfing the waves far away. I saw boats full of people, smiling and waving at times. What a joyful feeling!

As you keep going, the ocean gets deeper and deeper, waves hitting you hard and pushing you away to shore, telling you it is dangerous if you go further down the safety line. But some waves can suck you in and drag you deeper and deeper. If you don't know how to swim, you can drown and lose the pleasure and beauty of the shore. The ocean has limitless beauty. Its sentinel slopes, the ocean basin, barrier islands, estuaries where rivers meet the ocean, its shores, currents, and tides, its reefs and valleys—all is good, but it has strong waves, and if it gets angry, they are storms, which can cause havoc and destruction.

It gives rainwater, which gives us food and life. Without three-fourths of our world being covered in ocean, our one-fourth of land, our lives, would vanish, and nothing would exist. Its depth in the Mariana Trench reaches 36,070 feet deep. It gives us the feeling that we may never reach to the depths. Light does not penetrate as it gets deeper. The temperature drops as we get deeper to 0 to 3 degrees centigrade. Pressure keeps increasing as the ocean gets deeper by one atmosphere for every ten meters. Life and the shapes of living creatures change as we get deeper and deeper, some known but most unknown. Though we have tried and are trying to understand the ocean, we still do not know about its beauty and beastly nature or the moods of the ocean. Unpredictability is its nature. Changes in its mood are uncertain. It makes you feel relaxed and happy at one moment. And then it makes you feel like crying, angry at the devastating destruction and loss of life. It creates storms against which we living creatures have no force to stop. We hunker down. Some die, some get injured, some are left with emotional pain for their lives, and some lose everything and even loved ones. Though we human beings have developed advanced technologies to forecast and track the storms to give warnings, who can predict the emotions of the ocean? In the same way, who can describe human emotions, which fluctuate with time and events? We humans are full of emotions. We are just like a ship taking a journey of life in the vast ocean without knowing how and where it will end. We grow and learn about the journey through our experiences. Each ship has its captain. The soul is the captain; the cocaptain is the primary soul, and the crew is the secondary and tertiary souls (ibid).

When the ship sails in smooth, sparkling water, the beauty of the vast ocean is breathtaking and the journey of life is wonderful. We feel happy, we laugh, we relax, we feel pleasant, and we feel excited. We enjoy eating, drinking, sleeping, and joking and are playful with each other. We feel thrilled about each other's company. We remain alert and attentive.

Our facial expressions show our elation. Our desires seem to be fulfilled, and we look forward to new desires being fulfilled and share the pleasant memories of the past. We express love and liking for each other without any judgment, with heavenly aspirations of calmness. Our heart and soul are in harmony with a relaxed body. We look up to the sky and admire the beauty of the moon and stars in the blue sky at night. We want to share, care, and make love. Passion flows through us like sweet nectar. We take life for granted. Our soul feels in harmony with its cosmic soul, which we call God, and thoughts of ecstasy flow through us. We feel content and ignore the rest. But within a few seconds, a big wave comes crashing in and throws the boat fifty feet away, changing the direction and course of our boat. There is sudden turmoil, chaos, and confusion. We are frightened, agitated, and restless, gasping for breath. We feel tense, nervous, stressed, upset, fearful, and frightened, and we feel pain due to the fall. We feel internal and external bleeding. We may blame each other. We argue and blame each other, and we overreact in a rage for the safety of the lifeboat. We scream at the top of our lungs. We become judgmental, and our belief is shattered. We feel exhausted sad. We even cry and become depressed and bored. Fatigue sets in with psychomotor agitation. With loss of hope, there is doom and gloom until the boat is able to gain a state of equilibrium. Our primary, secondary, and tertiary souls work together to get the boat straight and able to float and look forward to having a comfortable sail. It happened quickly, but it takes a long time to stabilize the boat. Now we are hyperalert and take extra precautions. Our radar is on twenty-four/seven. We do not believe in predictability. We believe in unpredictability, which makes us hyperalert and sensitive. Our notions of future are uncertain. We learn from this experience by using our cognition and memory. A stunned feeling haunts us. We think about this most of the time. We compare the good and the bad. How does it affect us? I call it emotional prophylaxis. What is that? I describe it as follows.

When newborns come into the world and grow, we give them immunization shots for measles, mumps, polio, and other childhood illnesses, so that they develop immunity against infectious diseases and get their immune system to fight the devastating diseases. This strong wave that shook the boat developed enough strength that we learned to face any devastating events in our lives. I call it emotional prophylaxis, but we can call it emotional immunity to face future challenges. When confronted with disaster, this is how our emotions develop, react, and change with the change in situations.

There are numerous theories about emotions, but very few have been able to give us a clue what they are about. Emotions have not been seen or recorded. Emotions develop in the womb of the mother when the fetus is about eight months along or earlier. An infant can express his or her emotions by kicking or moving around in the womb. This was explained to me by my wife while she was pregnant twice, with a boy each time. My view, as described earlier, is that once the infantile soul is developed, it constantly interacts with the magnetic soul of the mother. As we say, when the mother is happy and content, so is the fetus. If the mother is in emotional turmoil, so is the infant. The emotions of the fetus are regulated or deregulated by neurochemicals or hormones, like adrenaline, serotonin, cortisol, and numerous neurotransmitters, which flow back and forth from the blood of the mother to the blood of the fetus. The emotions of the fetus grow as the nervous system of the fetus grows. I call it the infantile soul.

By the age of three weeks, infants imitate the facial movements of adult caregivers. They open their mouths and thrust their tongues out in response to the adults who do the same. Is this when mirror neurons develop in humans? Rizzolatti, Glacomoand, and Keysers(160,161) argue that mirror neurons fire both when an animal acts and when the animal observes the same action performed by another (160, 161). Once the mirror neurons are developed, one can observe the behavior of others as though the observer were self-acting. Such neurons have been observed in primate species. In human infants, at age three to four months, these behaviors are easily elicited. These imitative behaviors are believed to be the precursors of the infant's emotional life (159). Smiling occurs in two phases. The first is endogenous and occurs spontaneously within the first two months. It is unrelated to external stimulation. The second phase is exogenous smiling, which is stimulated from the outside, usually by the mother, and occurs by the sixteenth week. Stages of emotional development parallel those of cognitive development. The fact is the caregiver is responsible for both. The human infant is totally dependent on the adult for survival. Thus, healthy emotions develop with healthy emotions and social interaction. If an infant is emotionally deprived, this leads to unhealthy emotions and maladaptive behaviors, since neurons and dendrites grow at a faster pace and retain some of the healthy emotions. Assuming that the infant has a healthy genetic makeup and normal health (for example, the child does not experience Down syndrome, autism, and other disorders of childhood). In the first year, the infant's moods are highly variable and are intimately related to internal states, such as hunger, cleanliness, sleep, timely care, love, and affection. My experience raising two boys is that a well-fed and clean baby with adequate care cries less frequently compared to those who are not cared for properly. Food and appropriate nutrition are very essential. A colicky baby will keep you awake more often than a noncolicky baby. Neurons retaining such memory and emotions are developed. Toward the end of first year, the infant's moods and emotions grow rapidly in relation to external social cues. As they say, "a parent can make a hungry baby smile." When an infant is internally comfortable, he or she develops a sense of interest and pleasure and retains memories. Prolonged separation from the primary caregiver during the second six months of life can lead to depression that may persist into adulthood. There are studies that indicate inborn differences and wide variability in autonomic reactivity and temperament among individual infants. From infant to six years of life, there are numerous factors in the development of emotions, like whether the child is able to resolve separation anxiety from the mother and is able to resolve stranger anxiety. When you want to hold a child and kiss him or her, there appears to be an intensive stranger anxiety and the child jumps back to his or her mother. Once a child feels comfortable and is reassured that you are not a threat, he or she may sit in your lap and laugh and giggle rather than cry and want to run away from you. This is the stage of development of the infantile soul. That is not only due to neuroplasticity (generation, growth, and connections of dendrites) and neurogenesis but also to retention of important emotions and memories of the emotion, which explains the cognitive part of our emotions.

There are many theories about emotions and their various components. Some claim mood, temperament, personality, disposition, and motivation are the ingredients of emotions (163). Some believe that emotions are a state of feeling that results in physical and psychological changes that influence our behavior. Jean Piaget has written extensively about stages of intellectual development. According to him, there are four stages that lead to the event of cognition from birth to adulthood: 1) sensorimotor (birth to two years), 2) preoperational thought (two years to seven years), 3) stage of concrete operational (seven to eleven years), and 4) formal operational (eleven to the end of the adolescence) (164). Richard Carpenter and Benjamin Brady claimed that neurophysiologic approach like are as follows.

- *Arousal* describes the emotional state associated with movement of the organism (humans) toward a desirable goal or away from a source of threat, as in "fight or flight."
- *Conservation* is withdrawal. In situations like standing in the middle of a minefield, the only sensible response is to conserve one's resources, or when in a battlefield, where the soldier is trapped in the bunker, to do nothing, hoping the difficulties will go away. The result is stupor, loss of muscle tone, sleep, or even hibernation. If the situation is sudden, there may be an abrupt immobility or freezing. Snakes or other animals play as if they are dead. The associated feelings are of apathy, tiredness, and weakness.

According to Mark Pettinelli, there are three groups of life emotions:

- Thinking
- Feeling
- Emotions

All three are interconnected and may have the same origin. Some things in life cause people to feel. These are called emotional reactions. Some things in life cause people to think. These are called logical or intellectual reactions. In extreme emotional reactions, like crying, thinking is diminished. Sometimes you like some things or you are more passionate about some things. Some actions by others you do not like; you're disgusted by them. Sometimes, you see something out of your imagination, and you become curious and think about it more often. Sometimes, you see strange things, which make you curious about them. What a strange thing for a strange person. Thought is just a period of increased attention focused on a particular thing that is unclear and needs further investigation or clarification to understand whether it is a real or unreal, right or wrong. Is it practical or impractical? Thoughts could be triggered by our sensory system, or they could be triggered by the internal system of the primary or secondary soul. My view is thought is triggered by the soul, which acts as a reserve file, like cloud computation. Thought could be stored in the form of energy, which triggers the neuronal activity and continues the process of thinking. There is a lag period of neuronal action and the origination of thought or thoughts, according to current neuroscientific research (Dr. John Dylan Haynes).

Neurons are workhorses, sending and receiving electric impulses and using memory as a tool to drive any conclusion or discard the thought, thereafter sending feedback to our soul, which keeps all this in the back file in the form of magnetic energy. If the energy of a thought is strong, it remains in the soul file for an indefinite period of time and gradually fades away to be replaced by new thoughts, depending upon the strength of the magnetic energy produced. Neuroscientists call this "higher neuronal functions" (Penfield). Someday, they will find that a higher neuronal functioning does not exist in thin air. It is a form of energy, reserved and preserved, created by neuronal electrical firings for thinking and thoughts, which are infinite. Imagine in your lifetime how often and how many thoughts cross through your brain—approximately sixty thousand thoughts per day.

Jean Piaget describes a stage of formal operations in which the young person's "thinking" operates in a formal, highly logical, systematic, and symbolic manner. This stage is characterized by the ability to think abstractly, to reason deductively, and to define concepts and also by the emergence of skills for dealing with permutations (every detail matters) and combinations. Abstract thinking is shown by the adolescent's interest in a variety of issues, like philosophy, religion, ethics, and politics. Hypothetical, deductive thinking is the highest organization of cognition. It enables the person to make a hypothesis or proposition and to test it against deductive reasoning, which moves from the particular to the general and is a more complicated process than inductive reasoning, which moves from particular to general. Because young people can reflect on their own and other people's thinking, they're susceptible to self-conscious behavior, as they attempt to master new cognitive tasks. They may turn to egocentric thoughts but on a higher level than in past. For example, adolescents may think that they can accomplish everything or can change events by their thoughts alone. Not all adolescents enter the stage of formal operation at the same time or to the same degree. It depends on individual capacity and intervening experiences. Some may not reach the stage of formal operational thought at all and may remain in the concrete-operational mode throughout life if their emotions and feelings are strong about something or are focused on something else. Then, thoughts get weaker or maybe even blocked. For example, if you are emotional about your girlfriend and are attentive to her, then your other thoughts may not get the attention they need from you and these thoughts remain in a quiet mode (165).

In my experience of psychiatric practice, it is very important to understand thought content. Thoughts are limitless for limitless people. To describe all thought contents is impossible. I will focus on abnormal thought content and how it describes the underlying mental illness or underlying personality disorder. Some may ruminate on specific content of thought. In obsessive-compulsive disorder, there are obsessional thoughts that are unwelcome and repetitive thoughts that intrude into the individual's consciousness. They are generally ego alien and resisted by the individual. Compulsions are repetitive, ritualized behaviors that an individual performs to avoid anxiety or some dreaded outcome, like a ritual to wash hands repeatedly to avoid germs. Our thoughts control our emotions, like anxiety and fear, and our behavioral and emotional reactions. Another form of thought content that is frequently prevalent in psychotic patients and paranoid personality disorder patients is delusions that are false and fixed ideas that are not shared by others. They could be bizarre or appropriate. Common delusions are grandiose, erotomanic, jealous, somatic, persecutory, and suspicious. They are usually demonstrated by paranoid and psychotic individuals because of underlying causes, like schizophrenia, bipolar disorder, major depression, drug-induced psychosis, and organic mood disorder. The list goes on and on. Suicidal and homicidal thoughts are under the category of thought content.

Thought processes explain how a person is thinking, how thoughts are formulated, organized, and expressed. Normal thought processes are described as linear, organized, and goal directed, while in bipolar disorder, thoughts are fleeting from one thought to another. They may express thoughts about the mother and then shift to the president of the United States or the moon. We call it a "flights of ideas." These ideas are not linear but broken into different objects and different subjects. We cannot make logical sense of such thoughts. We in psychiatry use the term thought disorders. Let me describe briefly what they are:

As I have explained in discussing the abnormal pattern of thoughts versus normal thoughts, we all have our own thoughts and our own way based on our neuron and dendrite connections and our level of neurotransmitters at the synaptic cleft, where transmission of electric current is passed to the next neuron to produce the desired effect.

If there is an abnormality, then transmission will produce abnormal results and thoughts, based on our DNA sequences, which provided us the blueprint for assembling the proteins that make up our neurons so that they function the way they are encoded, for example, as written by Vargha-khadem et al. (2005). The FOXP2 gene is involved in the neural circuitry of speech and language. Though human genes have been mapped out, the information about emotions and their components have not been released.

Emotions can motivate social interactions and relationships and therefore are directly related to the basic physiology of stress and antistress responses. The strengths and weaknesses of our hormones, neurotransmitters, and neurochemicals are all based on our genes and their interactions with the environment, which bring on changes in our emotions or behaviors.

Dr. Ramachandran, in his book The Telltale Brain, raises several realistic questions about the meaning of knowledge or understanding and how 100 billion neurons achieve them (171). Dr. Ramachandran is a renowned neuroscientist, who has been called the Marco Polo of neuroscience in this era of advanced neuroscience. He explains that these are complete mysteries and cognitive neuroscientists are still vague about the exact meaning of "understanding or thinking." According to him, commonsense suggests some of the activities regarded as "thinking" do not require language. His example is intriguing. For example, I can ask you to fix a light bulb on the ceiling and show you three wooden boxes lying on the floor. You would have the internal sensors juggling the visual image of the boxes, stacking them up in your own mind to reach the bulb socket before actually doing so. It certainly does not feel like you're engaging in silent internal speech, like "Let me stack the larger box at the bottom, next smaller on the top, and the smallest on top of that." This is not a reliable guide to what is going on in one's head (stacking the three boxes). His notion is that what feels like the internal juggling of visual symbols actually taps into some neurocircuitry in the brain that mediates language, even though the task feels purely geometric or spatial. Where do these observations come from? Are these hardwired into the brain? Are they present at birth? Is it learned from our past experiences? Is it the silent internal language that mirrors and partially taps into the same neural machinery used for spoken language? Does language precede propositional logic or vice versa? Or is neither necessary for the other, even though they mutually enrich each other?

John Dylan Haynes has some answers to that. There is a lag period of seven seconds between starting a task and thinking about the task. The decision is already made seven seconds before the test started. Where is it? And who does that? Penfield called it the "higher neuronal function" of the brain. I call it the magnetic energy of the soul, which is constantly present in our brain and body. This energy starts the process of thinking and ordering the neurons involved in this whole process of action. This magnetic energy triggers the neurons in the respective areas of the brain, firing electric current, which spreads like a wildfire to complete the task. Our neurons are horses working for our soul, the magnetic energy; this energy is created by an electric current flowing from the neurons, the sensory system, and the rest of the body. The soul is a cowboy with one hundred billion neurons running around and following the command in an organized fashion. Thoughts are described by the different thinkers. Some claim it to be the product of mental activity that one thinks. Some claim it is a single act of thinking. It is the capacity or faculty of thinking, reasoning, imagining, considering, reflecting, meditating, contemplating, and recollecting. The conscious mind has reasoning and remembering experiences to imply one's mind rationally and objectively. We use the phrase think twice, which meanss to weigh carefully before acting or considering, and the list goes on and on. Thoughts consumes energy, whether it is electrical, magnetic, or chemical. It does not come out of thin air. Thought is an energy that is conscious. When you have a thought, you know it, because it is yours. If you are unaware, it becomes unconscious thought. Sometimes you want to do something, but you may not express it very clearly to yourself. Some thoughts are very clear to us, and sometimes they are not clear. Intellect and memory work hand in hand with thoughts or a thought. If you had no memory, then you would not have information to compare and bring up simultaneous thoughts. They sometimes follow each other and change one thought to another. Let's put ourselves in an examination room where we had to take a test with 350 multiple questions. Oh boy! Your thoughts are stormed and bombarded, moving from one question to another question until you finish the 350 questions in the test. You feel exhausted and stop thinking or change your activities, which preoccupy you. Attention is the bread and butter of thoughts. If you are not paying attention, your thoughts are fuzzy and unclear. Thoughts are also powered by feelings. When you feel nervous, your thoughts are weak, but you take a pause and reignite your thoughts and understand what it is all about. Those thoughts are functions of intelligence because that caused you to think and draw a reasonable conclusion. You made a decision and took action.

Thoughts are an integral part of creating a self. When you think about yourself, you become aware of yourself. For example, you thought of going to the beach and picked up all the essential things you needed, like a towel, a chair, a cooler full of water, and so on. You walked out the door and touched the doorknob to make sure the house was safe and locked up. You turned the car on and started to drive. Your friends called you, and you paused and answered the phone.

"Hey, what are you doing?" asked the friend.

You replied, "I'm going to the beach. You want to come?"

"Oh! Yes, I will see you on Sixty-Eighth Street. I will call you when I arrive there."

Now, what happened between the thought and the beach? You became self-aware of your existence and the existence of your other (friend). That is how you became aware of yourself. I am driving and listening to music. I see beautiful trees alongside the road. You see cars passing by. It gives you reassurance that it is not only you; there are others who exist too. While on the beach, you see young and old males and females, all kinds of people. You see a beautiful lady. It triggers the thought, Should I wave at her or go and say hi? Introduce myself? Your body and self and soul are altered. There is a surge of adrenaline and neurotransmitters. If you have courage, you may go and say hi or you my keep thinking, Should "I" or shouldn't "I"? Then the feeling of self gets strengthened. Thoughts keep you alert and conscious. You question within yourself, What if she has a boyfriend? What if she is married? What if she says, "Thank you," and walks away. Now others exist in your thought. Your cognitive thinking is churning inside of your brain. Neurons are firing at a higher rate. There is a strong surge of magnetic energy supplied to your soul. Your autonomic nervous system is not only firing electric current but all the chemicals circulating through your bloodstream. Courage, which resides in your soul energy, orders your primary soul to get up and go say hi with a smile. You approach her with warmth and appear very eager to know about her. You say, "Hi, I'm Mike."

She looks at you and scans you thoroughly—a handsome body, a wonderful smile, and an eager sense. She answers, "HI, I am Julie. What a beautiful day to be at the beach!"

Your neurons in the brain start firing more and more. Your thoughts are burning with the desire to know more about her. Her neurons start firing and give her enough magnetic energy to her soul. You triggered her thoughts and emotions. There is a pause because both of your souls and neurons are processing the next move. So you ask her, "Where do you live?"

Her answer is "In Norfolk and you?"

"I live in Virginia Beach."

"What do you do for a living, Mike?"

"I finished a master's in economics and plan on going to law school."

"Wow, I am in my final year of economics and don't know whether I will go for business management or a PhD in economics."

Your conversation starts bringing you closer. She has screened you, and you have screened her. But there is a higher mechanism going on in the brain. It looks like an early attraction. Your thoughts start racing, and you offer her a bottle of water.

"Sure. Thanks!" she replies.

You feel somewhat calm and reassured by her accepting the bottle of water. You are somewhat nervous, and so is she. You and she trigger enormous thoughts for each other, like what to talk about. You chose humor, which you think to be a decent way to continue a conversation.

"You know Dr. Schulman?" you ask. "I cannot forget Professor Schulman. Is he still there?"

She laughs and says, "Yes, that joker. He's funny."

"I like him too."

Now both of you get involved in a little conversation about the university and feel somewhat comfortable. You spend about half an hour together, and you ask her for a drink after five. Before you go home, she says, "Yes, that's cool."

You exchange numbers, and she goes with her friend, jumping into the ocean. She left by saying, "I will see you at five, Mike. Bye."

It is about three, and a friend comes. You talk only about her, repeatedly mentioning how smart, beautiful, and sweet she is.

"It looks like you are attracted to her," says the friend.

"Yes, but I don't know anything about her." You think about her and give her an occasional smile.

"She is the one?" your friend asks.

"Yes, wow, she is gorgeous!"

Now your thoughts and her thoughts have been validated. Both of you exist. You feel reassured that you have a self and she has a self. Now your thoughts go back and forth from insecurity to security. You have doubt about the questions you asked. Will she come for a drink? There is an argument between "yes" and "no." You pace back and forth on the sand to the water edge on the shore, just to get a glimpse of her; she seems to be doing the same with an occasional peek at you without you knowing that.

The time between 3:00 p.m. and 5:00 p.m. is full of turbulent thoughts and feelings.

You ask your friend what time it is frequently. He says, "Don't ask me. Look at your phone."

"Oh, I forgot that I could check the time myself," because your thoughts have taken over your attention.

When intentions and thoughts take over our conscious self, our cognitive attention is dull and numb to our surroundings. Our attention and thoughts are focused on one object, which obliterates our attention to our surroundings and other objects. Our soul is focused, and our magnetic attraction is overwhelmed.

At 5:00 p.m., they meet and have a beautiful conversation. She says, "Mike, it feels like we have known each other for a long time."

"Yes, it is amazing how that can happen."

"Maybe we have lots in common," she says.

Mike agrees and they have good emotional feelings. They laugh and joke, and she leaves with her friend. She says, "Call me tomorrow. Maybe we'll get together."

Mike sees some hesitation on her part at leaving, but her friends are pushing her to go. Mike goes home, and she is glued to his thoughts. He tries to shake them out by watching a football game. It appears to him as if time has come to a standstill. Tomorrow seems too far away. He has the irresistible urge to call her, but the cognitive forces of his soul prevented him from calling with "reasons, justifications, and excuses." Well, I just met her, and it does not seem right to call her now. It is 8:00 p.m., and she may be busy with her affairs. It is too late. I don't want to annoy her and make her feel as if I'm smothering her. I have an irresistible desire to listen to her voice. Oh well, forget about my reasoning, his thoughts tell him.

Mike's anxiety surmounts his calmness and tranquility. His impulsivity gets stronger and takes control over his reasoning. He finally calls her; she doesn't pick up the phone. He leaves a brief message. "Hope you reached home safe. I really enjoyed your company. Good night."

Mike's compulsion and impulse calm down and his thoughts are somewhat under control.

It happens to all of us when there are overwhelming thoughts that cause anxiety because of excessive autonomic activity. Time comes to a standstill. Hours become days, and days become weeks; weeks become months, and months become years. Thus, our impulses become stronger to perform an act that causes anxiety (make a phone call). Mike was attentive and learned that he had a sense of self and sense of another self. When there are feelings, emotions, and thoughts, there is an enhancement of self. He was more aware of himself than he had been the day before. They met again and started dating. They felt as if they were drawn to each other, like magnets, which was due to their strong magnetic souls. They acknowledged to each other there must something that was drawing them together. It was a sharing of a strong magnetic force. If you want friends, you must learn to love all unselfishly. To use anyone is wrong. You must express selfless love. Very few people love you for your own sake, but if you can love others without any motive, then you can have true love in your magnetic soul. A husband should love his wife out of friendship, not because of her physical beauty. You should think of your friends not because of their richness, attractiveness, or power, but because you love them. Because of your unselfishness, the magnetic force is positive and strong and not negative and weak.

Mike learned that she liked her space and needed independence, though the mere thought turns into love. He used his common sense to grow the relationship stronger. Common sense is someone's ability to put data points (facts) together. If one does this with facts that relate to oneself, one's consciousness is going to be increased. This tells us that consciousness is just the awareness of the experience of oneself. The experience includes one's actions, thoughts, feelings, and emotions, both short-term and long-term. More common sense (Mike and Julie) means more ability to organize the future life. It is an addition to their actions, which they take in an efficient and clear manner by connecting facts to them. The more people are thinking about themselves (experiences, emotions, feelings, and thoughts), the more they are going to be aware of their life experience.

Sometimes we have real problems, and sometimes, we think that we have a problem. This is a distortion of thinking. For example, 4 + 4 is 8. But when our thinking is 4 + 4 is 9, it is more distortion. How do we resolve that? When we think correctly and realize that nine is false and eight is fact, our thinking has created eight by mere correction. With acceptance of our correct thoughts, the problem is solved. Cognitive behavioral therapy is based on the principle of reconstructing the negative cognitive distorted thoughts into positive constructive reality-oriented thoughts. Piaget used the term equilibration. The notion is based on helping the individual to think that previous cognitive structures and thinking are inadequate. Thus, a therapist, a teacher, or a guru disrupts the old cognitive structure, and an individual experiences the old disruptive thoughts with new ones, which leads him or her to the search for more adequate cognitive thoughts. The new constructed thoughts are established by accommodation and reexperiencing them. When we experience reality-oriented thoughts as rewarding, pleasant, and realistic, then these thoughts are conditioned. With repeated use of such cognitive thoughts, we replace the distorted thoughts. This is called "reframing of distorted negative thoughts," which exist in depression, anxiety disorders, and other disorders. This requires thinking about the thinking. For example, in depression, feelings of worthlessness, hopelessness, sadness, and negativity about oneself are replaced by making the patient understand and think about positive strengths he or she has. Gradually, he or she reexperiences the positive aspects of his- or herself. As he or she experiences the reality-oriented thoughts, feelings, or emotions, he or she feels the gift of such thought. Feelings or emotions are thus replacing distorted negative thoughts. Practicing new emotions, thoughts, and feelings results in hope and positive feelings, emotions, or thoughts about oneself, thereafter disrupting the depressive mode of life. Maurice Nicoll (412) says that crystallized thoughts form attitude. If you have continually thought in a certain way, all these thoughts crystallize into an attitude. Let us suppose you have always thought that you did not get the attention you should have gotten. You have identified with this thought thousands and thousands of times. Eventually, these thousands of similar thoughts form a solid deposit in the soul. This is called crystallization. Such a crystallization of similar thoughts forms an attitude, so you now have an attitude toward other people, which has been formed out of thinking and thinking time and again in the same way that you never get the attention you should get from others. You will agree with me that such a crystallization forming this particular attitude is not uncommon and can be observed in many people. Now apply it to yourself and see what goes on with you at home, work, and in other social settings. It can make some happy and some very distressed. It can eat one's force up daily and produce an inner sickness of the soul if conditions are adverse—if not, there is contentment of the soul. At times, the attitude being formed becomes part of our unconscious and is not directly observable. It has become part of you and acts invisibly and automatically without your knowing about it. Now, thought will not make you act, but an attitude will. In the given example, you will not keep thinking and paying attention to your attitude and keep acting the way you did before. In some, it becomes beyond one's observation. In some, a genuine practice of self-observation gradually draws it into the consciousness, which brings thoughts and attitudes hidden deep in the dark shadows of our lives forth. Now, if you begin to increase your consciousness of yourself by observation of what is accessible, then, after a time, you will find yourself becoming aware of the existence in yourself (your psychological makeup) of things you had not attributed to yourself but only to others.

Negative emotions originate in the hypothalamus and an elaborated amygdala (part of the brain). Though we and others do not like negative emotions, they have some importance in our lives. These are recognized as a survival skill to adapt to an environment and in relation to others. Though it is all about "me" and "I," recognition of these help us to avoid such feelings. For example, if we are not afraid of lions eating us, we would walk just in front of the lion. Fear keeps us away and acts as a survival mechanism by prompting us to avoid the danger (174).

How do we feel or express such emotions? It is a burning question in the neuroscientific, philosophical, and psychological fields. Everyone has theories. This reminds me of my psychiatric residency days. Our professor asked eight residents to write a paper on bipolar disorder. I wrote twenty-four pages, while the rest of the papers written by other residents were six in average. At the end of the class, my professor asked me to stay, and everyone else left. He asked me, "Why did you write twenty-four pages?"

I answered, "Sir, I wanted to be thorough."

He smiled and gave me some advice. "Listen, if you cannot explain the paper in four pages, that means you do not have the concrete concept of the subject." He added, "Where are there more theories about the subject? There are unanswered questions about that subject."

I answered, "Got it. Thank you, sir."

The same holds true for the theories of emotions. We still do not know how, when, and what.

My view is simple. Let's say I touched the hot stove and felt pain. My burning finger sent an electric current to my pain center, which in turn created a magnetic energy, the soul, which created an archive of files for my life. It sent the order to my neurons to keep my finger away from the hot stove. In future, when I see the hot stove, I am careful not to touch it. Thus, the complex mechanism involves my sensory systems (vision, hearing, touch, smell, and so on.) It involves my cognition and ability to understand and feel pain and avoid any future event. Can it be memory? Fine, I agree with that. So there are specific parts of the brain that respond to negative stimuli and perceive negative concepts. Thus, our soul responds to the negative current created by the neurons, which create a negative form of magnetic field. This is stored in the form of negative feelings in our soul, to help us avoid future negative events or actions through our neurons.

Positive emotions are generated in the limbic system, and I'm sure there is involvement of the frontal lobe too in order to use the cognition to understand and create a positive magnetic field to be stored in the archives of our soul. Positive emotions are more expansive and help us to broaden and build our emotional strength. In future, they widen our tolerance for others in our lives and expand our moral compassion. This is especially true of joy and love. They make thought patterns more flexible, creative, integrative, and efficient. For example, meditation makes us relaxed through the regulation of the autonomic nervous system. Negative responses to the stimulation of the sympathetic nervous system causes excessive adrenaline, evoking a fight-or-flight response, anxiety, panic, and physical responses, like shakiness, apprehension, dryness of the mouth and anxious moods. The parasympathetic nervous system causes positive emotional responses, like a reduced basal metabolism and lower blood pressure, heart rate, and respiration rate and reduced muscle tension. Functional magnetic resonance (FMRI) studies of kundalini (a yogic term for internal energy) in yoga practitioners demonstrate that meditation increased the activity of the hippocampus and the right lateral amygdala, which stimulates the parasympathetic nervous system, causing deep peacefulness and tranquility. Positive emotions have a biological basis, which evolved with time as an evolutionary process, thus helping adaption. This led to survival of the defenseless Homo sapiens, children in the African savannah one to two million years ago (139, 125–126).

In reptiles, for example, the motor cortex reacts to sensory cues of vision, sound, touch, chemical, gravity, and the magnetic field of the earth, which leads to preset body movements and programmed postures. With the arrival of night, in inactive mammals, smell is replaced by vision as the dominant sense. It is a form of emotional sense and emotional memory. Loveheim proposed that in anger, there is low serotonin, high dopamine, and high noradrenalin (177). According to Harmon-Jones, anger is a negative emotion that activates the left prefrontal lobe cortex. If we are still arguing about emotions, then how could we disclaim mystics who emphasize the known of the unknown. At least we in neuroscience have some neurophysiologic understanding, which with the advent of time, shall get clearer and clearer. We will explore more, discard some ideas, and adopt others. I will stick to my theory of "soul" as the master combining mechanism of all functional events of our body and emotions. The mind is a figment of the imagination, which is a name given to the energy created by our body cells and neurons. Basically, our body is mindless but still operates on the basis of electrical and magnetic forces within and without. I have a burning desire to understand and relate to the fact that when I shouted or screamed at my son, his response was to get angry and cry or run away from me. He had the same ears and same eyes, sending signals to the brain areas concerned and processing my anger emotions. He was reacting to that. There were times when I would kiss him and praise him. I would tell him, "I love you, Son."

His reaction was very calm. He would be sitting in my lap watching TV and reply, "I love you too, Dad." He would smile.

Now, he had the same ears and the same eyes, which created an electric current and stimulated the areas of the brain specified for the same function. So how come there was a difference? Shouting caused him to get angry and loving words made him calm and loving to me too. Is there a different electrical current generated in our eyes and ears, or is it something higher that differentiates the two? If the brain has no sensation, then how does the brain feel the negative emotional behavior or positive, loving emotions? It reminds me of a fellow psychiatrist from Johns Hopkins, Leo Kanner, who wrote in 1943 about his son with autism. He wrote that positive emotions caused attachment in spite the fact that there might be minimal cognition. Dr. Leo Kanner treated eleven children and was the first psychiatrist to recognize autism. Remarkable studies have been done over the last twenty years. We have come a long way, and we have to go a long way. There are numerous studies using fMRI that have given us enormous functional information about our human brain. When a human experiences an existential state of fear, sadness, or pleasure, blood flow increases to the limbic system and decreases in many higher brain areas. This happens while the person is enjoying music, having a chocolate, winning money at a casino table or on the stock market, and even experiencing sexual orgasm. There are many areas of the brain involved in this part of life; I may mention a few more.

- Anterior cingulate gyrus
- Hippocampus (rich in dopaminergic innervations)
- Orbit frontal region
- Insula

The list goes on and on. I would rather keep it simple to help you understand and let neuroscientists bother about the details and duke it out.

The insula is the latest part of the brain to drawn attention all over the world. I respect and understand most of the connections and their respective functions. I have already written about the brain having no sensation and how it does feel sensations like pain, for example. Are we blindsided or too ignorant to understand it? In my view, it is a certain quality of the magnetic field that resides at a higher level of our brain that causes the neurological parts of our brain to coordinate the functional parts. Both the soul and brain work together. One cannot live without the other. One theory is that all the emotions are brought to consciousness through the insula (part of the brain).

What is the latest and most current thrust by neurobiologists to understand the positive emotions of joy, pleasure, empathy, humor, and trust? These are attributed to spindle cells, which are concentrated in the anterior cingulate cortex, the prefrontal cortex, and the insula. These are cigar-shaped neurons (also called "von economo").

Mirror neurons are situated in the anterior cingulate gyrus and insula, which are considered to mediate empathy (the experience of feelings and emotions of others). It suggest to me that the mind does not exist. It is the brain and the higher function of the brain that resides in the soul. There needs to be more work and research in order to prove my hypothesis. These are my views, without any experiments. It is my experience and wisdom from psychiatry.

Generally, emotions and reasons do not exist together. The emotions are the outburst of the state of tension and excitement caused by certain events and feelings, when a person is emotionally aroused. Any amount of deliberate suppression and care in thinking causes disturbances in the nervous system. Reasoning, on the other hand, requires a calm mind. At the same time, a person without emotions feels emptiness and loneliness. Keeping the emotions to a desirable level is necessary. They should always be balanced by reasoning, thus helping the person to evolve a state of emotional reason. Emotions are broad-spectrum descriptions of numerous components. Sometimes they are realistic, and sometimes they are unrealistic. It is our intelligence that ultimately makes our soul to understand the ability to redefine and manipulate our emotions. It differentiates between the reality and unreality of our emotional status. It differentiates between logical emotions and illogical emotions. People may experience positive emotions, but does that mean they are extremely happy and joyful and have ecstatic feelings? If they are unrealistic, they can develop cyclothymiac or manic behavior. If people experience negative emotions and are unrealistic, they feel sad, hopeless, and despondent. Chances are they develop dysthymia, depression, and anxiety or personality disorders. Let us say both are realistic as per our cognition. Then they are real feelings or emotions. But they are short lived, and we snap back and forth to the normal homeostatic status of our soul, our body, its reactions and adjustments to the environment, our surroundings, situations, and events.

Yesterday, I attended a wedding and met my friends. We all picked on each other laughed, joked, and had a good time. We all set limits on how far we would go. Everybody has their chance to express their feelings without offending anyone. But sometimes you will find a person dominating and continuing to pick on you or joking about one person.

My view about that is impressions created by others about me are created by others, for their own selfish needs, greed, and jealousy. My impressions are solely created by me and my soul but not for others. They are free of need, greed, or jealousy for anyone else. Hence, their impressions about me mean nothing, because they are theirs. I have no control over them and have no desire to have them. Let them delve into their own imaginations, beliefs, and jealousy. Let them deal with their impressions about me. Thus, I am free, since I do not have to deal with those impressions, because they are their own. What you think of me is none of my business because those thoughts are yours. This false notion of validation of your self-worth is useless, though we are taught from an early age to believe in the opinions of others, more than our own opinions of ourselves. The truth is "know thyself before you know thou." Our self-esteem stems from our internally held positive belief in our soul, not from the approval of others' souls or selves. Don't imagine that anyone can have true faith in you when he or she has no faith in himself or herself. Believing that who we are is defined by what other people think of us cripples the joyful spontaneity of our authentic selves; if others disapprove and their opinions define us, then we either modify ourselves or shrink from their view. If our image of ourselves is located in them, when they reject us, we no longer are ourselves. If they think we are stupid, we attempt to think otherwise by trying to be the person they want us to be. We cease to exist, except as a reflection of what others think. Others are important in our life in our quest to share, care, love, learn, and teach.

It is important that your emotions belong to your soul and theirs too. In addition, at times, we need others for validation as a result of our actions and decisions, which are our own. That is all that matters, because you have to live with them, not with the decisions of others (169). Your soul becomes stronger when you refuse to be offended by anyone, anything, or in any set of circumstances. By all means, state what you feel from the heart or soul. Then let it go. Do not hold on to it. When someone claims to be right, even though you know he or she is wrong, forget about your instant gratification in winning the argument and feel right. I use "You may be right" or "You could be right." I learned from a great Sikh saint of the fifteenth century Baba Guru Nank, who once said, "Never argue with an ignorant man. Pay attention to your thoughts and soul and rectify your thinking. Let it go because it is a waste of time and energy to argue with an ignorant one. When you judge someone, you do not define them. You define yourself" (170).

You do not own jealousy. Others have an exclusive right to know it. What difference does it make to you if he or she has something that you do not own or do not have rights to. Jealousy is perceived and assimilated by our senses (vision, hearing, touch, and so on), but the final process of understanding is through the cognitive process. It is all through neuronal processes, but still, it is stored in the files of the soul in the form of energy. Jealousy prevails everywhere. It could be from immediate associates or distant associates. To me, it means the same thing. How to deal with it is the question. Again, it is an individual response; some of us are sensitive and are emotionally affected. Anger, sadness, impulsivity, or your own jealousy can cause an emotional storm. It is common. It can happen in spousal relationships. It can happen between two siblings, neighbors, relatives, friends, and workplace professionals (professional jealousy) and in a variety of relationships in our environment. Jealousy usually refers to thoughts, feelings of insecurity, fear, concern, and anxiety over an anticipated loss of status or something of great personal value, particularly in connection to other humans. Jealousy often varies at times, depending upon the situation and the circumstances prevailing at that time. Some of them are anger, resentment, inadequacy, helplessness, and disgust. Hart and others have noted jealousy in five- to six-month-old infants (183, 84, 85). It could be cultural or unconscious influence. Sexual jealousy is fairly common, when attention is paid to another person, male or female, or where one partner pays more attention to someone of the opposite sex. Sexual infidelity is very harmful to both men and women.

Emotional jealousy is more dominant in women than men. Jealousy increases more in men over sexual infidelity. Jealousy is even common in animals. Bulls fight until one is the winner to mate with females. Even pets, like dogs and cats, have jealousy when their owner does not pay attention to them or pays attention to other pets. It makes it difficult to define jealousy because different humans express it with different emotions. Even killings have been reported by mere jealousy. One of my patients killed his wife and himself when someone told him that his wife was seen watching a movie with another man. That is extreme jealousy. My wife feels angry and anxious when she sees me talking to a pretty woman and paying attention to her or discussing any subject intellectually. She brought it to my attention many times by a question: "What were you talking about with that pretty-looking doctor?" I perceive it as an insecure feeling, which precedes a sense of abandonment. I usually tell her the truth.

With few friendly families, we went to Venezuela. We got off the ship and went to Caracas. There were beautiful women all around, walking on the streets and in shops. I could not resist but turn my neck to see. It went on for a little while, and my wife bought me dark glasses. "Here, put them on."

I asked why, and she gave me a smile and said, "I don't want your neck to fall on the ground. This way, you can move your eyes, not the neck."

It was a good joke, and my friends laughed about it. His wife told me, "Yes, she's right." I'm sure she felt somewhat jealous of my odd neck movements and odd fantasies.

W. G. Parrott makes a distinction between jealousy and envy through a common experience of humans (186, 187)

Jealousy is the following:

- Fear of loss
- Suspicion of or anger about a perceived betrayal
- Low self-esteem and sadness over perceived loss
- Uncertainty and loneliness
- Fear of losing an important person to another
- Disgust
- Envy is the following:
- Feelings of inferiority
- Longing
- Resentment of the circumstances
- Motivation to improve
- Desire to possess the attractive rival's qualities
- Disapproval of feelings (186, 87)

Scientists describe jealousy as in the following (188-189-190):

- Romantic jealousy is defined as a complex of thoughts and actions that follow a threat to self-esteem and perceptions of loss of attraction for a partner's relationship with another that is real or imagined.
- Emotional jealousy could be a cognitive, behavioral, or emotional response at the partner having or being imagined to have had a sexual relationship with another.
- Jealousy is perceived as being protective against a threat to a valued relationship.
- Jealousy is triggered by the threat of separation or loss of a romantic partner.

Once you retract or distance yourself, jealousy usually disappears. It may take six months to a year. As they say, "out of sight is out of mind," especially in those who have cognitive faculties intact and whose reasoning works through itself. In some cases, with mental illness and personality disorders, jealousy can develop into pathological jealousy and suspiciousness or even paranoia and delusions of persecution. For example, this can occur in paranoid personality disorder, passive-aggressive personality disorder, borderline personality disorder, and the list goes on and on. This is due to pathological negative and distorted, disintegrated, and fragmented energy of the soul, which generated in our neuronal mechanisms of the brain.

76

CHAPTER 4

BELIEF SYSTEM AND THE SOUL

A belief system is a state of mind in which a person thinks something is the case, with or without there being empirical evidence to prove it with factual certainty (348). Some define it as a mental representation of mental attitude positively oriented toward the likelihood of something being true. In the event it is represented as a negative mental attitude, we call it disbelief. Some define it as a map or view of the environment and the world around it. An individual is aware of himself or herself and that he or she is having those beliefs. When needed for any action or reaction, he or she can use that at will. Such awareness is stored as a form of thought or thoughts. Therefore, I can say every belief has a thought that initiates it, which is processed through the experiences and judgments. There is a long list of definitions because each individual has his or her own belief systems. Every culture, every religion, and every group of followers have created and accepted beliefs. So it is difficult to lump everything into one system. For example, Hindus believe in reincarnation, and Christians believe in resurrection. Muslims believe in the Day of Judgment after death. Islam's first requirement is a belief in Islam, and then the action to be taken is to lead the Islamic life. Out of one's beliefs and concepts, there is the development of attitudes toward one's life, society, and other human beings. This belief is so strong that some develop a certain kind of personality, a distinctive type of human interaction, a particular style of worship and rituals, a particular type of family life, specific manners and living habits, and particular relationships to all aspects of life, as defined in the Koran. I am sure it applies to all religious beliefs and teachings of their belief systems.

Those who believe in the teachings of the Koran would lead their lives with the concept that the entire world of creation and everything contained therein is sustained by certain definite laws inherited in each object and in harmony with each other. These laws of nature, the sunit Allah, are necessarily unalterable. Man's joy in life should lie in cooperating with these laws and imitating them in his or her own activity, assisted by the balance set in nature (Q 91:7). These laws constitute the "will of the God," and man should try to the best of his or her capabilities to conform to them for a life of peace and order. Whenever a person neglects to understand and conform to them, the consequences will naturally prove to be harmful to him or her. Law must have its course; a cause must produce its effect. One has to believe in the unity of God by recognizing that the entire universe, both visible and invisible, owes its existence and sustenance to one Supreme Being. Not one word in the Koran is believed by Muslim to be a thought created by Mohammed himself, although he is revered above all humanity as one of the most perfect of God's messengers (417).

Zoroastrianism emphasizes three basic principles as a belief system, which are good thoughts, good words, and good deeds. To me, these are very altruistic components of the belief system. Zarathustra was trained as a priest in an older unknown religion. He did not see God as an omnipotent being, as described in his hymns. According to him, God must grow, through the cumulative power of man's good thoughts, words, and deeds, which will eliminate the evil forces, giving rise to the omnipotence of God. Some believe that the earth will burn, and living creatures will disappear.

Every discipline has created its own definitions. Philosophers, psychologists, economists, and other disciplines have their own views. Psychologists define it as a form of mental representation of a view for survival and existence. The concept of belief presumes a subject and object, which means a believer and his or her belief system. Belief involves the existence of a mental state and intentionality. Beliefs could be core beliefs and dispositional beliefs. Core beliefs are strong mental forces and processes evolved as part of our life experience, which may persist throughout of our life. For example, I was a born-again Christian and grew up in a family where everyone was a born-again Christian. There is a high probability that the principles and structure of the environment I grew up in will become my core belief. So the environment has a great influence on my development and the course of my life's journey until death. Such core values are hard to influence with external factors. These core values become part of our genetic makeup. Someday, we may be able to find genes that will give us insight into how our environment of belief systems become an integral part of our lives. Once it becomes a part of our genetic system, it is very hard to change the basic core of such a belief system.

Some may have a transitory belief system as a part of their development and growth. Such systems adapt to the changes in the environment. For example, with the development of science and technology, we are presented with the facts and figures by which we live and thrive. We believe that there are cars we drive every day. There are airplanes we use to fly anywhere in the world. We have Internet, smartphones, Facebook, Google, and numerous other technical discoveries in our modern era. The days of riding in a buggy with a horse pulling it are gone. Information spreads in seconds across the world. Sending a message by tying a piece of paper around the neck of a pigeon is no longer done. So the time of spreading unfounded information and being blindsided by fearmongers is gone. We have to write new books about our belief system and other systems as well, as we move into the next phase of our lives. We define belief as a dynamic and changing system of our thought and acceptance of those thoughts. The experience of being rewarded by those thoughts when put into action can condition us with positive feedback and rewards. I can access my stock accounts with click of a button. Who can convince me to hire a broker to manage my account? Those who believe that brokers are the most intelligent and rewarding option for their clients. Those who believe they can make them money. They may believe that my view is wrong.

Those who never learn new things and put their trust in what has worked for them have a belief system that becomes what I call a "static belief system." One could believe in religion, God, destiny, luck, intuition, and a bright, wealthy future. One may believe he or she will live for a long time since his or her father and mother lived up to 102 years. Is there truth in their belief? The list is infinite.

Sonali B. Marwaha writes, "Having passed through of colors, I grow firm in my belief that the only way to end inter-religious prejudice and hatred is an exposure to different world views, which will enable us to realize that we all have truth of our own, the foremost truth being, we all belong to the species Homo sapiens" (425).

Beliefs vary in strength, longevity, and sustainability. We believed in change in the recent election in the United States of America and elected Donald Trump. I watched the whole dance in the primaries. Everyone I talked to about it and the media pundits and commentators presented maps and demographics supporting the belief that Madam Secretary Hillary Rodham Clinton would win the election. I am sure that she believed in that too. So when we got the results and Donald Trump was the winner, what did that tell us about the reliability of our belief system? We can believe in what we want to at our free will, but that does not mean that our belief system will predict the outcome of the future. I believe that the sustainability and reliability of a belief system is questionable. Even if we believe 100 percent in an outcome, it can turn into 0 percent. Now, if Madam Hillary Clinton had won, then the outcome would have been 100 percent. It means to me that sometimes we operate based on our instinct rather than our belief system. If I predict something, it may mean that I have worked through some possibilities and have determined the probability of success versus failure. I would say I have a 50 percent chance, which is better than 0 percent. In this situation, my expectations were within my capabilities. I would be able to deal with the successes or failures better than my beliefs. Let me give you an example. In one case, I keep my expectation one yard high, which is way beyond my ability. In the second case, my expectation is one-quarter of a yard. If I had fallen from one yard, chances are it would hurt me more than a fall from one-quarter of a yard. In the second case, it is easier for me to get up and go on to work. In the first case, I would be hurt, I presume, more than I would be in the second case. I will be shy of setting up my expectations according to the norms. The same holds true when I expect much more from others. If our expectations are not met, then we are disappointed and feel rejected.

In a belief system, chances are extreme, and expectations kept within reason are far better than a belief. I learned this from my friend who narrated a story to me about his belief and his expectations. He had plans and desires to visit a country and was led to believe by his best friends and online research that it was the best country to visit. I am sure his expectation were too high. When he visited the country, he was disappointed and blamed himself for spending all the money and time in vain. I asked him,

"You were disappointed that you believed in your friends or that your expectations were too high?"

His answer was both.

"How?" I asked.

He replied that his friends who had visited the country led him to believe in what they were saying, which made his expectations much higher.

If that is true, then our belief system has a direct relationship with our expectations. What if he reasoned it through himself rather than relying on his friends and Internet information? Chances are he would have kept his expectations one-quarter of what they were. Chances are his disappointment would have been less intense and he would not be blaming himself for such a mistake. I believe that if we work through our belief system by experience and cognition, chances are we won't become a victim of our own belief system. We will reason rather than follow it blindly. I have certain beliefs, and depending on those beliefs, I took some chances in my life, which we all do at certain points in our lives. Every time I worked through and thought carefully, my success rate was higher than it was when I jumped into something. If I go in blind, then my success rate is not 100 percent. Feelings and rejections are appropriately consistent with the outcome and results. I am able to deal better when I have processed an action, a venture, an investment, and a future plan, regardless of the outcome of success or failure. If a belief and sometimes blind faith lead to an outcome of failure, I have difficulty dealing with that. I feel bitter, angry, self-critical, and remorseful.

Belief started with the evolutionary process for survival. Let's look at the animal kingdom. A herd of wildebeests migrates with a belief that there are green pastures across the river for survival. They would change the course if they knew that crocodiles are waiting for them to eat. We humans went through that process as our consciousness emerged. We invented tools to kill crocodiles and cook them to eat—rather than them eating us. I am sure some of us were eaten by other animals until we figured out how to eat them rather than be eaten ourselves. If we did not grow out of our belief, we would still be eaten or would have vanished from the face of the earth. Therefore, my belief is that we can eradicate beliefs with our higher cognition, which is done through reasoning. That is how we developed groups and social living. Thereafter, smart humans invented a religion and created a belief system, which became so strong that our genes could not shake it off. So whoever was born in a Muslim family became Muslim, and whoever was born into a Christian one became Christian. The same is true for Hindus, Buddhists, Sikhs, communists, and so on.

Scriptures were developed, and philosophies were created. Myths dominated and became beliefs. Belief was promoted because it became an economic tool to exploit the system at that time and place. The more I got out of it, like power or monetary gains, the more I exploited it. I wanted to create fear among my followers and my group to protect my bounty and power. I thought, How can I do that? I found something called fear of god, and I wrote and preached about it because I wanted to protect my bounty in my absence. I magnified it so much that I left no choice for anyone to challenge that. As my group or common thinkers grew larger, I picked the smarter followers to elevate to a higher rank. Those who remained faithful and followed the beliefs, I rewarded. They did the rest of my job, because I could not do it alone. I created guidelines to be followed. I, along with my faithful, created rituals, which reinforced the belief I blessed them with. Those who questioned and refused to accept my blessed belief were either abandoned or were forced out of the group or sect. Some were killed, and that made my believers and belief stronger. As my power and following grew to the point I could rule, I created rules and regulations to be followed. I declared myself a king of the masses. Without my approval, nothing could be right. I was smart enough to understand the weakness of the masses, and I created means and ways to exploit them to the best degree I could. I failed many times, but the belief was reinvented time and time again. If one belief did not motivate the masses, I introduced the next one. I learned quickly that if a belief is passed on to the next generation, it gets distorted and even becomes stronger. After my death, mostly my immediate family got the power. They were taught to distort reality when the belief is threatened. Being loyal to me, they did anything I told them to do.

As a king, I could have anything available in that time and in the group. I could have as many queens as I wanted. I could have as many children as I wanted to continue my blessed belief. Whoever claimed I was a poised and generous man got a good chunk of my bounty. Who would not do so for money, lust, and power? They were the ones who would beat my drum and made my beliefs legitimate, because I learned fast that without others, I do not exist. Others were the ones who recognized me to be the great king. Now, from a ruler, I became a priest, the blessed soul. Once that happened, the sky was the limit. Once language was developed in written form, volumes and volumes were written about my miracles, since I learned that mysticism and the unknown are more valuable to common followers. I created an undeniable belief system. Some were accepted, and some were rejected and vanished away. I promoted the belief that was more acceptable to ignorant followers. Why waste time on something that may not be sustained? I used as much force as I could to reinforce my belief system. Some of the beliefs I created were accepted; some were created to either appease the masses, and some to annoy my competitors, to weaken them and take over their followers to increase the numbers of my followers.

I made my followers to understand, if you do this, that will happen, and if you do not, this will happen. If this or that happened, I was a spiritual man. Now, even if it happened as a placebo effect of 33 percent, I was still right, because every time, 33 percent of the time, they would multiply the number of times it happened to equal to infinity over time. So what happens to belief when 33 percent becomes infinity? Here is an example of the god.

At this stage of life, who can eradicate God and his power, other than atheists or communists? Three-quarters of humans believe in God. I don't think at this stage of our life, one-quarter has the power to change the beliefs of the rest of believers. Fate is an outside belief that what is supposed to happen will happen, regardless of your efforts, whether it is from a mysterious outside force or your inside developed belief with experience and coincidences. For a wise person who uses the right thinking and right living with cognitive reasoning, fate is like any event in life. For those of us who live with unconscious thoughts and actions, when undesirable events happen, we say, "Well, it was my fate, which means that a cause has happened and operated to produce an effect." For example, if we live a life of heavy drinking and smoking, knowing that they can cause diseases, then when disease happens, we blame it on our fate, rather than realizing and accepting the fact that if we had quit both, we may have at least had a chance of the diseases not happening. Fate is the result of our own karmas and our own deleterious actions and behaviors.

As humans developed their brain memory and problem-solving and prediction abilities, anticipations started emerging. Curiosity created inventions by trial and error. In my group, one day, I found that half of the followers had left to go far away to start their own venture in search of food and the good life. I asked the wise man who advised me occasionally. He told me that this is happening everywhere. When there is too much power and a lack of resources, humans have to search for food and resources to continue the species. He imagined and told me that they are spreading anywhere and everywhere, wherever there are resources. One day, they will be all over the world.

"But who will protect them from wild animals?" I asked the wise man.

"Don't worry; they have their own instincts of survival. The stronger ones will survive. Some will eat, and some will get eaten. They will have their system in place. They will have their group leader who will do almost the same thing you did. They will develop their belief system, which will guide them to survive or vanish. Some will be smarter than others by virtue of their intelligence. Their learning will be infinite, because there is so much to learn. Inventions will guide them to invent more and more. They will never run out of inventions, because they are infinite. They will continue marching to their goal, which again is infinite. They will create more, because creation is infinite. They will develop their own societies, cultures, groups, sects, and religions, and some will trade with each other. Some will conquer others. Some will be good neighbors, and some will tolerate each other. Some will vanish, and some will flourish to the point that they will have dominance in the group. They will be cohesive and learn to work together. Some will have mutual interests, and some will carry on with vengeance. Those who believe in progress and the welfare of others will grow. Those who become greedy will someday self-destruct. Those who realize death is the final destination after the entire journey of life will create their own belief system, which suites them. They will learn how to create art, culture, social norms, science, and medicine to cure their diseases and find their ways and means to be happy after suffering and losses. They will find love, respect, mutual help, understanding, sharing, caring, and altruism and then tolerance, patience, desire for the well-being of each other, nurturing, and respect, and empathy for others will become the norm by trial and error. They will learn love and mutual understanding, which will reward them more than anger, jealousy, aggression, punishment, and harm to others. They will learn not to kill, not to harm, not to steal territory or wealth, not to exploit or take advantage of others, and much more."

I was amazed, startled, ashamed, anxious, and angry, but I understood the wise man's response, which gave me something to ponder. This shook me up, for days and months, until I thought, What I have done wrong? I kept myself away from the rest because of shame, guilt, and feelings of worthlessness and despondency. For days, I was not able to sleep or eat, which made me realize that I have feelings and emotions, so others must have them too. Time flew by fast and furious, without waiting for a moment. This loneliness was a blessing for me. I was able to learn that there is something higher than I that controls everything. Days went by, and months went by without any account, which made me understand there is time, there is value to it, and if I used it properly and productively, the reward could be enormous. I learned my control makes no sense, especially when I heard many of the group members had died because of a lack of food and other causes (diseases).

One fine day, I came out and gathered the courage to address my group to apologize and pass on my experience. "I declare today, after days of isolation, that I have found that there is something higher than me."

There was a sudden calm—then everyone got up and shouted, "Long live the king!"

It went on for a while; I saw the joy and happiness. I saw the strength and sadness was gone. Togetherness was back again with smiles, joy, power, and strength, which echoed everywhere. The wise man beside me addressed the crowd and claimed, "The wind, sun, food and water, mountains, sky, animals, and the group as whole are more powerful than our king."

We all started worshiping these every day in our spare time. Our group flourished again day by day. We had an abundance of food, and we produced more children. The group grew stronger than ever before. We all agreed that it was due to worshiping the wind, sun, food and water, mountains, sky, animals, and the group as a whole. This became our belief, and the belief became the norm of our life in that group. Nobody could shake this in our group, and we lived happily. The wise man developed a protocol, which included worshiping these factors for our prosperity, like meeting frequently and worshiping together as a group, teaching our children about this belief, hunting together, and finding plants to cure diseases and illness. Together, we found that emotionally, we felt strong and happy. Sharing and caring enlarged our group. We started learning about nature and found everything existed in nature for our survival. Only belief could do that, but taking action was essential. Because of that, we kept on exploring and flourishing, and our future generations kept the belief intact, which reinforced the prosperity. This news spread like wildfire in the neighboring group.

One fine day, a wise man from the other group showed up to meet the wise man from my group to learn how they could flourish in this famine-ridden harsh area. The meeting was set up with me; the wise man asked me, "How you could do this?"

I shared my belief and the actions taken according to this belief, which included information sharing among the group members and children. Work, worship, and give to charity became the norm of our group. Monogamy, responsibility for the raising of our children, and respect for our women became the law and order of our group. Exploring nature became the soul of our group—loving, caring, and sharing. Belief became our breath. Aggression, hostility, vengeance, brutality, and hatred were our enemies. The meeting was amicable, and the wise man of the other group left with a friendly gesture of offering us some animals to sacrifice in the honor of this friendship. My wise man refused this offer and gave him enough food to take with him to feed the hungry in his group with an abundance advice and love. My wise man praised my cooperation, the attainment of my belief, and the implementation of it for our group, leading to health, wealth, and prosperity for our group.

The wise man of the other group went back and revealed the entire secret of our success and implemented the same belief in his group. This belief spread like a hurricane to an unknown distance through the neighboring groups—far beyond my imagination. Those who stuck with this belief survived and carried on surviving to this day. News about me and my vision were perceived as miracles. Someone and others wrote about me after forty years, two hundred years, and four hundred years. Every event was described as a miracle with powers to heal and create sanity. My isolation from my group became a symbol of revelation.

As time passed, new wise people were born, and they became curious to find out who I was and wrote about me. Every story was distorted, depending upon the need of the time. This went on until the modern human was born. By this time, there was nothing left to challenge my authority. Belief became the genetic code scripted in the genes of humankind. My principles, my beliefs, and the actions taken to protect my group were glorified to the point that if not accepted, hell was the only answer for their lack of acceptance. I did not know then that it would happen. Who knows what I would have done differently?

I wonder myself, reflecting back on what happened to me when I isolated myself from my group for days and months, according to the modern calendar, because I had no concept of time. I asked myself this question after learning from modern man. Did I have a revelation? If I did have a revelation, then what was it about? Was it that I was malnourished and had a chemical imbalance that caused hallucination? I never mentioned that I heard voices from external sources telling me to do good and be kind to my group. Was it my guilt, remorse, and shame that made me to realize that bad is bad and good is good? Doing good things and good deeds brings forth good results, and others like and accept you better and trust you more. Was it my soul that ordered me to accept defeat and turn bad, empowering behavior into kinder, gentler, more loving, and more caring behavior toward others? Was it my self-actualization and recognition of my self and other selves? Was it a blessing from an unknown external force, which created enough strength in me to face the facts and deal with them appropriately by acknowledging my unacceptable greed and lust for power over others? Was it that I grew wiser with time by learning that cruelty and domination of others to fulfill my desires is not realistic? Was it accepting that there exists more power in nature than I had? Was it incipient belief that turned into mature, full-blown belief, which led to prosperity and welfare for my group members and then spread like a wildfire across the deserted barren land for the welfare of others whom I never knew. I do not know which one was true. Maybe all.

I will ask this question to a new man who may teach me something new. I better not ask this question because they are doing worse than I did and continuing the same. At least I confessed and realized I had to give up my power and trust my belief to continue the prosperity of my group. The new humans are gifted, and their knowledge is beyond my expectation. The inventions they have made are unbelievable. The myths they created, I can never understand. The dominance and control over others they have created is unacceptable to me and my group. Truth is distorted and covered with a sheath of lies. Truth is ashamed to be called truth. The new humans believe in this kind of truth, day in and day out. I call truth a truth and a lie a lie. They disagree with me, because they call it stretching the truth or politics, which I do not understand. They created wonderful beliefs, like "If you vote for me, I will do anything for you." They call it democracy. I asked the wise man in my group what that is; he called it demagoguery, which he explained to me means an appeal to people that plays on their emotions and prejudices rather than on their rational side. This just started to create more curiosity in me and my wise man. I told him we better come back with real and genuine questions so we do not look like fools of the past.

A meeting was set at different parts of the planet to which we all belong; we learned that nobody owns it. Death was the teacher for us. We claimed and believed that a piece of the earth belonged to me or us, which was not true, because when we died, everything was left behind for others to claim. All that was left behind was a fake claim with a nonexistent name and fame. Death is not a belief because it is true, which destroys the belief that is blind and false at times. We went back to our caves and trenches where nature was at its bloom, flowers everywhere, trees lush and green, some in the process of blooming, some blooming, some full of juicy fruits, and lush green grass and shrubs. We had full smiles, while looking at the beautiful full moon. Streams swirled with clean water, hugging the stones and pebbles, making soothing noises without any need, greed, or demands. Birds had their own space in the sky, flying without any restrictions. Some were sitting on the beautiful trees, singing songs, some to mate and some full of joy and entertaining with their talent. Some were dancing, fluffing their feathers and spreading their wings to show their art, strength, and might. I wondered to myself, Do they believe in the bright summer ahead?

Hope and belief are essential ingredients to add spice to our lives. Hope helps us to look forward to having something positive. Hope is a motivating factor in our lives. For example, I am looking forward to seeing you. I am looking forward to starting my new job. I am looking forward to summer arriving; I am tired of winter. The key phrase is looking forward. It's a powerful phrase or a belief, which makes us believe that summer is coming soon. This helps us to ride through the winter and spring without distress or anxiety. Looking forward is a motivating factor for all of us. Imagine when you feel hopeless. It generates negative energy of the soul, which impedes our initiative and impacts our motivation negatively. Hope reinforces the belief system directly or indirectly. Those who lack the capacity to look forward get stuck in their negative thinking and self-derogatory behavior, which can cause depression and negative frames of thinking. An unhealthy way of living is a negative frame. Lack of hope is the worst thing that can happen; it makes people give up and creates doom and gloom. People get down in the dumps. It can feed on itself and cause rumination, which is recurrent negative, obsessive thinking. Those who believe in hope tend to excel in their lives. They may fall or fumble, but they pick up the pieces and move to the next act, action, decision, or venture. As mentioned earlier, I, along with the wise man, am looking forward to meeting with the new humans. Our hopes are high, but I doubt our expectations will be met.

Both of us believe that we will learn a lot from a new man, who is far more advanced than both of us.

I, along with the wise man, went to the Far East in early summer. We were lost in the large crowd of people and saw too many humans, which was overwhelming for us. Poverty was rampant. People were distressed, and hunger was everywhere. Happiness did not exist. Nature was destroyed. There were many classes of humans. Some were outcasts, and some were in the middle, working for rich, happy, and wealthy people. There was chaos and confusion. Women were supposed to burn themselves with the dead bodies of their husbands to fulfill his desires after his death. The sky was brown due to pollution instead of blue. There were no wild animals; they had all been eaten or killed. Rivers were dried up or polluted. There were too many temples everywhere. People were taking food and gold to these temples to enrich the elite ones. They called them gurus. Nothing could happen without the approval of those gurus. Malnutrition and sickness were everywhere. The stronger ones were ruling the weaker ones. Wise people had left the crowd and lived in caves for meditation in search of the self. The streets were full of trash and filth. There was no motivation or desire. Everywhere, there was sadness and hopelessness. The only belief they had was that a higher power would solve their problems. Men would leave women behind with children to take care of and feed. People would get up early in the morning and rush to temples for prayers and to find hope for the day.

Rituals were performed with offerings to their gurus of gold, grains, and vegetables. Humans lived in small mud huts. Horses were used for transportation and for farming. It all depended upon rain. If it rained, everyone could feast. If not, there was famine and the deaths of humans and animals. They had developed a language called Sanskrit. They had developed social skills, but because of their caste system, there was segregation of societies. Jobs were assigned by elites to poor, caste-ridden people. There was a hierarchy among humans. Blessed ones lived a high, prosperous life at the cost of the lower classes.

Our curiosity led us to understand what this was all about. We went to see a colony of untouchables. These humans had the job of cleaning up, including human waste. If anyone touched them, it was believed that he or she had committed a sin. There were humans walking without arms, and some were sitting without legs. They called them lepers. Some had inhuman-looking faces because of leprosy and unknown diseases. Smoke and fire were everywhere. Some people lived under trees, and some slept on the roadside. Nobody would touch them or help them. Some were begging for help and some for food. The second colony was a little better than the previous one. They called it the labor class. The third colony belonged to the warriors. Their job was to fight with intruders or to protect the higher class. The fourth colony was very impressive, and there were lights everywhere, called the lights of devas. Bands were marching, singing songs about superior humans. They were dancing on the street with chanting and the noise of beating drums, praising someone who was superior to all the humans. Everyone was offering food to each other. Nature was beautiful, with manicured gardens. Beautiful women wore garlands of flowers. Smiling and love were shared by everyone. This was the colony of the higher class. We had never seen such a division of humans in our entire lives.

The wise man and I decided to meet the wise men of this land to learn what we were missing. We were led to cave where a wise man who had hidden himself to meditate away from regular human suffering. We were lucky to meet him and to understand where and how far humans have come in understanding themselves. We asked, "Oh, wise man of the East, teach us. We are hungry to know what and how we the humans are doing with ourselves?"

The wise man knew who we were and what we wanted. He started with this statement. "It is all with your blessing who we are and what we do. Without you, we would not be here. You gave us love and misery too. What you saw is what you have given to us. We have to live with that and move on to the next mile of our lives. We believe in soul. We call it atman, which means the eternal self, the spiritual essence. It is not the body you have and the material you have in your possession; it is the self and your soul that will prevail after your death. Atman is the spiritual essence of who I am. It is the atman, which leaves the body and is reincarnated. This is the belief in our religion of Hinduism. Karma is the Hindu belief that the actions of a human will determine the fate of that human. Good deeds in this life will be rewarded in the next life. Those who do bad and evil things will be punished in the next life, which means you will reap what you sow. Dharma is the Hindu faith and a moral force that keeps the world in motion and the universe alive. Every Hindu has to follow the law and order of dharma. It is the duty of each Hindu. Moksha is the final stage of a Hindu. It is the final stage, the liberation of the soul, which blends with the almighty paramatama or super soul. It is the liberation from birth and reincarnation in the process of a Hindu's life." He mentioned the Bhagavad Gita, Upanishads, and numerous other books and Parramattama.

We left the wise man of the East in search of another wise man who believed in Jainism. The wise man described Jainism as an ancient religion dating back three thousand years. He called it Jain dharma. He believes God is the creator and the universe exists on its own, as does everything in it, including the soul. He said that the soul is eternal and has its states, shapes, and sizes; it exists in animate and inanimate objects, like in animals and vegetables, which are underground, and even in bacteria and insects. This religion is very close to Hinduism and Buddhism.

Now we learned that humans in this part of the world had developed religions and believed in them. We met a wise man who educated us about Buddhism. He described it as close to Hinduism with a belief in reincarnation. The difference is that Buddhism believes in rebirth, but a person does not necessarily return to earth as the same entity ever again. For example, when an old leaf falls off, a new one grows. It is not the same as the old one, though it is similar to the old one. After many such cycles of birth and reincarnation, if a person gives up attachment to desires and the self, this leads to a state of liberation and freedom from suffering, called Nirvana. The Buddhist wise man added that they follow three practices: sila, which includes virtue, good conduct, and morality, meaning that all living entities were equal, and when you do good to others, they should reciprocate and vice versa; samadhi, which includes meditation, concentration, and development of the mind, leading to a path of wisdom, good conduct, and control over the mind; and prajna, which means insight, wisdom, enlightenment, and the ability to judge truth from falsehood and have sharp perceptions. Wisdom will only emerge when your mind is pure and calm.

The Buddhist went on, explaining about four truths of suffering in humans. Dukkha means we humans suffer because of loss, pain, sickness, failure, and impermanence (without exception, existence is transient, evanescent. and inconstant). Samudaya is when the desire to have control, which can lead to sensual pleasures, and the desire for fame and to avoid unpleasant sensations, like fear, cause suffering. Nirodha is when the mind feels complete freedom and liberation from attachments. There is a state of Nirvana (which is the end of suffering). Megga has eight paths (349):

1. Discernment
2. Concentration and meditation
3. Mortality
4. Do not kill.
5. Do not steal.
6. Do not lie.
7. Do not misuse sex and others.
8. Do not consume alcohol or other drugs.

We understood about the new path of humans in that part of the world. It looked like they had developed belief in something that we did not know or believe in. It seemed to us that humans had developed some insight about themselves. Some things remained the same. My wise man and I will discuss it at the end of our vast journey. In the meantime, we changed our direction toward the vast desert.

We met a wise man of the desert. He welcomed us and knew who we were and what we wanted to know. This was a tough, ever-lasting, vast desert with no lush green grass and tall mountains, but it had its own beauty. Bushmen were still fighting and killing. Animal sacrifice was a common practice to make the higher power happy. Humans were taller and darker. Sandstorms were frequently blinding our eyes. A few humans were living high while others were living with animals like camels. Barbaric behavior was the norm and expected all the time. Everyone seemed alert, ready to rob and steal. Groups of humans were spread everywhere in the vast desert. The sun was scorching hot during the day, but humans were adapted to such a harsh environment. Small groups had merged with each other with a common belief. The wise man explained to us that they called it Islam, which was summarized to us by the wise man of Islam very patiently. It was a belief in God, which to them meant that their god was the only true god. He had the most magnificent names and sublime attributes. No one shared his divinity or his attributes. God alone was the almighty, the creator, the sovereign, and the sustainer of everything in the whole universe. He was the all-hearing, all-seeing, and all-knowing. He is the most gracious, the most merciful, and the most beneficent. The wise man mentioned the name of Prophet Muhammad and the Koran.

"We call God by the name Allah in the Arabic language. We believe in angels." The wise man told us whoever follows these beliefs is called a Muslim. He added, "Angels worship Allah alone and act only by his command. Among the angels is Gabriel, who brought down the Koran to Muhammad. We believe in God's revealed books. One of them is the Koran, which is protected by God from any corruption or distortion. We believe in the prophets and messengers of God. The last one sent was Muhammad. We Muslims believe in the day of judgment. After death, there will be a day of resurrection, and God will judge us for our deeds and beliefs. Muslims believe that God has given human beings the right to choose right or wrong, and they are responsible for their actions. The belief in divine predestination means God knows everything; he knows what has happened and what will happen, and whatever he wills will happen" (350).

My wise man, after listening to all this, was astonished and amazed. He asked me to continue exploring the new humans and their beliefs and new thinking, but I do not understand anything they say. My wise man laughed and told me, "I will explain everything at the end of our journey."

I agreed, and we continued our journey for an indefinite period of time. We landed on a piece of earth that was beautiful with lush green trees, mountains, and valleys, where the river roared with the mighty strength of waterfalls and nature was respected. Humans were small-statured with small noses. They spread across the vast range of mountains, where animals and birds were free to roam. Humans had learned how to grow food and had flourished in numbers. Because of the abundant food and favorable environment, the population had grown. We hunted the wise man of that land. He believed in Taoism/Daoism, which taught humans that living in harmony with the source, using the source appropriately, and respecting the existence of everything around leads to prosperity. We learned about jing, which means the essence of the physical body; qi, which means matter-energy or life forces, including thoughts and emotions, and shen, which means spirits or generative powers. The wise man of the land mentioned the name of their book as Yijing. It was made clear to us that there was no existence of God. They had developed their own shamanistic rituals, and they did not use or recognize the religion. They appeared to be a different race of humans compared to what we had seen before.

Our quest continued, and we landed on a piece of land, which was strange and cold. Humans were nice, but with cold, frozen rivers, they preferred to stay indoors and developed the means to survive. Animal furs were used to stay warm. Humans were tall and white with blue eyes. We met the wise man of the followers to enlighten us as to what they believed in. The wise man called it the community of Christ and followers were called Christians. They believed in a vast range of events and facts about their lives. Their belief system dictated that they believe in God.

"We believe in one God, who was revealed through Jesus Christ and moves through all creations as a Holy Spirit. All things that exist owe their being to God, mystery beyond understanding and love beyond imagination. We worship him with our heart and soul. No one can take him away from us as long as we live. Jesus Christ is the son of God and savior of the world; he is fully human and fully divine. Through his life, death, and resurrection, God brings the world together and breaks down the wall of division. The Holy Spirit is the giver of life, holy wisdom, and the true God. The spirit moves through the sustained creation, endows the church for its mission, and frees the world from sin, injustice, and death. Whenever we find, love, joy, peace, patience, kindness, generosity, faithfulness, gentleness, and self-control, the Holy Spirit works to attain all that. Creation is an expression of divine love, which explains the belief that God created heaven and earth and everything in them. Everything belongs to God, who sees creation as a whole without separation of spirit and element. God invites everybody with joy to join him in this graceful world. Every human being is created as an image of God, who has blessed us all with the gift to choose whom or what we will serve within the circumstances of our lives. God created us to fulfill our duty to love and care, but some of us deviate from the path of truth and end up committing sin and crimes. Sin is a universal phenomenon due to the separation from God and one another. God forgives us in the event we join him, and with his grace, we are free to love and be part of his goodness. The gospel is the good news of salvation through Jesus Christ, who forgives us of our sins and heals us. He frees us from agony, pain, brokenness, and the power of violence and death. This happens through our faith and full belief in him. Baptism is the final commitment to him to yield our lives to Christ, who accepts us as a part of his community with the promise of salvation. But we affirm that God's grace has no bounds and his love is greater than we know. God wants Christians to believe in companionship with Jesus Christ and for other disciples to serve the world. All will have a revelation affirming that the living God exists and prevails in the entire world. The faithful feel him to be with them all the time. The church of the Jesus is for all humankind to join and create communities. All will be welcomed and brought into renewed relationship with God, and there will be no poor. Scriptures are written through the inspiration of the spirit of God and are accepted by the church as a normative expression of its identity, message, and missions. We affirm the Bible as the foundation for the church and all believers of Christianity. When responsibly interpreted and faithfully applied, scriptures provide us with divine guidance and inspirations and insight into our discipleship. Sacraments are special ministries given to the church to convey the grace of Jesus Christ to his followers and all those he yearns to touch with his compassion. The sacraments are baptism, confirmation, the Lord's supreme marriage, the laying on of hands for the sick, ordination to the priesthood, and the evangelist blessing in these ministries. God sanctifies common elements of creation to bless human life and to renew and form the church to seek the peaceful kingdom of God.

"According to the model of Jesus, ministries are humble services provided to be shared by all the disciples in the world. Some disciples are called by God and are ordained to priesthood offices to serve the missions of the church in specialized ways. The Holy Spirit gives complementary gifts and abilities to all disciples to equip the body of Christ for its witness in the world. The reign of God is the coming triumph of love, justice, mercy, and peace that one day will embrace all creatures. Jesus taught his disciples to pray for the kingdom's full coming and sent them out into the world to be believing emblems of the new creation. There will be Christ-centered communities in families, congregations, neighborhoods, and cities and throughout the world.

"Jesus preached on the name of God that there should be peace, righteousness, wholeness, and the well-being of the entire creation of the universe. The Holy Spirit empowers us for the pursuit of peace and justice. We believe Christ has risen and God is for life, not for death, and will overcome all of those who demean and who degrade the creation and even death. We believe the Holy Spirit will transform all of creation to share in the glory of God. Jesus is the advocate and judge of all living and dead. It is important to know that God cares how we treat everyone around us, like the poor, sick, strangers, and people of different colors, creeds, and nations. Our labor is not in vain; neither is it for those who oppress, dominate, and destroy us. With faith in God, Christ, and the Holy Spirit, we will have peace, love, and hopeful longing" (351).

We learned a lot from the wise man of Christianity, who suggested we meet another wise man of that land who had his own belief system.

We met a wise man who had a belief system he called Judaism. There are thirteen principles of orthodox Jews. Those who do not believe in them

95

are not considered Torah-observing Jews. He referred to Rabbi Moshe ben Maimon, who compiled these principles:

- Belief in the existence of the creator, who is perfect in every manner of existence and is the primary cause of all that exists
- The belief in God's absolute and unparalleled unity
- The belief in neither God's noncorporeality, nor that he will be affected by any physical occurrence.
- The imperative to worship God exclusively and no foreign or false gods
- The belief that God communicates with man through prophecy
- The belief in the primacy of the prophecy of Moses, our teacher
- The belief in the divine origin of the Torah
- The belief in the immutability of the Torah
- The belief in God's omniscience and providence
- The belief in divine reward and retribution.
- The belief in the arrival of the Messiah and the messianic era
- The belief in the resurrection of the dead (352)

Orthodox Jews, including Orthodox Jewish scientists, condemn the theory of evolution and strongly believe that the world was created 5,771 years ago. They believe in creation. The ultraorthodox Jews believe that the Torah is above science. Many of them do not want to even know or may not have heard the name of Charles Darwin. Modern orthodox Jews do believe that the world was created by God (Hashem). The important thing to learn is the belief in the origin of the Torah. It is believed that Torah is a divine work of God (Hashem). The Torah was revealed and given to Jewish people at Mount Sinai in front of a crowd of six hundred thousand Jews loyal to the Torah for the past 3,300 years (353).

After having such an experience, the wise man suggested we travel to a land unknown to us. The people called themselves the Mayans. We had to cross the desert, which was full of cacti and bizarre terrain. Then we crossed the mountains with all their wildlife. Neither of us had ever seen anything like it before. The lay of the land was different, with a different look, shape, and size of humans. They were shorter and darker than the humans that we had seen before.

Their wise man gave us a tour of the land and realized why we were there. He was open and honest, revealing the truth of the land and the humans of that land. The Mayans believed that their rulers could communicate with the gods and their dead ancestors through the ritual of bloodletting. Their belief and common practice was to pierce their tongues or cut them with a stone knife. They fought wars in order to capture high-ranking prisoners who could be sacrificed to satisfy the gods. Mayan kings were the most important priests. They were seen as a link between humans and the gods, and when the kings died, they themselves became the gods. Their belief system was vast, full of rituals, and complicated.

The Mayan landscape has ritual topography, with landmarks, such as mountains, wells, and caves being assigned to specific ancestors or deities. Rituals were governed by the projection of cylindrical models onto the landscape. They had given a day name and number to their specialized shrines in the mountains with the appropriate time for their rituals, which included offerings of maize, honey, liquor, incense, flowers, and cigars to establish new relations with the other world. Their offerings were even buried below the houses. The sacrifices were made by sprinkling the blood of turkeys, deer, dogs, and other animals. Cannibalism was rare, but bloodletting was common. They would cut an earlobe or the tongue, which was burned afterward (354). The Mayans had their own priesthood from local villages. They performed their own specific rituals, which involved the ritual of healing for the sick, like shamans. High priests lived in bigger towns and lower ones in little villages. Mayans believed in self-purification rituals, such as fasting, sexual abstinence, and confession before any rituals and usually before entering into the areas where deities lived.

Sacrifices and offerings were usually before meetings with the holy man. Some used group hypnosis. Pilgrimage was an essential part of the Mayan tribe's lives. They would travel far away to visit designated holy places, and some would even go to nearby villages, which created a social interaction and reciprocal visits. Periodic feasts were held, as were performances with the impersonation of deities, especially by the kings. Feasting was common and sponsored by wealthy men of the village; dances were also very common in this tribe. Mayans created a calendar with a 260-day cycle, which replaced the 365-day cycle other humans created for calculations. Healing was done by performing rituals, which were focused on the retrieval and reincorporation of the lost soul or souls, whose particles were imprisoned somewhere by specific deities or ancestors. Shamanic techniques were used to cure ill people, which varied from tribe to tribe in different villages. Rain dances and other rituals were performed to control the change in weather. They would hunt frequently for animals and dance with deer skulls painted blue.

Territories were marked by shrines. Wars were held during any dispute. Jaguar gods were adorned for any act of war. Kings were the rulers, and the land they owned was called the kingdoms of the kings. Numerology and calendars were believed to log a time unit from one divine unit to the other divine unit.

Astrology was a priestly science resting on the assumption of an influence exerted on the earthly events by the movement of heavenly bodies and constellations. Their observations of the sky and horizon, Mayans relate chiefly to celestial signs of seasonal changes relevant to agriculture. They even believed in the collapse of the sky and subsequent flooding.

The wise man concluded and advised me what would be the future of the new humans.

The new man is far more intelligent than we were. Their intelligence will become a constant threat for themselves and other groups. They will have better tools and inventions for their luxuries in life. Inventions will be infinite for them. They will always look for something new. Their satisfaction will never be fulfilled, and they will compete with each other like we did, but the magnitude of their intelligence will continue to grow to infinity. Contentment will not exist. Hunger, thirst, and lust to conquer other groups will be to the point of extinction of some groups. We did compromise with each other and learned to live together and tolerate each other. We learned to live with the minimum and made the best of what little we had. The new humans will never find themselves happy and satisfied. At times, they will have too much, so that they do not know what to do with what they have, which will lead them to encroach on other groups, steal their beliefs, destroy their belief systems, and impose theirs on the humans they have conquered. They have invented religion, which will be a double-edged sword. It will work both ways, good and bad, right and wrong. When used in the right way, it will develop cohesiveness among them. The rule and order will be appreciated. It will create morality and honesty. Fear of God by itself will create self-regulation and promote best behavior when nobody is around to watch. The belief in God by itself will monitor their actions, attempts, greed, needs, and malicious intent toward other humans and animals. It will create respect and honor for others. This belief will create self-monitoring guilt in cases of malicious harm to others.

The existence of others and self will grow. When good deeds are rewarded, such as good behavior, it will be reinforced and repeated. Guilt, remorse, and self-reflection on bad deeds will haunt them with the belief that God is looking at us and watching us all the time, which will be reconditioned and will reinforce good behavior and good deeds.

Some will learn, and some will not. Belief in God will promote law and order in the humans, which will promote family values and value for others. There will be collective consciousness and collective unconsciousness and tolerance. Love will be enhanced, and this will give birth to karma.

This reminds me of a story about karma. In a small village of now India, there was an honest farmer who needed money to feed his cows. He went to a rich man who lent him some money at a high interest rate with the understanding that if the farmer could not return his money with interest, the rich man would take away his cows. After a while, the farmer paid him what he could but not on time. The rich man took his cows and auctioned them to other farmers. The rich man had exploited almost everyone in that village. One day, the rich man got sick and could not keep up with his exploitation of poor farmers. Slowly and slowly, he lost everything he had. He approached most of the local farmers, but nobody came to his rescue. The farmers had flourished with good weather and the bounty of their farms' products. He was miserable, distraught, and depressed, asking, "I have helped everyone, and nobody is here to help me; what is wrong?"

He went to seek advice from a wise man who was well respected for his good deeds, honesty, wisdom, and timely, sincere advice to all in that village who sought it.

The wise man asked, "Why are you here?"

The sick rich man told him the whole story.

After listening, the wise man asked him, "Have you ever done good and helped anybody in the village without your greed, need, and lust to accumulate wealth?"

The rich man said, "No, never."

"Well, if not, how can you expect the other farmers to help you? You had bad deeds and bad karma, which is haunting you now; it is your own doing. You reap what you sow; your own actions and deeds will pay you back when your turn comes."

"So what should I do?"

The wise man asked him to give up his pride, power, and greed and go and apologize to everyone he had exploited. "I am sure some farmers will help you to get back on in life."

The rich man went to everyone in the village, and the farmers came to rescue him by lending him the money without interest and without any time limit. He thanked everyone and learned the lesson that your karma will follow you wherever you go, no matter how big or how powerful you are. We the cavemen gave the new humans these important things:

- Genes
- Curiosity
- Soul
- Fire

Genes will give them a road map for their physical and psychological shaping while interacting with the environment. There will be constant mutation of their genes, which will change their strength and adaptability to their ecology for survival. Some will adapt to cold, harsh weather. and some will adapt to hot, scorching heat. Genes will dictate who they will be and what they will look like. I was born in Africa, and my color was black. I was tall and full of strength. I wonder what happened to the new humans, because I saw white, brown, and short people. My nose was big, and my lips were broad. I saw new humans with tiny noses and lips. I believe it was due to lack of sun, which changed their color, or it could be a genetic mutation that changed their color, height, and looks. I will find it when I come back in three thousand years to see how they are doing.

New humans will find the answer for themselves. Curiosity is a gift to new humans from us. It will cause them to test and check everything they like or dislike. The magnitude of their curiosity is infinite. New humans will test and learn out of their curiosity to infinity. They will fall and fumble; they will have successes and failures, which will make them learn more and more. With such stimuli, their brain will grow and change with the times, needs, and things to achieve. This curiosity will increase their memory, intelligence, and value of each and every thing. New humans will test the dangerous, harmful, harmless, pleasant, and loving behavior, just to see what this is all about from curiosity. Thereafter, they will learn. With memory, there will be thoughts that will become actions, which produce reactions and retain them. Some of their sensations will grow, and some will fade. Those needed less frequently for survival will weaken.

Their brain will grow rapidly. Those who will use theirs more will find their growth faster. Those will be the inventors among new humans for the future. New humans will discard old things and hold on to new, comfortable inventions. They will use them to the best of their capability. They will exploit anything to their advantage. They will use less energy and get more out of it, while we spent more energy and got less.

New humans will be bound by their beliefs given to them and some forced onto them from the supreme power of the group they belong to, like kings, gurus, saints, and leaders of the religion. This process will continue for a long period of time. The belief system will be distorted. Some will vanish without any trace. Some will become fixed beliefs, some with proof and some without any proof. For example, the earth moves around the sun, and the moon moves around the earth. Myths and mysteries will be used and reinforced by writing and speaking to the followers for gains and at times for exploitation of the followers.

Books will be written with full of mysteries and myths about the dead holy men to convince the followers to believe in them. These books of religion will become the gospel truth for their followers. Saints, prophets, kings, and holy men will be created in written books, which will become the treatise for new humans. Some will question the validity of such books and treatises. Those will become outcasts. Money and wealth will be dispersed to the poor and needy to adopt the principles of such treatises. The sick humans were provided with myths and mysteries of cures until the new man invents new medicines that are proven. These leaders will be called messengers of God for the betterment of the new humans. The treatises will be written to show proof of the existence of God. New humans will be convinced to follow such religions and make them an integral part of their daily life.

Principles will be described for daily life and prayers. New humans will learn to pray to God and to occupy their free time, and they will find peace and tranquility either by placebo effect or by occupying the time away from the daily agony of the stress created by the instinct of survival.

New humans will get structured and conditioned to the daily routines of life, like work every day to earn and feed their families and themselves. New humans will find that morality, truth, sincerity, humbleness, and respect to other believers of that religion are rewarding in the long run. It will create social awareness, and religion will flourish and grow. For some, it will become a blind faith, which will enhance the blind belief in the need to avoid distress and anxiety about life and death. Work, worship, and giving to charity will become the norm of their lives and to run an organized religion. Over time, more than 15,000 religions, sects, and organized groups will be created by the new humans. They will learn fast that religion is the best way to create a business; some will treat it like a business and gather fortunes for themselves. New humans will learn fast that the power of suggestion can influence others who are sick, poor, and needy. They will be easy prey to such organized groups to profit from. New humans will learn that building exotic buildings and monuments where worshipers will gather will attract more and more followers. Such monuments will have everlasting glory in the life of a new human.

Poor and skilled humans in that group will be used to create such magnificent and glorious monuments with carvings and figures depicting the glory of their god. These architectural marvels will be declared as sanctuaries of their god, where humans will pray and gather en masse. They will donate valuable metals, like gold, until valuable currencies are created. Holy men will have exclusive rights to continue such ventures and expand as the number of human followers increases and revenues are abundant. There will be competition among religions. Who is the best, and who has the power and wealth to expand? Powerful ones will dominate and grow. They will have a belief that the more they have, the more they want to increase power and might to control human capital. The weaker ones will get weaker, and some will vanish along with their belief systems, which to me means that belief systems can change and vanish according to the needs of the time and adverse conditions prevailing at that time. Survival of the fittest will become the norm of the new humans; stronger ones will get stronger and thrive. New humans will develop tools and lethal weapons to conquer other religions. I will call these war and wars of religion with the passage of time. Those who develop the lethal weapons, better than sticks, stones, and swords, will rule the rest of them or will be killed or will merge and adopt the belief system of the ruler. Some will run away hoping to survive. Some will perish, never to be seen again. Those who challenge the authority of the belief of their religion will be tortured to the point of submission, or they will be killed with the gunpower. Spoken and written language will become the common denominator of spreading the news and miracles and the belief system, which will strengthen the religions. This process will continue forever, I presume.

The curiosity of new humans will be diversified. Some will focus on inventions and learning new things about nature because everything existed way before new humans found it. For example, the law of gravity existed way before Newton found it; light, fire, oxygen, water, metals, magnetic energy, the soul, the solar system, and every form of energy existed before new humans found them. Those who found and stumbled upon them got the name and fame with their tests and the passage of time. Some of the new humans who stumble on things against their religious belief will be killed and tortured. They will be punished by holy men and their organizations to protect their fixed, unrealistic beliefs. No one will ever exist or has existed to challenge the belief of the religion of that time, which I call a holy belief—for example, the death sentence handed over to Copernicus, Aristotle, and many more. We will never know from the holy men of the religion who created the belief system of that time—the unrealistic and unfounded belief that the earth is flat. The idea that the moon circles around the earth was dismissed, and a death sentence was handed over to the one who changed such belief, though the fact is the earth was round and circled the sun way before it was claimed.

Some new humans may ask me where curiosity came from. It was handed over to us through our genes, and it became the function of our magnetic energy created by the neurons of our brain through the stimulation generated by our sensory system, like vision, by which we see, hearing, or the sense of smell by which we can tell what and where something is, through our sense touch, by which we can feel what something is.

Curiosity is the form of our magnetic soul's energy, which creates thoughts. Our thoughts create actions, and our actions produce results, which are stored in the form of memory and magnetic energy of the soul. Upon our needs, such energy is available on demand to take action and produce results we have to live with or without. The decision is made or to be made by the magnetic energy of the neurons of our frontal lobe (explained in detail in the chapter on the subsoul). Curiosity found fire, which existed before in the sky, the mountains, the ocean, and all around us in the form of lightning and lava. This was a monumental discovery by the new humans. It was a revolutionary discovery through investigation or by mere accident, I don't know. All I know is that it existed way before life ever existed on the earth or in the universe. Some have claimed and will claim that there is a form of fire called electric current, which was instrumental in creating life from a soup of amino acids that existed in the ocean or water. I will find it and learn about it in the future, thousands of years from

103

now. Fire changed the life of new humans by cooking the undesired food into a palatable, delicious taste, by denaturing the tough carbohydrates, proteins, and fats, which had great influence on our evolution and the mutation of our genes.

Once the digestive system of humans adapted to cooked food, our life expectancy increased, not only by the change of taste and learning to use the abundance of food products never known before, but also by killing the bacteria, viruses, and other noxious infectious agents, which caused diseases. Cooked food changed the entire physiology and anatomy of humans; I would say that if cows had invented cooking they would not have to have cud and regurgitate the food to chew it for digestion. They would not have remained cows; they would be like a new intelligent person in the society of new people who will write theories about evolution and provide the proof of evolution of new humans. I would say you did not invent fire; it existed way before your curiosity stumbled upon them. This reminds us of the ancient men and Rishis of so-called India, who said it as it was, with all the knowledge expressed in the Bhagavad Gita, Upanishads, and other books written about the philosophies of Hindus. Knowledge existed way before they found it and wrote about it. Curiosity and the fire provided the ingredients, which enhanced the energy needed for our brain and body to grow in an efficient way to adapt to a new way of life. It also contributed to an increase in our intelligence by increasing the growth of our brain in size and shape to accumulate and store the knowledge at a rapid pace, which enhanced the new curiosity to venture out more, take more risks, and learn from them, which led to efficiency and use of caution when needed. Caution and efficiency became the dominant forces to be effective without the constraints of time. Curiosity and caution led to the exploitation of fire. New humans looked for new things, like metals, which existed in abundance in on the earth. They stumbled upon them and with trial and error learned about the use of such metals. Humans learned by process of elimination to shape the metal to float the sheet of metal in the vast water of the ocean, after floating on a piece of wood to cross the rivers. Humans will learn to fly the metal by creating the size, shape, and structure using fire. Fire revolutionized the creation of new things and objects beyond the imagination of the new humans themselves. They used fire to create machines for their convenience and learned about commerce and trade. Various goods, machines, and tools were exchanged with other groups of humans for goods needed by the group of humans for themselves. Humans will learn how to protect themselves and the group as a whole by developing tools to destroy others and defend themselves from aggressive animals and groups of other humans based on the principle of fire. Humans will put fire to the ultimate test.

Fire was not only used to scare and keep animals away, but could be used in any form of energy require to produce effective and powerful results to achieve what was desired. Humans will learn how to hunt and kill animals from a distance without having close contact, which will cause a decrease in mortality, based on the principle of fire.

Frustration and distress caused by failures made new humans think about emotions and feelings. Restful days and nights made them feel comfortable and tranquil, which made them think that running after material things and the constant urge to achieve more and more are not the ultimate answers to life; after they saw sickness and death in their families and peer groups, it made them think about mortality, and they realized there is more to life then curiosity and fire. From thoughts, they developed the thought process, which when it runs amok causes very uncomfortable feelings, with loss of sleep, appetite, and unknown fears haunting them without knowing what they are. Sadness, anxiety, insecurity, guilt, remorse, and a sense of worthlessness started erupting day after day with occasional tears rolling down their faces. They collected them on the petals of beautiful flowers just to see what they were; those looked like beautiful droplets of rain. They tasted them to feel what they were. They tasted like salt and blood. They smelled them, and they smelled like their own bodies. They felt relieved after they stopped rolling down their faces, which became a mystery to be solved.

The quest to know and learn continued. Some came early, some slowly, and some remained a mystery for their entire lives. This was the time when the new brain started developing at a fast pace. We call it the neocortex or cerebrum. The external stimulus was so much that the new human had difficulty keeping pace with the connection between the limbic system and cerebrum.

Neurons and dendrites increased in numbers, and synapses kept forming new connections and relaying messages from one part of the brain to the other quickly and creating thoughts in fractions of seconds. In this process, new humans continued exploring and storing information. The frontal lobe became the executive center, and the old-brain-like sensations started diminishing and decreasing in their intensity as new humans started

105

using the limbic system to process the emotions and cognitive functions. In layman's terms, new humans started using their head instead of their hands. This must have been a frustrating and amazing time in the life of new humans. There must have been millions of questions to figure out what is going on with them and why. This must have been an exciting time of life to feel the feelings and emotions. Old things must have appeared vague and useless. It must have been gratifying to know that new things are there. Things appear to make sense, like a little child when he or she grows wants to touch everything around and wants to put everything in his or her mouth to test. How great it is when a child learns to walk, talk, and run. How great it is when a child learns to speak and demands the things he or she wants. How great it is for a child to remember things and repeat them. I wonder and cannot explain. Were new humans happy, sad, excited, angry, or anxious. As time passed, they got more confident and contented with the gift of their brains.

One day, a new human man decided to go and hunt by himself and saw a saber-toothed tiger snatching a baby from a bison herd. He was amazed to see the emotional reaction of the mother bison. She fought until exhaustion and kept looking with sorrow and helplessness. The new human learned it was a great loss and emotional trauma for the bison mother. He went to his cave and picked up his son, and out of the blue started kissing him and hugging him. His baby was happy and very comfortable with contented looks and frowning faces as a gesture of love. This day, kissing and hugging was born in this new human's life, which got stronger and stronger and became everlasting. It felt very rewarding to him, which stimulated his limbic system and frontal lobe to grow faster and store that emotional energy in the form of the magnetic energy of his soul. This event created the thought, and he showed affection and gestures to the new human woman and her response was unbelievable in return. The foreplay and sex were beyond his expectation. This was the day he learned that passionate love is gracious and full of joy and pleasure. He extended his affection to his groupmates, and again, the response was beyond his expectations. This was the day he gave birth to social interaction and love. He continued such practices, and the rewards were phenomenal. He held on to those, which enhanced the growth of his brain parts just mentioned. Every day's and every year's thoughts increased, and with that came the worries.

Once the new human went hunting and hid himself in the bushes, watching carefully. He saw a saber-toothed tiger trying to catch a baby elephant. He was surprised to see all the elephants attacking the saber-toothed tiger, to the point they almost killed it and it ran away, limping with its one leg broken. He thought to himself, What if we get tighter and hunt together? He went home empty-handed and told the story to his groupmates. They agreed to hunt together, and then all of them were successful and never went hungry for a day. They were able to produce more children and grow closer. They learned that sharing is key to mutual success and beneficial to the whole group. This was the day altruism was born, which gave birth to collective and social strength. It was much stronger than a single man; thereafter social norms were created and trust bonded them together, which was registered in the frontal lobe and hypothalamus region of the brain, which grew with leaps and bounds.

One day, he went with his female partner and his baby to drink water and was excited to see his reflection in the clear blue water pond. He turned and looked at his child and female partner and then looked at the water and saw their reflection. He started yelling and dancing to figure out what that was. He looked in the water and saw the same child and his female partner, because he had never seen himself. He had seen them all the time, but it was different. He touched himself many times and saw himself touching his face to feel if it was real or just a dream. Sure enough, he felt it was real. This was the day his occipital lobe was connected to his frontal lobe and midbrain, which could differentiate and recognize himself, others, and process the reality. This gave birth to the self and others. Now his limbic system's frontal lobe and occipital lobes were connected and worked together in harmony whenever needed. What a wonder in his life! He could see himself and recognize others. These small milestones would keep growing to an extreme in the future human. He started becoming self-conscious and conscious of others. His brain's neurons were firing the electric current to stimulate other parts of the brain to grow faster because of excessive stimulus from outside environments, which were partially perceived. His genes were triggered and wanted him to master the concept of life, which was beyond his reach. Time was on his side to achieve whatever his genetic mutation dictated him to be. All he could do was keep trying and learning as he went.

One fine morning, the sun was ready to rise, and he could hear birds singing and leaves rattling due to the strong wind. All of a sudden, he heard screams from his female partner, who was in agony and distraught due to labor pains. She was ready to deliver the baby. All the new human could do was be there and watch and hold on to her. He could feel her pain and could do nothing. Tears rolled down his face because of her agonizing pain. There was a sense of empathy and deep-seated desire to help her. All of a sudden, he felt his heart beating fast and felt restless. He was irritable with a dry mouth, with fear of losing his partner. His eyes were wide open, and the hair on his body was erect. He felt confused. He held her in his arms to make her more comfortable, reassuring her that she had his support and protection by touching and even kissing. This was the day his sympathetic and parasympathetic nervous system was connected to the limbic system and to the frontal lobe. What a new tool to work with. Now all of his senses could talk to the frontal lobe and make some decisions. It was a blessing in disguise. He would realize that this came with a prize. Nothing is free in nature or in real life. He would feel more stressed, anxious, and nervous, and he would be easily startled with feelings because of the effects of fight or flight. After excruciating pain, she gave birth to a baby girl. All said and done, the mother picked up her pieces and was full of joy. She expressed her love, care, and protection for her newborn baby. He could not comprehend how it was possible that she was in such pain and agony, but now she was caressing and feeding the baby with joy and contentment. She seemed to him to be happy and as if having achieved the goal of her life. He scratched his head to figure it out. His frontal lobe ordered him to reflect back and go back to the imagination of the time he was born. It reminded him of his mother in pains of labor while she was pregnant with him. He had storms of emotions and the thunder of recollections. This is what my mother went through. This was the day his memory was born, and he could relate to the birth of the baby of his partner. This was the day he had the capacity to think and relate his birth to the newborn baby's. This was the day his cognitive functions were born. They kept growing with experiences, sufferings, pain, and pleasure. He experienced them again and again, which reinforced the cognitive functioning with the passage of time.

Humans never stopped venturing out and kept exploring the environment all around them. With the development of cognition and memory, the sky was the limit. One fine morning, the group humans went hunting and came across a pack of wolves. They were all hiding in the bushes, watching carefully what was going on. They hid together and were amazed to see that the pack of wolves were chasing a single wolf, who was running until he could no longer run and gave up and lay on the ground with gestures of submission. The wolves did not kill him or harm him. Everyone in the group was surprised and amazed to see that submission was the key to avoiding harm to the individual. The group thereafter would submit to each other and resolve any conflict. This was the time for submission to prevail forever in humans. This experience changed the anatomy and physiology of the connections between the amygdale and the frontal lobe forever with the passage of time. The amygdala is associated with aggressive responses in humans and animals, while the frontal lobe is associated with reasoning, cognition, and many more functions in humans. It is highly developed in humans. This learning event created the surprise part of the emotions of the human beings.

While continuing their hunt, they were confronted with thunderstorms, lightning, and heavy rain, which made them realize that all this came from above, from the sky. They looked up and developed a sense that there was something up there that controlled everything, like life, death, and prosperity, which created a belief in a supernatural force. They had no power to control anything. After the rain fell, they saw a raging mountain with an eruption of fire in the sky. The tremors were shaking the ground and trees. A boulder rolled down the small hill. This was a terrifying experience, which reinforced the concept of fear and danger. They still had not made any kills, which gave them knowledge of patience. It was not easy or comfortable; this was how patience became the reasonable part of their lives and of the social group. After the rain and the storm stopped, they went on with their venture of hunting in the plains.

Before they could hunt, they saw a gruesome scene. A group of saber-toothed tigers were hunting in a pack. They were all over a giant woolly mammoth. Finally, they were able to get it on the ground. They watched very carefully and observed that there was a hierarchical system in this group of saber-toothed tigers. After killing the mammoth, a big male saber-tooth was the first one to fill his belly. After that, the rest of the pack was free to share the bounty of their hard work. This stirred the curiosity of a group leader, who would command the leadership and lead with a cohesive force. This was the time for humans to accept leadership, risk, reward, persistence, and perseverance and for the future of that group to ensure success and law and order and to gain wisdom, which would guide them for the future generations.

They got enough food for their group. Since dawn was setting in, the journey back to home was called for. Because family and little ones were waiting for the food. On the way home, they had another learning experience. They saw a pack of baboons, jumping and running around, except one mother, whose baby lay on the ground. She was trying to wake him up. She was sniffing and turning the body of the baby again and again but all in vain. More of them gathered around the baby, sniffing and touching him to wake him up with no response. Suddenly, the pack leader screamed with the signal of danger. The mother baboon picked up the body and ran to the woods.

They reached home and fed the group. Thereafter, a strong man with some knowledge of the terrain was nominated to be the group leader. He shared the experience of the baboon monkey and her dead baby. Everyone paid attention to the group leader and learned about death, respect, and disposition of the dead body, even if danger lurked around. At this stage of life, humans learned and believed in death and respect for the dead. Thereafter, all the knowledge and experiences were shared with the group, which grew stronger and stronger. This stimulated the growth of our new brain to store infinite information and process it in a fraction of a second. This went on and will continue to infinity.

Humans kept on growing their knowledge at a faster pace with time and the changing environment of the surroundings. As the concept of self and others grew, the worries, anxieties, and sense of attachment to the family, group, and belongings grew stronger too; this came about with certain sufferings, which led them to look for cures in the jungles, investigating all the plants. They preferred the fruits and plants that monkeys ate and survived on. Besides that, they kept looking for medicinal plants, which at times were poisonous and at times relived their anxiety, making them high so they forgot the worries of the past. Some plants made them feel happy after they went through a spell of depression. This was the era of drugs and their use versus abuse. Life went on, always with new inventions and the growth of the human brain, behaviors, and emotions. This and more went on for millions of years.

My wise man and I decided to leave humans here and visit them in a few thousand years.

Belief in the modern human's world has expansive elaborate explanations and meanings. Personal attitude is associated with true or false ideas and concepts. Some have described it as a simple form of mental representation, which creates conscious thoughts. The beliefs are the collective perception of fundamental truths governing behavior. The adherence to accepted and shared beliefs by members of a social system will likely persist and are difficult to change. Some justify beliefs with their own beliefs, whether they are real or not to others. For example, one person may believe in witches and ghosts, and children believe in Santa Claus.

In psychiatry, we learned that some of us use a defense mechanism called internalization, which begins at childhood. I used to sit down with my father while I was growing up and recite prayers written in the holy book of the guru Granth Sahib. Over time, it became a defense mechanism to believe in what I was taught about a belief. Nobody could change it or steal it away from me, though I always liked when somebody else followed the same idea as I did. Psychiatrists use the term an oral incorporation, which means we have interjected an object or a belief that has become an integral part of our thinking. It is hard to get these ideas out of our system. Beliefs can be changed in some cases by the believer weighing the set of truths or evidence against an alternative, which can revise the belief. There are several ways to change the belief of an individual or group of individuals by persuasion and by raising consciousness about unrealistic beliefs. An activist or a politician can change the view of some individuals. Even the experience or outcome or failure could modify the belief and replace it with a more realistic and practical one. For that, cognition and thought processes are essential.

Once the changed belief brings on success and positive outcomes, the individual will repeat his or her action, depending on the adopted belief. If success is achieved, the conditioning of behavior or behaviors takes place. Old ones are gradually deconditioned. Stephen Pirie (356) eloquently describes the belief system as an autopilot. You automatically take it for granted. Your autopilot makes you to do what you do and is the root source of all the wonderful things in your life—love, fun, money, and the pleasant surprises, as well as all the drama, conflict, frustration, stress, and other negative situations. Some examples, as per Stephen Pirie are the following:

- Eating healthy foods will bring me good health.
- Smoking is bad for your health.
- Earth is round, and the sun circles around the earth.
- Money can't buy me happiness.
- Money can buy me happiness.

- Men who wear beards are untrustworthy.
- Women who wear makeup are shallow.

The list goes on and on. There is no end to it. In my view, the belief system does not exist in a vacuum or come from thin air. There are neurophysiological mechanisms behind the scene, some of which we understand and some that remain mysteries to be solved. We learned this from scientific studies of schizophrenic patients and psychosis due to any cause, like psychotic depression, bipolar disorder with psychosis, and organic disorders (delirium, Alzheimer's disease, drug-induced psychosis, and head trauma). The simple explanation is based on an increased level of dopamine and aspartate and decreased levels of serotonin at the synaptic junction, which causes alteration of the electric current and leads to delusions. Such delusions are defined as false beliefs about an external reality that are firmly sustained despite counterevidence and rational counterargument (357). Both argue that this may be the accepted definition of the delusions. Sometimes, they may come true. For example, a patient has a delusion that Miss X is in love with her or him. He or she may fall in love with Miss X, and then the delusional belief is true. Well, this is rare but possible.

My experience with patients after years of private practice of psychiatry is that this is rare. If it does occur, it usually happens in the case of shared delusional disorder. In such cases, both partners have a common delusion, which becomes a way of life for them. Some are able to live with the delusion for their entire life, as long as it does not interfere with day-to-day normal factions of their work and the social norms of their culture. For example, a couple who lived together thought that eating raw broccoli prevented cancer. All they did was make sure they ate broccoli every day.

One of my patients believed he was a dog and would walk like a dog and eat like a dog. I asked his mother why he had developed corns around his knees with thickness of the skin on his knees and on his hands.

The mother replied that he believed that he was a dog and he walked with his four limbs for the last thirty years. This was a real delusion, which is a false belief due to his mental illness. He was diagnosed as having schizophrenia.

One of the patients believed that the FBI was taping his phone conversations, while another believed that he was controlled by the aliens. These delusions caused his inability to function in a normal social setting because of the unacceptance of such beliefs, which interfered with his functions, like having a job, having a relationship, and having trust in others. He had a fear of being abducted by aliens and being investigated by the FBI.

Many neuroscientists have used functional magnetic resonance imaging to study the brain functions of these patients. Their conclusions are a malfunctioning of the frontal lobe, temporal lobe, and limbic system, with possibly more to be known. I am of the opinion that there is certainly some neurological and physiological basis of a normal belief system. There could be levels of dopamine, aspartate, and serotonin that are not enough to cause psychosis but enough to cause a belief system that becomes an integral part of our cognition and memory; therefore, we act on them, and when we have positive results, these beliefs become part of our behavior because of a conditioning mechanism that reinforces learned behavior and belief systems. I would add to such a hypothesis that abnormal neurochemical stimulation causes abnormal electric current for the transmission of the information among our neurons, which in turn causes abnormal generation of a magnetic field in our brain. The higher neuronal functioning causes an abnormal or normal belief system, depending on the strength and the nature of the magnetic field generated. I call the magnetic field the soul; therefore, my view stands firm. I postulate that the belief system is the function of our soul in the form of magnetic energy, which is with us twenty-four/seven and the rest of our lives, availed on demand at any time, anywhere we want. We want it at will, and it is there and will be there with us. all we need is to trigger our thoughts, since belief started with a thought.

CHAPTER 5

MEDITATION AND THE SOUL

t was one of the hot days in summer, a Friday, and I came home with a
full day of scheduled and all-day events. We had many incident reports
to write and a meeting in the hospital because one of the patients of our
unit had killed his wife and himself. The news was everywhere, since that
patient was discharged from the hospital three weeks ago. I went home,
and my older son came running up to me.

"Daddy, Daddy, I want you to see what I learned today."

Well, though I had had a stressful day, I had no choice but to listen
to him. He had learned meditation. His demonstration looked like to me
it was never going to end. While he was sitting with his eyes closed, I ran
to my bedroom to change out of my monkey suit to more comfortable
clothes. Sure enough, when I came back, he was somewhat upset. After
cooling him off, I spent some time with him to understand what he had
learned. He started all over again and kept going until it was suppertime. I
was fascinated by his enthusiasm and his belief, which was created by his
teacher. I was intrigued by his suggestion, "Dad, you should do it every day,
and you will never complain about your work." He must have heard me
complaining about my work.

I was aware of meditation, it being an integral part of Indian culture, and
was trained in psychiatry, but I did not know what it did or how it worked.
I researched online and found amazing work done by different programs

developed in universities to use it as an adjunct therapy in different sets of patients. My interest developed, and I learned that we have to have a certain set of rules, which were described in Jon Kabat-Zinn' s book Full Catastrophe Living, which to me looked like a big book with 640 pages. It gives an extensive description of meditation and the wonders it has done for humans with programs like Mindful-Based Stress Reduction (MBSR) at Massachusetts General Hospital. There were numerous articles written in psychiatric journals about adjunct treatment of psychiatric patients and their effectiveness when used with medication. This became my personal treatment for rough and tough days of my routine, days of private practice. As I grew into it, I wanted to explore more and share my experience with others in my book, which mainly explains our soul and its structure, physiology, anatomy, and functions.

Meditation became a norm of my life, and I learned that meditation is one of the mechanisms to go from the exterior to our interior, which works through our soul. So I decided to write and explain it as I understand it. Kabat-Zinn's book is a treatise and the gospel for my research and for writing this chapter. I feel honored to use him as a reference. I start this chapter by understanding what meditation is all about and how it integrates with our processes of soul, which is extensively discussed in the rest my of book. Meditation requires the following:

- Being nonjudgmental, paying attention to changes from moment to moment and gradually adjusting with the new ways of thinking. If you have driven conclusions that meditation is not going to work for you, then you have already judged the onset and outcome. Once you feel the change, your judgment automatically alters.
- Patience. Patience is a pretty thing, especially in stressed patients. We want quick results and quick responses. Patience is a part of our wisdom. If we are wise enough, then we do what is good for us. Wisdom tells us to meditate, which enhances wisdom itself. People who lack patience tend to be prone to stressful situations and overreact to trivial situations. Meditation takes time. Results grow inch by inch to reach the desired goal.
- Attitude. It is very important to understand that a positive attitude creates positive results, and a negative attitude causes negative results. Some of us have our own beliefs and our own lifestyles, with some biases of our own, which could change as we go through

the process and have some control over our feelings and emotions. It not only applies to our attitude but also to how we value others. Once you get hold of your attitude, you could apply it to your relationships with a fresh outlook. The fact is, your mind and brain are all that you have. They possibly could be at peace even in difficult times. Being wisely selfish and being selfless can be the same thing. There are centuries of anecdotal studies and testimonies on this point. There is no doubt about that. How one uses one's attention moment to moment largely determines what kind of person one becomes.

- Commitment. It applies to anything in your life. For example, you joined medical school to finish one day. You joined the army and are committed to fulfill your honorable duty assigned to you. If you do not fulfill your commitment in medical school, no harm is done; nobody is going to punish you or terminate you from medical school. It is your own loss of the benefits of meditation if your do not meet your commitment.

- Honesty. Whatever you do in your life, it is better to have an honest approach; being honest with meditation is a good approach. It will teach you to be honest with yourself, since it is for you and nobody else.

- Acceptance. It is an integral part of meditation. You have already accepted yourself for whoever you are, but obviously, you may have some doubts about yourself. Meditation gives you a chance and tools to look inside of yourself from outside of your own perceptions. If you have pain, accept the fact that you have pain. If you are obese, then accept the fact that you are obese. Acceptance is the recognition of the facts about oneself. Meditation will help you to resolve your defense mechanisms, like denial, rationalization, isolation, and many more. Acceptance does not mean you have to give up your principles. What it means is whatever your need is, your recognize it and accept it. That will help you to move forward.

- Attention. It is an essential aspect of meditation; we are all used to paying attention to others, like family, friends, our job, and so on. They are all important, but there is something called you, me, or I, who deserves equal attention. Without your well-being, others will suffer too. Your good life spreads the fragrance of your rosy life to others. Paying attention to yourself does not mean you

116

ignore others; as a matter of fact, you teach others how well you feel and are contented with your life. You become a role model for their inspiration. I had all the excuses for not having time for myself while in private practice. I finally figured out when to meditate. I would spend some time meditating right before going to sleep and would have sound sleep. If you do so, you will wake up fresh and ready for a productive day. Attention is not only an act of meditation; it is a process of meditation. Those of you who started for the first time must have experienced that your brain wanders in a million directions, and it is hard to hold on to a focused thought. I had the same problem, thinking about what went on whole day in the hospital, in my office, with the family, and paying bills. I thought about meetings and work the next day. It went on some weeks; finally, something told me, "This is nonsense. What is supposed to happen? Tomorrow will happen, so what is the point of punishing myself." Reasoning crept through my mental processes. I started paying attention to what I focused on; usually, I would take myself to Virginia Beach. We have to do what we have to do. For some, it is easier to say that we in Western culture focus on material things. Why not? It is simply true that if I do not pay my water bills, I cannot use the bathroom. I can eat and drink all I want, but if my bills are not paid on time, I am on the streets. To have a good quality of life, you have to pay. Nobody from Eastern philosophy will pay my bills, even though they think we are materialists. But after having done what you have to do, pay attention to yourself, because you are the only one for yourself. The rest of them are others. They have to do what they have to do. As you progress in the process of attention, you will be surprised to see how attention changes the neurochemical and neuroanatomical structures, which I will discuss as we go along.

I mentioned that meditation is cold ice water to erupted lava. What did I mean by that? My friend read that, and he did not like it. He explained that there are fumes, smoke, fire, fog, thunder, and vapors all around. When there is volcanic dust, it is horrible sight. "How can you make such an analogy to meditation," he asked. "It is a minor action and situation compared to the mammoth event of volcanic eruption. He advised me to delete this comparison, because I could not justify to readers giving this example. I listened very carefully and smiled. My friend is well educated, well rounded, and comfortable in his life. I know him well and his past.

I asked him, "How did you feel when your father died? And how did you feel while you were going through your divorce?"

He went on describing his experience of anger, distress, confusion, agony, pain, sleepless nights, unhappiness, vengefulness, worry over financial losses, disbelief, distrust, physical pain, the pain over the loss of his relationship with his loving daughter, the stress of attorney's fees and lawsuits, the pain of losing his beautiful house, and the list went on, until he realized why I had asked him this question.

"How did you deal with that?" I asked.

He replied, "I had to see a therapist, and my doctor prescribed lots of medications for sleep and depression. He finally paused and asked me, "What do you think?"

I answered, "Your volcanic lava erupted, and your confusion was due to the lava. Medications did help you to cool off. Meditation and paying attention to what was going on around would have cooled the eruption of your volcanic lava." I suggested to him, "You still carry the scars of the pain and loss. Go and start meditation. Your scars will be gone, and your tormented soul will heal in the rest of your life, but make sure you pay attention to what you are doing."

Three years later, he started enjoying the beauty of life, sharing his life with a loved one. He realized the truth in my analogy of the cooling effects of water and ice on the erupted volcanic lava. This reminds me of a great wise man of the east, Baba Bulleh Shah (1680–1758), a Punjabi Sufi poet. I have translated his words into English. Sometimes, it is hard to express them exactly, but I will do my best.

You read and read; you search and search till,
    You become a scholar, learned and wise a man.
    Then you keep searching and reaching for the highest things,
    Which are beyond your reach high up in the sky and around you,
    But you never tried to enter inside of yourself and catch the one who is within you
    Waiting, for you to catch him or her (soul)

This is what happens to those who are either afraid or never pay attention to their inner world. That is their way of life, and they choose their path on which to lead their lives. To them, I would say, self-awareness is the most important thing to understand. When we have our eyes open, all we see are externals and others, and when we are asleep, we see nothing but dreams. I tell them a lot that when they are awake, nothing else tells them about them. Who are they? Unless their inner eyes open, they remain ignorant of themselves. Meditation is a tool to look deep into the inner self.

- Authenticity. When you have a fear of meditation, look to your belief or faith, because meditation has no religion, no color, no caste, no creed, and no worldly name fame or wealth. It is free for all. Nobody owns it. You are the only one. This will help you to overcome your fear and defenses, like generalization and rationalization, to avoid acknowledging anger, guilt, shame, violent thoughts, deviant desires, greed, and need.
- Will. All humans have the free will to do or not do. Meditation should be a free choice. Those who meditate freely will be blessed with the glory and bounty of it. Let your free will be the master and guide for you to find your inner peace at will. The only savior is our willpower. Will is the only button that controls everything in this universe. If you don't exercise your willpower, you will be a weakling, easily influenced by your environment. The development of willpower is the only secret of our magnetic soul. Men and women of success are have great willpower. When you develop willpower, no matter how you are pounded down by life, you rise again and say, "I am successful! I can win!" Suppose you tell yourself, "Now, today, I will find time to meditate." Do it. Sit for at least a few minutes. The next day, resolve to stay a little longer in meditation, and the next day, inspire yourself to clear obstacles. Make a little effort. Accomplish something by your will. That is how your magnetic soul gets stronger and stronger to enjoy the tranquility of the meditation.
- Thoughts. Meditation is food for thoughts. When you meditate, your thoughts are rational and free of anger, vengeance, aggression, corruption, and evil acts, which leads to rational desires. Rational desires lead to rational actions, which create rational results, soothing your soul. This leaves you anxiety free, painless, and

pleasant with no guilt or shame. Oh man! Instead of thinking how to relate, fulfill the first requirement. Meditate, and then relating will arise out of it on its own accord. You become one who is silent and blissful, one who starts having overflowing energies, becomes a flower, who has to relate. It is not something you have to learn to do. You start relating to people, animals, and nature. You can relate to earth while you are walking. You can relate to the beauty of the moon and the stars. You can relate to the ocean when you are swimming. You can relate throughout your life to whatever you want to relate to.

- Perceptions. Some have false perceptions of themselves or of others, who they are and who others are. Merely by name, fame, or wealth, all is good and fair in the game of our world. My friend told me one day that I will be a famous man, because I am a doctor, actor, and writer. My answer was, "No, I am not, but someday, when I find my fame and name within myself, I will be the most famous of the famous men in the world." I told him others do not own my fame; I own it. When I attain my inner fame, it will be mine. Others will never see it or find it. Through meditation, I will be rewarded someday. There is no hurry or lust for that.
- Illusions and delusions. Some of us remain buried under the illusions and delusions of life with false perceptions and beliefs. Without existence of those and not tarnished with rusty impressions of those, you will not be living a blindfolded life. To those people, I say lay the wreath of meditation on the grave of ignorance and arrogance. Then and there, you will deflate the fake air of their balloon to realize the power of wisdom and peace.
- Suspicion and paranoia. Some remain drowned in the burning thoughts of their own, never to find an exit of freedom from them. They remain engulfed and suffering in the dark shadow of their lives. They will find an exit from the enclosed black box by the enlightening of glowing meditation. Their suspicions and paranoia will be replaced by trust and love by reflecting on their inner self. Unrealistic fear and distortion of reality of self, others and unknown will dissipate by understanding and unification with their self.
- Hope. This is the antidote for hopelessness, despondent feelings, and worthlessness. When you find your inner strength, hope

will dominate such unwanted feelings through the wisdom of meditation, liberating you from the shackles of such torments. Hope at times brings joy out of nowhere, though joy may be due to outer factors and fruits of external events, like winning the lottery. In human experience, certain events are required to bring forth joy, but the joy itself is the perennial native of the soul. Love brings joy to our lives, which is felt and appreciated by our soul. It is the power of meditation, where love and joy are strengthened in our soul. Sometimes you wake up and feel happy and full of joy for no reason. You don't know why. When you sit in the silence of deep meditation, joy bubbles up from within, roused by no outer stimulus. The joy of meditation is very overwhelming for those who experience it for the first time, and then it becomes a way of life.

- Wisdom. Wisdom and meditation are brothers and sisters, whichever gender you want to pick, be my guest. Spirituality is the father, and soul is the mother of all, which gives birth to all, nurtures them, feeds them, guides them, loves them, shapes them, and helps them to grow. Without mothers, brothers, sisters, and fathers, no one is ever born. It is the mother who is the creator of all of us, which I will discuss. Wise people meditate, and meditation helps wisdom to grow. It is the love of wisdom, meditation, and spirituality that makes the love of the mother (soul) to be content. She sees her children happy, healthy, and enjoying the fruits of their labor. On the eightieth birthday of their mother (soul), wisdom, meditation, and spirituality wrote their mother a birthday card, which read,

Oh! Mother the sweet, with your acceptance our seeds were sown,
You bore us with passion, love, and our fate was grown,
We ran our course with the care and love you had shown.
You nurtured us with your blood and flesh till we were born,
Our love, loyalty, passion and dedication are forever sworn.
Lovely mother let us know, when you want to go,
We will hold your beautiful hands and end our show.

It is the mother soul who puts up with the naughty games and silly tricks of wisdom. It is the mother soul who understands the hide-and-seek game meditation plays and the secrets of spirituality.

Consciousness and unconsciousness both play an important role in meditation, depending upon the stage of meditation. Various stages develop as meditation progresses. Let me describe some of the techniques briefly. First of all, there is the conceptualization of mediation, followed by action taken. By now, you have learned to sit quietly and attain full relaxation of your body in whatever setting you choose to be in, as described by Richard and Patricia (269) and by John Kabat-Zin (268), Osho, yogis, yoga asana instructors, gurus, and countless modern yogis of the world. The basic principle is the same: focus on the breath and breathing process. Acknowledging the breath and attention paid to the breath is the key to the process of meditation. Some of you may ask, "How does breathing start meditation?" When you sit comfortably and focus on your breathing, other sensory stimuli are diminished in their strength as you ignore them to pay attention to breathing. After that, you close your eyes, which cuts down the sensory stimulus. Ancient Buddhist, Hindu, and other texts emphasize breathing. Awareness of breathing is the start and end of the meditation. Sit comfortably. Close your eyes and mouth and breathe through your nose. Nature has provided us with an alternative route of breathing. If you cannot breathe through your nose, it is fine to breathe through your mouth. Close your eyes if you are comfortable doing so. Feel the air as it moves in and out of your nose. Start breathing slowly, gradually, and deeply. Feel the air go deep into your lungs and then back up and out again. Feel the rise and fall of your belly and chest, the movement of your rib cage. Now you are becoming aware of breathing. Some feel comfortable sitting and some lying down. Make sure you are comfortable, because the comfort of your soul is the goal. Stay with it until the end of the life. Start relaxing your chest and belly muscles. It is not necessary to push your belly muscles or chest muscles artificially.

Nature is the goal of your attainment in the journey of your meditation. Learn to put your best foot forwards, right from the get-go. If you cannot do that, put your hands on your belly and let the sensation of your hand tell you that the rhythm is perfect and in harmony. Start paying attention to the muscles of your body and attain the relaxation of your muscles, starting from your toes and going to your legs, pelvis, chest, face, and arms until you feel like a rubber doll with no tension or stiffness. Slow, rhythmic breathing is the start of the healing process. Let's look at a patient with hyperventilation syndrome. If that patient pays attention to breathing, it is possible to avoid the distress of the hyperventilation syndrome—tingling numbness, dizziness, anxiety, fear of dying, and many more symptoms. Some scientists claim that conscious breathing is helpful in increasing lung capacity to provide sufficient oxygen to nourish our lungs and blood, which supplies oxygen to each cell of our body at the molecular level. Some claim the everyday practice of breathing makes them calmer and calmer.

After making the rounds with patients, some of the doctors used to meet in the doctors' lounge to briefly look at the news and stock market, talk or joke to break the ice, and get ready for outpatient treatment. Some would take a quick lunch break and gobble a quick sandwich without giving a thought to it or what it was. I was one of them. Now I call it swallowing, not enjoying or tasting it by chewing, breathing slowly, and giving yourself the chance to feel something that needs to be felt. One day, I was discussing the stock market with an old wise surgeon who had meditated all his life. I went on babbling continuously, and he listened. After a while, he told me, "Can you please slow down and take a breath, so I can understand what you are saying?" He added, "I hear you talking but not breathing. If you breath slowly, your speech is slow and comprehensible and understandable."

I stopped and asked him, "What do you mean by that?"

Politely, he said, "Try breathing. Slow down and pay attention to that. You will find it easy to talk without rushing to explain too much. You will enjoy it, and others will listen and appreciate that." Patiently and humbly, he said, "I understand the stock market."

We went on our way, saying, "Have a good one."

I thought then, Well, he seems to be an arrogant, grouchy, burned-out old surgeon.

We met again after a year or so, and he was the same arrogant old man about whom I had already made an opinion, so I was quiet and greeted him. He slowly, with his compassionate voice, said, "You look wonderful and calm. Have you made enough money in the stock market in the past year?"

I thought he was being sarcastic so why even bother to pay attention? I left as soon as I could, thinking of the old surgeon as a sarcastic man.

A few years later, we met again. By then, I had learned and had heard about him and about his wisdom and dedication to meditation, besides him being one of the best surgeons in Virginia Beach. I had started learning about meditation, having been motivated by my son. This time, I needed his advice and acknowledged his qualities. How selfish of me! I changed my thinking and attitude. I no longer thought him an arrogant and sarcastic man, but rather a wise, learned man. Judging someone is a reflection of yourself. To this day, he remains my teacher of meditation. He has recommended many books and studies on wisdom. Every time, I meet him, he jokes about it. "Are you talking slowly and listening to your breath?"

Thereafter, I became an observer, not just an observed one. This is the power of breathing during meditation. If you master paying attention to breathing, you will learn to pay attention to everything around you, and with the passage of time, it will lead you to the path of wisdom of your soul. That wisdom will guide your outer shell to be strong through yogic exercises and will give you healthy tools for your internal organs, which are wise. They talk to each other, and their wisdom will relate to the wisdom of your brain to develop a common understanding with the soul. Breathing exercises can help many individuals who need to hold their breaths for a longer period of time; they can achieve such control by concentrating and paying attention to their breathing—for example, deep-water divers and musicians who have to sing for a long time. Athletes can increase their endurance and keep playing for a longer time, skiers on high mountains can breathe more efficiently, and golfers can maintain full concentration. Paying attention to new things leads to new experiences. Some you apply to yourself, and some you ignore. According to the Buddhist philosophy, mindfulness is the key to reaching the goal of mediation and its attainment. Mindfulness is a way of paying attention that originated in Eastern meditation practices. The four foundations of mindfulness are the body (breathing, posture, and activities), feelings (the sense of pleasantness, unpleasantness, and neutrality), the mind (in particular, its moods and attitudes), and the object of the mind (all the five senses). Pay attention in particular way, on purpose, in the present moment. Be nonjudgmental, and bring complete attention to the present moment.

Full enlightenment is a misunderstood achievement of our mental faculties as described by some authors. My view is that it is the internal achievement of our senses and neuronal functions, which generate the appropriate magnetic field of our soul to enrich our understanding of the processes that govern our life events and deal with wisdom and spirituality. It is not a transcendent energy or form revelation. The question of whether enlightenment is a permanent state should not fool us. The crucial point is that you can glimpse something about the nature of consciousness that will liberate you from the suffering in the present. So the repeated process of meditation will continue reinforcing this through the rewards your soul attains. To me, it is a continuous process, not a one-time event. It also helps and influences in the fields of education, law, and business, policy making, and running the government. Some have defined it essentially as being about relationality, which means how we are in relationship to everything, including our mind, our body's thoughts, our emotions, and the relationship of our present, past, and future.

Practicing mindfulness teaches us how to live our way into every aspect of our life with integrity, with kindness toward ourselves and others, and with wisdom. Mindfulness is not only a good idea or a nice philosophy; it is a value we need to embody in our everyday lives, to whatever degree we can, with a gentle touch, thereby nurturing self-acceptance, kindness, and self-compassion. The troubles are always troubles. There is no escape from them. Escape creates problems that just multiply. There is an art to facing troubles and problems with effective solutions and inner peace and harmony. There are times in our lives when we feel completely overwhelmed by numerous factors, like job stress, money, relationship problems, illnesses, and catastrophic events like earthquakes, wars, flooding, terrorist attacks, death in the family, and many more events noxious to us. It is very easy to fall into depression and anxiety. We feel helpless. Nothing seems controllable or even worth trying.

At that point, it does not matter whether they are real or unreal; they will have a harmful effect on your soul and body. At times, a threat by itself can easily lead to feelings of anger and hostility and go from there to outright aggressive behavior, driven by the instinct to protect ourselves and keep things under control. When things do feel under control, we might feel content for a moment, but when they get out of control again or seem to be getting out of control, our insecurities overwhelm us. We might then self-destruct or hurt others. We lose our peace of mind and contentment. Some of us have chronic illnesses or disabilities, which make us lose our control because of physical pain that has not responded to medical treatment. Then our physical distress is compounded by emotional distress. At times, there is a distortion of cognition, and our smallest problems appear to be enormous. Even those can cause emotional turmoil. Some of us can reason it through and understand that there is love as well as suffering, hope as well as despair, calm as well as agitation, love as well as hatred, and health as well as illness. Cultivating mindfulness can lead us to invent a deep realm of well-being, calmness clarity, tranquility, peace, and insight about ourselves. Sometimes, it appears that something is unreal. There is a new light of wisdom and positive energy for understanding and self-healing. It is just close to your soul, body, and breath. This domain of pure being and wakefulness is always accessible to you. It is always there, whether you have heart disease, cancer, pain, or just a stressful life.

Mindfulness, if attained, can provide energy that is of great value to you. Besides mindfulness, interconnectedness and wholeness are the building blocks of understanding the soul, brain, and body. John Karat writes,

> Learning how to suspend all your doings and shift over to a being mode, how to make time for yourself, how to slow down and nurture calmness and self acceptance in yourself, learning to observe what your mind is up to from moment to moment, how to watch your thoughts and how to let go of them without getting caught up and driven by them, how to make room for new way of seeing old problems and for perceiving the interconnectedness of things—these are some of the lessons of mindfulness.

This kind of learning involves turning toward and settling into moments of being and simply cultivating awareness (369).

These are all conscious efforts and methods. Once you are fully attentive to your rate and rhythm of breathing, you start diminishing your sense of touch, taste, pain, temperature, and all other sensations, including hearing. The bottom line is you control all your sensations by the rule of attention—attention to breathing—at your comfort. In the beginner stage, your thoughts start wandering from conscious to some unconscious thoughts. Never be afraid of these thoughts, and never be discouraged by these thoughts, because they are your own. This will give you some insight into your own thoughts, which are wandering and wandering. You wonder if you have such thoughts that you have never experienced. Call on your patience, self-control, and commitment. As you progress day by day, you are pouring water on the erupted lava of thoughts, which causes steam to evaporate.

Evaporation causes cooling, and this holds true in your case. As thoughts cause confusion and chaos, there is fear. It is caused by both conscious and unconscious thoughts, which are your own. There is no external threat, so relax and reason it through. Fear is internal. You have never dealt with it. This is normal fear caused by your autonomic nervous system, especially the sympathetic nervous system. At this stage, you may feel your heart rate going up. Your internal sensations may be more pronounced, and you may feel nervousness and a tingling sensation. Bring your courage to bear at this stage, because you are not insane. Some people open their eyes. It is fine to do that to reassure yourself that everything is fine around you so that you can overcome the fear. Confidence overcomes the fear of the unknown. The process keeps going on for a while. Every time, it gets easier than the previous one. This stage differs in time from one individual to other, because we are wired differently. Those who respond to suggestion overcome this stage faster than those who do not, as proven in the theories of hypnosis. The difference is that in hypnosis, you respond to the suggestion of others. Here you are responding to your own. Some of it may be true in self-hypnosis. I have no problem accepting that. This is the crucial stage, as I learned. Self-blame, self-depreciation, and discouragement are triggered by the old, familiar statement, "I cannot do it." You are right. I went through this stage. Many people quit here because of fear of the unknown. It is okay to do that, especially for those who are prone to psychosis or who have personality disorders due to their brain synaptic connections or excessive dopamine levels. When the person is stimulated, this can cause hallucinations, which are enhanced by sensory deprivation, as per new scientific studies.

The moral of the story is that meditation is not meant for everybody. If it were, everybody would be meditating all over the world. Meditation is meant for those who can tolerate understanding themselves and their thoughts based on the structure of the brain and the soul. I believe meditation is for higher neuronal functions rather than only neuronal functions, which I will discuss as I write more.

Let us presume we have grown out of the turbulent stage and want to progress further in this journey of life. Some will argue there is much more involved, and I give credit to them and call them individuals with enhanced personalities and spiritual wisdom.

- The Early Stage of Coherence

I purposely avoided extensive descriptions of the beginner stage to have a brief and concise description, since I am writing a chapter and not a book on the subject of the soul and meditation. Those who want to learn details, please refer to the books mentioned earlier. Some yogis or sages call it a quiet stage, in which you do nothing but sit quietly without any harm to yourself or to others, without gain or loss to yourself or others, without uttering bad words or insults to yourself or others. Isn't it nice that peace is all around you and you are by yourself? We learn that there is no selfishness, no motivation, no desire, no gain, and no loss; only the self prevails. Once we get a chance to master that, we pay attention to our body parts, starting from our toes and going to the top of our head as a whole. I call it the external shell or apparatus. It is easier to start focusing on body parts once we have gotten ahold of our wandering thoughts.

Some yogis recommend you start focusing on the toes and relax each part of the body, ascending all the way to the top of the head. That is fine for those of you who can do that in coherence with your breathing, which by now is automatically regulated and starts working in harmony with relaxation. It took me a long time to make them work together, because I learned that my thoughts were wandering more and more as I started relaxing. As I was concentrating on relaxing my body parts from toe to head, I would lose track of controlling my wandering thoughts. Do what makes things work. There are no hard and fast rules to be followed step by step. There is one goal: achieving the practice of meditation by any means you can, whether sitting with your eyes closed or open, standing or lying in the bed before going to sleep, or doing a headstand with your legs up in the air and head on the ground. The path of the journey may be different, but the goal is one and the same: to reach the destination of meditation. It took me a while to achieve this state with my brain and the external apparatus or shell of the body.

The second task was to have coherence of breathing and the external apparatus and to bring my internal apparatus (including all of my internal organs) to work in harmony in a single unit and single form united together. It again took a long time. Sometimes, they worked together, and sometimes, each one dictated its own terms. I used the experience of my wisdom to make them work together. Sometimes, I failed, and sometimes,

I succeeded. My wisdom was my savior. It scorned the discouragement and overshadowed the disharmony, thus achieving the early harmony.

Coherence leads to conditioning; mastering the different aspects of the early coherences, as described, leads to the conditioning of behavior, according to scientific experiments done in the different disciplines in the field of neuroscience. We have learned from animal models and the study of human behaviors. This part of the development of meditation then gets reinforced once the rewards of tranquility, peace, calmness, serenity, self-identity, true perception, and many more aspects of a complete sense of life are engraved in our soul. Reinforcement of a behavior keeps going by itself. Gradually, it becomes a registered part of our soul. Some yogis have voluntary control over their internal organs, which can enhance the function of their organs. Some can wash their stomachs and run water through their one nostril to the other. Those are yogic mechanical controls.

Meditation has higher neuronal functions beyond the function of neurons, axons, dendrites, synapses, and various neurotransmitters. Our internal organs are regulated either by their own nervous system or by the neurochemical system (details are explained in the chapter on the secondary soul). I will explain as I discuss meditation and the soul. This coherence with our internal organs is very fruitful in attaining a sense of satisfaction and getting hold of our desires, needs, expectations, and wants.

- Attainment of Meditation

Some attain the art of meditation to a level of their satisfaction. Some attain it to the level of their comfort. Some attain it to the level of their capabilities, enough to enjoy the fruits of their endeavor. For some, it becomes a belief. For some, it is the way or routine life. For some, it is the basic structure of their principles, coupled with and incorporated within their structured life, without which, a description of life is incomplete—for example, yogis, Buddhism, and Hinduism. Nobody has ever claimed the full degree of meditation in this ever-changing life of humans. If some have, it is they who know it better than anyone else. Let us presume that we meditate every day and it is our lifestyle; what happens to us, and how are we different? Paying attention to new things is a healthy experience, like mindfulness, which means a way of paying attention that originated in Eastern meditation practices. It is paying attention in a particular way, on purpose, in the present moment and nonjudgmentally bringing one's complete attention to the present internal and external experiences on a moment-to-moment experience basis.

Mindfulness is not only used in meditation but also could influence many aspects of life, like in education, law, business, technology, leadership, sports, economics, and politics. It could be used to develop law and order and policies to interact with other governments of the world and to avoid wars and destruction in the chaotic world we live in. Jon Kabat-Zinn adds to it heartfullness and explains that we are in relationship with everything, including our mind, body, thoughts, and emotions. It is not a philosophy for its value. We have to be embodied with it in every day of our life without forcing it or straining it. If you use a light and gentle touch, it can give you a sense of nurturance, self-acceptance, kindness, and self-compassion. Cultivating mindfulness can create a sense of well-being, calmness, clarity, and insight about the existence of self and others. It gives you insight to experience good again and again until you master the art. Meditation teaches that there is no moment away from our body, mind, and breathing. Mindfulness is a part of the wisdom of our soul. When attained, it gives us knowledge of how to practice a healthy lifestyle and mental health, by giving birth to wholeness and interconnectedness.

For humans and all living souls, stress is inescapable, no matter how much luxury we were brought up with or live in. Some of us use avoidance to deal with stress, and some of us use denial. Some of us run away from it, not realizing this is our own shadow. For some, this becomes a way of life, a way to deal with stress. Some suffer and have learned that suffering is the only way to live. Some of us tranquilize ourselves with pills, alcohol, and drugs. Some of us are completely overwhelmed to the point that we fall into depression, and some of us become hyperalert to the point that we are extra cautious, which makes us anxious and even paranoid, moody, and resentful all the time. At times, some of us feel threatened and overreact, which can make us angry, hostile, and aggressive just with the instinct of protecting our feelings and emotions. This can result in the development of maladaptive behavior, which could be repeated again and again.

When we get hold of such a feeling and calmness sets in, if stress appears again, we repeat what we learned before. This becomes a chain of events, never to go away. Such a learned behavior is distraught and stressful. Some of us have chronic illness, chronic pain, disability, and cancer not responding to medication or conventional treatment which leaves us with paralyses of the will, with failures of the desire to explore more. Some of

130

us have minor problems, but our reactions are magnified to the point that a small mouse looks like a big bear with the distortion of our thinking. Some of us do self-reflect and find that we have contributed to distress and pain in others as well. It might include cruelty, violence, ignorance, greed, mistrust, and deception. Those of us who lack self-reflection continue such acts without guilt or remorse. We fail to develop insight to accept the change in our lives. This usually is the case in individuals with personality disorders, as discussed earlier. In summary, we must understand the fact that joy has a companion called suffering, hope has despair, calm has agitation, love has hatred, health has illness, high has low, up has down, and so on, like two sides of a coin.

You have to learn to sit down and sometimes do nothing but look at yourself. Let your thoughts wander. Some will be ugly, some pleasant, some foolish, some good, some bad, some fearful, some fearless, some sensible, some senseless, some full of love, some full of hatred, some full of wants, some full of the desire to give, some full of rejection and some full of acceptance, and so on. Let them flow freely. Some will make you fearful, some fearless. Some will make you wise, and some will create a sense of insecurity, anger, and shame. Some will be full of lust, some full of passion. Some will be suspicious, and some full of security. This will go on. Make yourself aware of each one of them.

The goal is to know them all, see them all, and acknowledge and accept them all. If you fail to know them, sit alone by yourself again and again until you know them all. This is the first lesson for us to achieve the path of meditation, wisdom, and spirituality. Do not force yourself to act on them yet. Wait until the time of acceptance is part of your soul. Without acceptance, you will be irrational, incomplete, ignorant, impulsive, and despondent. You will be quick to take action, thus drowning the truth in the ocean of doom and gloom never to be found again. You do not have to be a PhD, MD, scientist, or wise man of the West. All you have to be is who you are as a human being. Do not pay attention to your behavior. Do not call yourself ugly and sinful. Do not judge yourself in any shape or form. Rich, poor, famous, criminal, cruel, or saintly—our thoughts are so powerful and overpowering, especially during the time of crisis or emotional upheaval, which is pretty common. They easily cloud our awareness of the present. Even in the relaxed moments, they can carry our senses and numb them, like driving on the ramp without being conscious of that. Instead of driving in the lane we are supposed to, because of a lack of attention, which is hijacked for that moment, we drift. Just sit quietly as much as you can and as many times as you can, only you and nobody else. You are nobody, but you are everybody and still you. Screen every thought, every action, every reaction, every result, every moment that crosses through your mind. But, remember, you are not judgmental of yourself because you are helpless in the process of exploration, which will never stop in your life, so do not rush.

Let your soul work for you. It has enough energy to work tirelessly. Let it run amok until it finds the answers for itself. You sit quietly without any effort. Let it wander like an aimless cloud, air, or stars in the galaxy to find its destination to settle down. Let it run amok like a storm, creating havoc in its path, only to find the end.

Oh, Human! You hunker down and wait for this storm to
go away,
only to find calm after it is gone.
Oh, Human! Look around you and learn what this storm
has done.
It has destroyed some and created new landscapes and new
shapes around us.
It has killed some and injured some.
It has left nothing but devastation, agony, pain, and
suffering.
It did not discriminate rich from poor, good from bad,
right from wrong.
Some cry. Some hold on tight and focus on cleaning and
rebuilding the destruction left behind.
Some seek help from others. Proud ones do not.
Look around you and see what you have lost.
You may have lost your friends, your loved ones, your
house, your wealth, your pets, your crops, your peace of
mind.
Look around at what the storm has done.
Learn to call it destruction, and do not forget it.
Don't forget that it can strike again without warning.
You will pick up your pieces and build your life again,
even better than before after the calm of the storm has set

in. If you learn from it, you will learn how to deal with it better than before.

We call it rebuilding life again.

You will find lush green crops will grow again. Trees will bloom again to give you the bounty of fruits due to your hard labor.

You will be happy again and will have friends and loved ones again.

Now, sit again and look at the storms of your thoughts again.

Use the wisdom of your experience, and get rid of your evil thoughts, which were destructive and harmful to you and others.

Take your time, and use the right ones.

You will have prosperity and happiness again.

You will know what is wrong and what is right when you apply those thoughts to the actions.

Sit back, and get rid of and ignore the ugly and ruthless thoughts.

If you do not learn to control your ugly thoughts and continue putting them to action only to hurt others, do not forget, the storm can hit you again.

This is the stage of rebuilding and controlling your thoughts for yourself and others.

It is important to know that in meditation, we can never force our thoughts to disappear. I learned that if I let my thoughts run wild, they are just like a butterfly, which dances from flower to flower and in turn gives birth to fertile seeds of the flowers, which keep giving life to the species. In the same way, wandering thoughts give us clues about how and what we think. They inform us of who exactly we are. They will come to rest like a butterfly comes to rest after she is satisfied or exhausted from venturing out to seek for the nectar of different bright and beautifully colorful flowers. Being attentive to breathing helps us allow our wandering thoughts to settle. Thinking is essential during meditation, because the thoughts you have ignored all your life become alive and noticeable. What a nice thing to happen to a deaf and blind man, to be able to hear his thoughts and see them alive. It is the first wonder of meditation followed by countless others.

It is the blessing of thoughts by themselves that you are a human and alive. My thoughts gave me the desires and pleasures of my life. They always reassured me of my existence and validated my actions and reactions. They are the best companions of my life, so I respect them and they respect me too. If I treat them badly, they treat me badly too, so our understanding is mutual and graceful. Why should we be alarmed about their existence? They proclaim your existence. I always respect my thoughts because I keep good ones and let go of the bad ones. They never argue with my will to let them go. I entertain them if they come back. I do not argue with them. I let other thoughts argue with them. That way, they never blame me, and I am a free man. Meditation widens the room for the thoughts to be in there so I can see who is who and what is what. I can see their colors, shapes, sizes, and form. If they remain hidden, there is nothing I can do. I remain ignorant of them, and they know about my ignorance and play hide-and-seek to win over me.

My meditation makes them visible in real form, not hidden behind the sheath of pretention. My thoughts laugh at me at times because they have control over me and my ignorance, but they need to know I have developed a tool to abandon them at will by meditation. By now, I understand that they are shining stars hidden behind the dark clouds and show up when the sunshine is gone. I reveal them even while the sun is shining, and I lift the veil of clouds through the power of meditation. I am aware of their tricks. They come and go, leaving behind their tracks, and make me believe that they control my willpower, as they did in the past. The present is mine, and I am looking forward to them coming in the future only to be surprised that I will pick and choose. They will have no control over my mood or actions. I will dictate them to follow me and my actions. I will not work for them; they will work for me. I call it the second stage of meditation, by which I mean the restructuring and screening of my wandering, wild thoughts. If you think about it, how could this happen? Think for a moment, and ask yourself, "Who can do this for me?"

I would say nobody but you. They will be yours forever, and nobody can steal or rob them from you. Someday, you will be honored to share with others who will need your knowledge, experience, and wisdom. No matter how much other people want to help you and can help you to move to this stage of your life, the basic effort has to come from you. After all, no one is living your life for you, and no one cares about that for you anyway. It is fine to have a guide. In Indian culture, a guru is the only one who passes on his or her knowledge to the followers or disciples. To my utter surprise, in India, every corner is full of such self-proclaimed gurus, and people are flocking to them with offerings of large amounts of money.

The rich can buy a guru for a certain amount of money if the guru is just out of fashion or for a show of power and wealth. Last year, a guru died, and under the room where he used to sleep, they found a room full of rupees, an uncountable number just donated to him by his admirers and followers. Some of them have grown so wealthy that they even control politics and politicians. I said to myself, "Well, they are smart, intelligent businessmen gurus."

Now, however, I can go on YouTube and watch a video about meditation anytime I want to. Generations Z, X, and Y have taken care of that and will take care of the rest. The new generation, I call generation "Q." It is the generation on the quest for artificial intelligence with the new concept of meditation, wisdom, and spirituality based on scientific knowledge, proof, and evidence. I will address this toward the end of this chapter. Meditation to this neogeneration sounds like an alien creature. For them, their phones and apps are their tools of meditation. Why should they believe in meditation when they have everything available in their hands? Google Facebook, and Amazon are their religion and meditation. A simple click gives them any information they want. They can contact anyone they want to contact and can see them on their phones. Memory is stored somewhere else by someone else. When you need it, click the button, and you will have it.

Screening the entire body both internally and externally is sometimes a cumbersome process, but my experience relies on my commitment. The principle is basic and simple. Start screening by paying attention to each body part from your toes to the top of your head, including genitals and the rest of the internal organs. As you learn to pay attention to the whole skeleton and to your heart, you will eventually be able to pay attention to your brain. Since you are not trained in medicine, you cannot focus on each and every part of the organ, like an MRI, X-ray, or ultrasound of the body could. You don't have to worry about that. You can do it by focusing on the region of the body. Focusing on your brain is a little complicated if you cannot just sit quietly and let the process begin. Sometimes, repeatedly looking at the pictures of the brain given in this book makes the mental image more visible. It may take time. You do not have to remember the names of the parts of the body or brain; an image of the part is sufficient for nonmedical individuals. There is no mysticism about it. It is all real because you are real.

We normally do not pay attention to our body. For example, when we have pain or an ulcer or injury to the foot, it is the pain sensation that draws our attention; otherwise, we keep on going with our usual routine of life. Screening each part of the body will teach you anatomy by localizing the region that hurts or itches. Keep screening and breathing together in harmony; this stage is crucial to reaching a higher level of meditation. Let us presume you have reached to the level at which you have localized back pain or knee pain. Soft and slow yogic exercise and meditation will be highly effective. At this phase of meditation, you will be able to concentrate and pay attention to the region of the pain. Now the question arises, "Who feels the pain?" Please understand it is not your knee or the back that feels the pain; it is the sensory pain center of the brain that feels exactly where the pain is. Pain could be due to numerous causes, but pain is pain. Your doctor will explain the cause of the pain to you and treat the cause. Our goal is to get rid of the pain when conventional treatment is not working. You had all the surgeries and have taken all the pills in the world for pain. At this point, you are frustrated, and so is your doctor. Sometimes they refer to it as a psychogenic pain disorder or a malingering or chronic pain disorder. Many more names are given, but let us understand what pain is. It is felt by the one who has it. I am no one to measure it or label it.

Pay attention to the region every time you have completed the drill of meditation. You will wonder how paying attention and concentrating on this region could cure your pain. It sounds too good to be true. Yes, it is. It, all depends on your technique and attainment of the meditative state of your life. How does it work?

The first mechanism starts here. As I mentioned, it is the sensory part of your brain that perceives the pain and tells you that pain is in your back or knee. By meditation, this sensory center receives constant electric current from your back and knee, so your sensory center is fully alert and listens to you constantly. This center generates enormous amounts of magnetic energy constantly from the constant electric current generated by your attention and focus on the region of pain. This electromagnetic field energy orders almost all the mechanisms involved in the chain of command of the pain system. Our pain-control hormones are secreted in abundance (endorphins, encephalin, and numerous painkillers, some we know and some don't know). To learn more, please refer to the chapter describing pain. If it is psychogenic, then serotonin, dopamine, cholecystokinin, and many more neurotransmitters are secreted, which act on the synaptic cleft of our brain and create new synapses and neuronal growth processes. This is called plasticity and neurogenesis (explained extensively in the chapter on the neurology of the soul). The second mechanism is through yoga exercises, which cause stretching and increased blood circulation, removing bradykinin and substance P (along with many more neurochemicals, some we know and some we will know), which cause pain. The third mechanism is angiogenesis and regeneration of new small nerves to supply the injured area, which causes pain. This means there is generation of new blood vessels, supplying that area of pain and initiating regeneration of new tissue in the healing process. Old rotten tissue is gradually replaced by new healthy tissue; believe it or not, our body is a great healer. Sometimes, it works on its own, and sometimes, we have to work with it to bring healthy changes. For example, when there is a small cut, blood clots first to stop the bleeding, and then there is regeneration of new tissue for scar formation. This goes on every day in our internal organs, where old cells die and are replaced by new ones through angiogenesis, which supplies blood, oxygen, and nutrition.

Some scientists have suggested that the hormone (chemical) that inhibits angiogenesis is sometimes not able to stop the growth of cells, which can cause cancer. Some cancer cells are shed off at a certain point, and we are cancer free. Some claim that we produce cancer cells that die down, and we do not develop cancer. The debate is ongoing. If that is true, then one day, we may be able to control cancer by the process of meditation, the healing power of our body.

The fourth mechanism is acceptance of the pain. It is not a foreign agent. It is your companion in life as long as you are alive. Please refer to the chapter on pain. While meditating, your thoughts go wild in the wilderness as you attain the stage where reality prevails if you are having psychogenic pain, which is very common, because pain is constant, annoying, and exhausting. It is a noxious irritant to your body and soul, which can cause a sense of despondency, low self-esteem, and depression, which enhances the pain by lowering your threshold of pain. For example, minimal pain appears to be enormous, and you react with agony and perceive it to be unbearable. Pain causes anxiety. It seems like a never-ending process and brings uncertainty about the future, like if you cannot work, how you will support your family and manage other responsibilities. It is a fact of life, which we have to deal with. You feel inadequate and inefficient. You are self-derogatory and preoccupied with intrusive thoughts of loss of functioning. Anxiety does not relieve pain but adds to the pain, as you are thinking about it all the time.

Meditation will give you a perspective on life to do what you can do. Some of us indulge in to too much with previous expectations before the pain or disability. Sometimes, we have to learn to live with less or within our means. If you are malingering with secondary gains, the purity of your thoughts and sincerity of your action will change the perspective of your life to deal with reality.

Some of us have histrionic personality behaviors or disorders. Attention-seeking behavior is predominant and enhances pain. Magnification of symptoms is the trademark of such behavior. A child cries to get the attention of his or her mother. In the same way, we adults moan and groan to get sympathy from others, like a spouse or any loved ones. Some of us lie about the pain as an excuse to avoid confrontation as a defense mechanism, as described earlier. It is an unconscious or conscious mode of action or behavior.

Chronic pain is a serious underlying cause of painkiller or heroin addiction. Listen to your soul and self. There is no one else who has time to listen to your complaints and excuses. Just meditate and listen to the voices coming from within yourself. You are the one who is the best listener of all beyond and above all, including your loved ones and your doctors as well. When you are in deep meditation, you feel a great serenity, a joy that is known to you and a mindfulness that is a new guest. Soon, this mindfulness will become the host. When mindfulness becomes the host, it remains with you twenty-four hours a day, and out of this, there comes wisdom, which will give you clarity, purity, spontaneity, and grace. Your wisdom gives you the gift of knowledge, compassion, and insight about how to handle yourself in the event of pain, misery, agony, and addiction. This is the Buddhist wisdom of meditation and the self.

The fifth mechanism has a long chain of events and is complicated. It involves the sympathetic and parasympathetic nervous system, which supplies the arteries and veins and carries the sensation of pain to our limbic system and other parts of the brain, which upon stimulation sends messages through the electric current to our limbic system. It sends messages to the sensory part of the brain. Please refer to the chapter on the sympathetic and parasympathetic systems. Both systems are alerting, soothing, and relaxing. They restore the functions of the nervous systems. These systems counterbalance each other. The sympathetic system, when activated, gets us ready to do things we need to do as well as to respond to threats or danger, the fight-or-flight reaction, through the secretion of adrenaline, which speeds up the heart rate and increases the breathing rate. It raises blood pressure and redistributes blood to the muscles of the arms, legs, and the rest of the body. This stimulates our adrenal gland to pump cortisol and numerous other hormones into our bloodstream, which burns a lot of energy to complete the action. The parasympathetic system slows down our heart rate and respiration rate and relaxes the smooth muscles of our body. It reduces inflammation. We need both systems, but they should be in balance. Some claim that coherent breathing stimulates the parasympathetic nervous system by increasing lung pressure (370). That may be a factor, but this mechanism involves the limbic system and hypothalamus. We all agree with the fact that learning breathing techniques could strengthen the alveoli of the lungs to transfer more oxygen to our bloodstream, which is essential for our health. It may prevent pneumonia and other respiratory infections. Both systems mentioned are key parts of the nervous system for stress and stress responses. They include functions like regulating the heart rate, respiration, digestion, and the hormonal, glandular, and immune systems. They send information to our brain from moment to moment about the state of our body. Our breathing has an immediate response to any changes in the status of our body, including thoughts, emotions, and behaviors. These regulatory responses are accomplished through the information received from the organs or parts of the body. They send information back to the sender by a feedback loop. In physiology, it is known as homeostasis. It maintains a tight range of variability in the physiological system that promotes immediate survival like in oxygen and glucose levels, body temperature, and more. Keeping the fluctuations in the body within the needs of normal functions by checks and balances is called allostasis. It has ongoing processes like blood pressure, cortisol level, and fat storage. These are all controlled by our brain and by how we adapt to the ever-changing environment and changes in our lifestyle, depending on the situations in our lives. Both of these systems can be affected by chronic stress due to any reasons or factors. These mechanisms keep our survival and existence intact. They are responsible for us eating and drinking when we are hungry and thirsty or craving certain foods when we are deficient in any vitamin or essential amino acid. These systems have mechanisms by which we can screen out wasteful substances or chemicals through our kidneys and liver.

Without any doubt, our body has developed the techniques to heal ourselves from some injuries, like minor cuts and broken bones. There is a sudden rush of red blood cells from our spleen in the case of severe bleeding. We have endorphins as painkillers, mechanisms to get rid of cancer cells in our body, and much more beyond the scope of this book. This all is done by our brain and all the organs working like a cohesive family, as a whole team, with full coherence. We still have much to learn or find with time. Even if we abuse our body by drinking, taking drugs, or smoking, it will forgive us to a point. After that, it gives up. If we abuse food or do not provide what our body needs, it will work until exhaustion. After that, there is no apology. We have to work with what we have left for ourselves and our body. If we ignore our inner language, which always gives us warnings, then we cannot blame our organs or our body. Our body has learned a wonderful language with wonderful communicative signs and symptoms, like throwing up, headaches, heavy shoulders, constipation, abdominal pain, chest pain, and at times, pain referred to other parts of the body, signaling something is not right. If you keep ignoring it, then your body feels helpless.

The brain even signals us with anxiety, panic attacks, depression, obsessive-compulsive behavior, generalized anxiety attacks, restlessness, changes in moods, anger, aggression, crying spells, grief, and countless other symptoms. Do we listen? Those who listen do something about it and those who do not lead miserable lives and make others miserable too. Our body has all the mechanisms in place to take care of all of these symptoms on its own if we keep up our patience and learn to give it a rest for its own healing without drugs. This is the wisdom of our body, which has learned from millions of years of adaptation supported by genetic mutations to adapt to harsh environments for survival. Our automatic responses and habitual routines for avoiding new changes and behaviors put a damper on our enhancements and understandings. Automatic reactions trigger unawareness of the circumstances, which sometimes can be life threatening. Kenneth and his coauthors have given us enough insight about transcendental meditation (introduced by Mahesh Yogi to the United States from old Indian Vedic traditions). It emphasizes deep breathing and chanting. It is a quicker form of meditation, which can be learned from a trained, certified individual in that field. We all know that stress can cause heart disease. More than six hundred studies have supported the fact that heart disease could be prevented by this technique. It can prevent high blood pressure, reduce the use of alcohol and tobacco, lower cholesterol and lipid oxidation, and reduce psychosocial stress, which contributes to myocardial ischemia, plaque formation in the arteries, thrombosis, and arrhythmias (375).

Sant Rajinder Ji Maharaj is a modern teacher of meditation and has contributed to the teachings of meditation and connecting with our soul. His Holiness describes meditation as the surest way to spiritual growth. It is a personal, verifiable experience. His teachings lead us to progressive unfolding of the higher self with concrete goals and milestones along the way. The outer expression of the soul is the attention, which is scattered throughout our body and exits into the world through the five senses. To be aware of the inner light and sound, we have to withdraw our attention from the world outside and collect it at the seat of our soul. Radha Soami, in Indian language, means "lord of the soul." Satsang describes a group that seeks truth, and Beas refers to the town near which the main center is located in northern India. Radha Soami Satsang was established in 1891 and has followers in ninety countries. It is called Radha Soami Satsang Beas (RSSB). The central philosophy is based on a spiritual teacher who explains the purpose of life and guides and instructs members in a method of spirituality based on daily meditation practice. Members are vegetarian; abstain from alcohol, tobacco, and recreational drugs; and are expected to lead a life of high moral value; there are no cultural or religious restrictions and beliefs. Any one is welcome to join the path to spirituality.

Meditation is very useful for individuals with chronic dysregulation of control or cooling off of the sympathetic nervous system, either due to genetic predisposition, as seen in some families where siblings or parents have a short fuse and overreact to minor situations beyond the proportion of the given stimulus or situation, or to birth trauma, which is unnoticed. In some cases, it can be caused by early traumas, like physical abuse, sexual abuse, rape, or any distressing event. Such individuals have an unrealized flow of adrenaline without knowing what is going on. There is constant anxiety, restlessness, overreaction, some degree of cognitive impairment, uncertain feelings, defiance in younger adolescents, and the need to always be on the go, the urge to do things constantly. Their brain starts racing upon the slightest stimulation, visual or auditory, by association with past trauma. They experience some physical symptoms like palpitation of the heart, dryness of the mouth, anxiety, and some attention deficit. At times, they have an inability to pay attention, and at times, they feel their brain is driven by a motor that is uncontrollable. They have difficulty following directions (this is especially true in children and adolescents). They almost appear to have symptoms of hyperactive attention deficit disorder. I wonder about that, but I had an excellent treatment response to Ritalin while treating some of my patients. Should future psychiatrists think about that and introduce meditation or other nonconventional treatments to control such disorders?

Some have claimed controlling the intake of sugar and its products helps ADHD patients. For children, should we develop games that can induce relaxation to the point that these children learn to relax and get conditioned gradually to overcome the symptoms? In this electronic age, can we create computer programs that can address such issues to help such children?

It is hard to teach meditation to children, but can we develop new therapeutic techniques with the assistance of modern electronic gadgets, like TMS (transcranial magnetic stimulus), which is used in adults frequently? I am just curious and want input from my colleagues with open minds.

It may be easier in adolescents, since their frontal lobe is developed to have some control over the amygdala, which is the controller of the sympathetic nervous system. In adults, the same mechanism takes place, which in some causes generalized anxiety disorder (GAD). It is a chronic anxiety disorder, and at times, these people have anxiety attacks. Some individuals develop type-A personality disorder. (I will discuss GAD later.) Such individuals self-medicate to remain even keeled, since the frontal lobe functions remain in control. We use all kinds of reasoning to convince ourselves what we are going through is common. We tend to use defense mechanisms to justify our suffering, which is an excellent tool for our unconscious to use to keep us from going crazy. Denial is one of the major defense mechanisms. "I don't have any problems. I'm not crazy. I am not tense. I'm a strong man. Pussies have such problems!"

But deep down, their soul is crying, and they are drowning themselves in alcohol. Denial is very unhealthy, but it is a temporary tool used to help one pass through the difficult times and survive for a short time. It is very hard to release tension if you do not even admit that it exists and it is there. If others challenge you about your denial, you are unwilling to accept such challenges and refuse to look inside of yourself to see what is going on. It is pretty common in an alcoholic who makes life miserable and hard for his or her family. Resistance to seeking help or looking inside of you can cause resentment and anger in you and your family. Some of us avoid our friends and families by working excessively, which is justified by the increase in income. It is fine. When we have to do what we need to do, we should, but using it as a defense or avoidance strategy leads to becoming a workaholic. As long as it does not become an addiction to work, it is fine to work in your younger days. We all have do it. After we finish residency from medical school, we have to work hard. There is no free lunch. I survived by playing tennis for two hours and felt relieved by getting my tension out at the tennis court. We used to laugh about it, saying, "Either someone is going to beat the hell out of me, or I will beat the hell out of someone." Some of us take our work home. To me, that is a no-no. Limit setting for you and for others is a sign of loving yourself and loving others, as described in the limit-setting chapter.

Some of us use smoking as a stress reliever, and to change the monotony of work or as a stress reliever from the boredom of sitting idle. It becomes an addictive behavior. In teenagers, it may start as a sign of acceptance in a group or being cool, which gradually leads to marijuana use. Deepak Chopra describes smoking being like a monkey gnawing on a piece of wood in a cage. Excessive eating is a sign of stress in some and a sign of rejection to loved ones. Looking obese is a rejection of love to a loved one. Binge-eating, bulimia, and anorexia nervosa are linked to neurophysiologic malfunctioning in the satiety center of the hypothalamus; stress is a major contributor for those people. Many people tend to eat when they are depressed or are anxious. It is a red light for inner emptiness and a green light to fill that inner emptiness. It is a recipe for feeling bad afterward. Some have suggested that foods that relieve stress are rich in sugar and fat, like ice cream, French fries, chicken nuggets, and other fast-food products. The same holds true of other chemicals, which can cause impairment of frontal lobe functioning and reasoning. For example, we know smoking causes high blood pressure, heart disease, lung disease, emphysema, cancer, and sexual malfunctioning, but we still smoke. Drinking causes liver cirrhosis, but we still drink. Cocaine causes heart disease and brain damage, and we still use it. I guess we can live for our short lifetime without realizing the truth and not only live with stress but cause further stress in our lives due to our frontal lobe malfunctioning.

When you have attained the full experience and mastered meditation, the things that used to bother you are less bothersome. You respond well to external pressures, which are empowering to you. At this stage, you are able to maintain and deepen the balance to maintain the homeostasis of your body and be able to face various challenges in life candidly and without creating unnecessary stress.

There are many studies done on the effects of meditation on the brain. An article published in Frontiers in Human Neuroscience, published in February 2012, reported that there is an increase in gyrification in the right fusiform gyrus, right cuneus, and right and left anterior dorsal insula. Gyrification was more pronounced in the insula. It was presumed that the insula was the key structure involved in the aspects of meditation. What is gyrification? It is the patterns and the degree of brain folds, which means the depth and thickness of the neurons in the folds of the brain. These folds increase in size with the time of meditation, the longer the time, the thicker the gyrification (271). In addition to that, there was gyrifications in the parieto-occipital region also. This was all established by fMRI. Pagnoni et al. 2008 proposed that the regular practice of Zen meditation enhances the capacity for voluntary regulation of spontaneous mental activity; they attribute this to altered gyrification in the right insula. Damasio and Critchley (2004) suggested that meditators are masters in introspection and awareness, as well as emotional control and self-regulation. Moreover, meditators often practice techniques oriented toward enhancing the unconditional, positive emotional state of kindness and compassion (372). Hoffman added that alteration in gyrification of the right anterior insula in meditators might be linked to these singular abilities or dedicated practices (373). There is some evidence in these studies that there is gyrification in specific areas of the brain that remain engaged in the process of meditation. It is just like our motor area where a pianist, violinist, or a gymnast has motor areas that are well developed because of repeated use of the parts of the bodies involved, like fingers and toes. Repeated stimulus and use of these parts of the body increase the neurons of the motor area of the brain. The same holds true in meditation.

In my view, there are many parts of the brain used in the process of repeated yoga and meditation. Bartly suggested that over a long period of time, meditation can cause neuroplasticity changes on a microanatomical level, like synapses and dendritic connections, and regeneration by increasing connections, which can cause changes in the growth and thickening of the gyrus of the brain (274). This was the first extensive study conducted and published. Brain neurons and the mass of axons and dendrites are developed more in the areas that are used more often than those that are used less frequently. In response to actions and experiences, the connections are developed in the areas designated for those particular functions. The same holds true in meditation, which can induce neurogenesis and neuroplasticity, as explained earlier.

Full Catastrophe Living describes the world-renowned program Mindfulness-Based Stress Reduction (MBSR), which was developed at the University of Massachusetts Medical Center, where more than twenty thousand patients were treated for stress-related diseases. Several research projects reveal fascinating data in the area of neurophysiology and the recovery of patients who attended that program for eight weeks. I recommended this program to several of my patients and still recommend it to anyone who needs to learn about stress and healthy living. There were several studies mentioned in the book, which give us enough insight into the neuroscientific world to get some answers about the aftereffects of meditation. Holzel, using fMRI in patients who had attended eight weeks of the MBSR training program, showed that there was a thickening of a number of different regions of the brain associated with learning, memory, emotional regulation, the sense of self, and perspective taking. They found that the amygdala, a region deep in the brain that is responsible for appraising and reacting to perceived threats was thinner after people attended the MBSR program and that the degree of thinning was related to the degree of improvement on a perceived scale, which is attributed to neuroplasticity (377), (279).

To me, this evidences suggests that in humans, if the amygdala is thin, it sends a less-intense electric current, thus producing a weak electromagnetic field, which has a calming effect on the sympathetic nervous system and may have a stimulating effect on the parasympathetic nervous system, or it creates a balanced effect on both, which prevents overreaction to prevailing threats. The response is then appropriate. Or the amygdala sends a weaker electric current to the frontal lobe, just enough to create an appropriate response. This will provoke a debate in future neuroscientific research, which may have a positive impact and beneficial results in the research of the area of mental illnesses and personality disorders. It may tell us a lot about aggressive behaviors in various disorders and define some etiological causes of anxiety disorders, panic disorders, PTSD, and even terrorists' brain malfunctions, along with many more disorders and their treatment and management.

Another study conducted at the University of Toronto using fMRI by Farb, Nas, and colleagues found that people who had completed the MBSR program showed increases in neuronal activity with networks embodied in the present moment. Experienced people can learn functions, such as how not to get caught up with thoughts or wanderings of the mind. People who associated with the self as experienced across time had the most wandering of the mind. These studies suggest that by learning to inhibit the present moment in an embodied way, people can learn how not to get caught up with the wandering of the mind, and when they do get caught up, they can recognize what is happening and return their attention to the most salient and important part in the present moment. They also suggest that nonjudgmental awareness of our wandering mind may actually be a gateway to greater happiness and well-being right in the present moment, without changing anything. In the network of the self, there is an ongoing story of "me" and others, which gives us a clue that how we manage to live and function to live as an integrated whole being is grounded at least sometimes in self-knowing.

Studies conducted by Rosencrantz and colleagues that compared two programs, HEP, developed at Southern Connecticut State University, and MBSR showed smaller blister sizes of the skin due to stress-related skin lesions in the patients from MBSR because of the mindfulness of the meditation. These are called neurogenic inflammation (278).

A collaborative study at the University of Wisconsin, investigating MBSR, indicated that electrical activity in certain areas of the brain known to be involved in the expression of emotions (the prefrontal cerebral cortex) shifted from the right side to the left side of the brain and also added to the finding that a flu vaccine given to participants in the MBSR program had significantly stronger antibody response in the immune system within a few weeks (38). We are aware of that left-sided emotional individuals are more organized, concrete, and logical thinkers, while right-sided emotional individuals are more analytical, adventure-seeking, less concrete, and more flexible, which tells me that meditation could induce some discipline, logic, and concrete thinking so action could be taken based on logic. These were the first findings of the MBSR program as claimed by Jon Kabat-Zinn in his book.

There was an important finding in a study conducted at UCLA and at

Carnegie-Mellon University by Creswell and his colleagues. They showed that participants in an MBSR program were less lonely, especially the elderly, fifty to eighty years of age, in whom the C-reactive protein was reduced. This is a gene-related factor of the immune system response to inflammation, which is a core element of cancer, cardiovascular disease, and Alzheimer's disease (381).

During my research for this book, Charles Sherrington attributed the mind as having a function of its own. W. Penfield, my idol, was the one who wrote that there is an unexplained phenomenon going on beyond the neuronal functions in the brain, which he called "higher neuronal function." Sharon Begley (367, 131–132) wrote of His Holiness the Dalai Lama,

> Something had always bothered his holiness, that even if we accept the idea that the mind is what the brain does, and that feelings and thoughts are expressions of brain activity, isn't two-way causation possible? That is, maybe in addition to the brain giving rise to the thoughts, feelings and other cognitive activities that together add up to this thing we called mind, some aspects of the mind also act back on the brain to cause physical changes in the very matter that created it. In this case, the arrow of the causality would point both ways, and pure thoughts would change the brain's chemistry and electric activity, its circuits or even its structures.

It has been my quest for my entire life to find answers to this question. My hypothesis is exclusively my own. I formed it after years of thinking and learning about neurology and psychiatry. I have discussed it extensively in previous chapters. The answer to His Holiness's question is yes; there is a two-way streak. The neurons and the rest of our body function on the basis of electric current from our brain to every part of our body and back to our brain. Electric current generates an electromagnetic field, which is present all around our body and brain; this magnetic field is our cloud computation, which is specific for each function of our body, like sensations, motor functioning, and so on and so forth. This magnetic field feeds back to neurons to create thoughts, emotions, desires, wisdom, spirituality, and the rest of our functional components, like consciousness and unconsciousness. Please refer to earlier chapters in the book for more information. This magnetic field I call the soul. It is the energy used for various functions to make us a human being or an animal. How does it work in meditation? After all, in the studies described, we have concluded that there is a growth of neurons and regeneration of neurons as discussed in this chapter.

When we meditate, there is total focus on our frontal lobe. For example, once we close our eyes, our sensations are gradually decreased, like hearing, touch, and the rest of the sensations. There is total concentration, which localizes our electromagnetic field in the frontal lobe, where all the cognitive functions and the rest of the decisions are made. This concentration of the electromagnetic field gets stronger and stronger as we meditate. This energy leads to neurogenesis and neuroplasticity, creating thoughts, actions we want to take, lifestyles we want to lead, and the rest of the goals we want to achieve. Meditation creates more than an average electromagnetic field, which keeps enhancing until the stage of wisdom and finally spirituality is attained. For details, please refer to the section on the structure of the soul.

Meditation has been defined by many wise people and will be defined in the future by many more. My definition remains the definition for me and for those who believe in me.

Meditation is cold ice and cold water to volcanic hot lava. What do I mean by that? Here is an example. When we face the sudden death of a loved one or when there are catastrophic natural disasters, like storms, flooding, earthquakes, fatal disease outbreaks, nuclear bombs causing devastation, terrorist attacks killing innocent people, wars, or any other kind of devastation in our lives, there is an eruption of emotional reactions, which are similar to the eruption of a volcano. Snow in the arctic or water in the ocean, rain has a cooling effect on this lava, In the same way, meditation has a cooling effect on the fire burning inside our body and in our soul. There are fumes and clouds of evaporated water, which have a cooling effect because evaporation causes cooling. In the same way, our emotional cathartic reactions, like anger, confusion, and chaos cause fumes inside of us, but after we react to these events, there is a cooling effect once we realize something needs to be done. We pick our pieces and save others with a prevailing cool head. Others help us, and we feel somewhat reassured. There is debriefing, which gives us tools to deal with catastrophic events. In the same way, when our stresses and desires burn us, meditation has a cooling effect on our brain and soul to continue the path of a peaceful mind. All of these take time and coordination and action. So does meditation. Those who have adopted it as a way of life remain content with its wisdom. Others have resorted to other means of compensating, by substituting external means, like in this modern world, a game of golf and walking eighteen holes, swinging, going to the gym, jogging, and yoga. This is a meditative experience because it involves intention, commitment, concentration, continuation, and consistency. Eyes on the ball, head down, and execution of a learned swing—it is a meditative event for a golfer. Some call it walking meditation. Millions play every day. A few climb the ladder of their goal to the top. They learn to keep quiet and think of the next shot with full concentration and zest, leaving behind their anger, rejection, mistakes, and frustrations, looking forward to something new and good. Like a meditating man, who wants to achieve the same every time he meditates, a golfer uses his or her wisdom for the next shot. He or she has learned from the previous one. A golfer never gives up. If the score on one hole is bad, so what? The next one is a few yards away. Hope is the key. It walks just besides him or her; the same is true of a meditating person.

A golfer takes the best care of his or her health, nutrition, and exercise to be in perfect shape and strength, so does a meditating person. If one style of swing learned by a golfer does not work, he or she is flexible to learn from his or her coach a new swing, so is a meditating person. A golfer believes in a restful sleep and practices repeatedly to master the art, so does the meditating person. A golfer learns to be humble, pleasant, honest, graceful, charming, well-dressed, and willing to take healthy criticism and learn from it, so does a meditating person. Discipline is the building block of any athlete in tennis, football, baseball, cricket, or any other field of sports. This is true also in meditation.

Modern humans have learned to meditate while playing video games, watching an interesting movie or a sporting event, or texting on his or her phone. It is the new form of meditation. Should a modern person and thereafter new humans play a sport of meditation? I would say if they do not, I would inform them that every part of their life involves meditation directly or indirectly—in school, at home, or in interactions with anyone intellectually or socially.

It is a fresh breath of air to my lungs and to my soul. When I discuss breathing and meditation, it will be quite clear that a breath of fresh air is a soothing feeling for our soul. A good amount of oxygen is life for our body, brain, and soul. Without fresh air, we cannot survive. Just ask those who have a lung diseases how they feel when they gasp for a breath. We breathe through our mouth when our nose is blocked. Ask congested people how they feel? Fresh air is life for them and for all of us.

When we meditate, learning breathing is the first step to paying attention, which controls sensations to divert your attention to multiple thoughts. Therefore, breathing is not only life; it is life beyond life. It gives you a life to live. What could be better than that? We are pronounced dead if breathing stops. Our primary, secondary, and tertiary souls are unable to sustain and survive. Meditation is a breath of fresh air to me and my soul.

It is shade under a tree on a hot summer day. When we are in a scorching hot desert or any other place, what is our desire or need to cool our body? I use the metaphor of shade under a tree. When our brain and body are burning with anguish, anxiety, depression, pain, anger, frustration, and torture, we look for relief. Who could give fresh air and the solace to my burning soul? It is the calmness and peace of meditation that will cool off the burning fire of my soul. It is the cool shade of a tree through meditation.

Meditation is medication for my rapid heartbeat and electrocardioversion for my arrhythmias. Frustration, anguish, and stress causes my heart to beat fast and even irregularly at times, especially when I am having a panic attack and am fearful of dying. It is the calmness of meditation that will regulate my heartbeat by calming my sympathetic nervous system. Meditation gives me hope to live and abate the danger of death and anxiety I perceive. Meditation gives an electric jolt to my heart and asks it to beat regularly and calm down. I feel reassured and hopeful. Thoughts of death are fearful and painful while we go through an episode of panic attack, anxiety attack, or any dangerous threat in our lives. Meditation lessens the excessive electric current generated to stimulate the heart, which has to obey the orders of the sympathetic nervous system. Meditation reduces and regulates the excessive current, by regulating the adrenaline and reducing excessive stimulus.

It is an anticoagulant to my bleeding wound. By programming me for harmonious breathing and reducing my heart rate, meditation regulates the clotting factors, therefore healing the wounds of my body and the scars of past abuse and torture. It gives me insight into how to avoid rumination about the bleeding of my soul because of painful events of the past and present by enhancing reality and the strength of my coping skills, like a trained therapist or doctor would do. Meditation gives me strength and creates tools for my soul to deal with my bleeding, as a result of my jealousy and sinful acts and the harm I have done to others and myself.

Meditation is an ointment to my infected wound. When my soul is polluted by noxious acts and cynicism, meditation helps me get rid of infected thoughts by providing the guidance on how to do it. It gives wisdom and knowledge of how to clear out the putrid smell of an infected soul.

It is an antifreeze for my cars and other machines that operate on the principle of heat and fire. When a running car or a machine runs out of antifreeze, there is a fire, which produces fumes. My body and soul run on the principles of electric current, which when short-circuited cause a sense of fire in my body and brain, which deranges my brain and behavior. Dear meditation, you ask me to sit down and stop running like a mad elephant, to pay attention to what caused the lack of coolant in my body and soul. The gift of spirituality provides the coolant to my soul to put an end to the burning fire in the furnace of my brain and body so I can function and run like a normal car again.

It is an extinguisher, a truck full of water to spray on my burning house. When a house is on fire, we need a fire extinguisher or a fire truck full of water to put out the fire in the house and get us back again. It saves the rest of the burning house. If you give honest meditation, you get honest guidance to approaching the losses and gains in life. Meditation teaches me how to rebuild a better house than before to live in. It teaches me the value of life and the value of material things. They are there but never last forever. They come and go. With the power of your suggestion and the creation of wealth, my wisdom lives in houses beyond my expectations of satisfaction, contentment, needs, and possessions.

It is an evaluator to my burning desires before and after their fulfillment, the soothing love of a mother to a child and of a lover to the beloved. It is food for my body and soul to curb my hunger and thirst. It is a hope against hope, the wisdom of my soul, the opium for my pain and suffering. It is a stimulant to my immune system to protect me against any disease or illness.

Neurotransmitters and chemicals in my brain antagonize the ones that cause burning pain in the brain. Meditation is an antidote for my poisonous thoughts, actions, greed, needs, wants, and the rest.

It is a belief to hold on to. Time is on my side, and I make use of it whenever I want.

Meditation is soothing music and a song to my ears and to my soul. It is an insight into the existence of galaxies after galaxies beyond my reach and imagination, beyond after the beyond, a body of water bigger than any sea—the universe.

It is a soul mate I can depend upon in good, bad, and ugly times, a lover of lovers, a passion for the passionate, and an orgasm of my soul, which satisfies burning sexual desires. It is an idol of worship, an institution of education, and information for my soul. It is a tranquilizer for my sleep and sweet dreams, so I wake up fresh and alert the next day.

CHAPTER 6

WISDOM AND THE SOUL

Wisdom has as many definitions, as many as you are able to define and accept. According to the *Oxford English Dictionary*, wisdom is "the capacity of judging rightly in matters relating to life and conduct; soundness of judgment in the choice of means and ends; sometimes less strictly, sound sense, especially in practical affairs, also knowledge, enlightenment, learning and erudition (The quality of having or showing great knowledge or learning; investigation, observation, or experience)."

Wisdom is the ability to think, act, and use knowledge, experience, understanding, common sense, and insight (357). It makes me encouraged to learn that common sense is one of the criteria of wisdom. I do agree with that concept of wisdom. At the same time, I also emphasize common sense is the beginning of wisdom. Without common sense, there is no enhancement and growth of wisdom. As a matter of fact, common sense gives birth to wisdom. Without common sense, the enhancement of cognition, understanding, and desire to acquire knowledge is limited. That is why the saying goes "Common sense is not common." Wisdom needs the highest degree of adequacy in any circumstances with the least errors. Wise people are to apply acquired knowledge to understand other people and the situations prevailing in the surroundings at that particular time or times. The judgment, perceptions, and knowledge acquired by wisdom require proper and acceptable actions to be taken in the appropriate time with a follow-up of the results of the action taken. Wisdom requires appropriate control of one's emotions and feelings and of others' emotions, whenever needed. It is not limited to one's wisdom but requires understanding of others' wisdom or lack of wisdom with truth, sincerity, and honesty intact. The five D's—determination, detection, discretion, divulgence, and demands—are the key ingredients of wisdom.

Nothing is absolute or perfect in the universe. How can we expect wisdom to be absolute and perfect? I have to confess that without our neurological system being sound and on its normal path, which gives birth to our soul, wisdom does not and cannot exist. If it did, it was primitive wisdom, which unicellular organisms do have to survive and carry on their species. We got our genes from the cave people, who gave us their wisdom, knowledge, information, and experience gained with time. The definition of wisdom changed with time. It depended on the facts and situations, conditions, and environment prevailing at that time; therefore, the definition of wisdom remained dynamic, not static. What wisdom was to a cave person was different from what it was to a new human. What wisdom was to new humans is different from what it is to a modern human. With the invention of different religions in the world, wisdom relied on the belief system adopted by that religion, which forces me to believe that the belief of the particular religion defined the wisdom, depending upon their belief system and the cultural norms acceptable to their believers. The wisdom of those religions gave rise to wise new humans who were held in high esteem and worshipped, as grounds were laid for the followers and believers by them. Holy men were declared to be the wise men of that time. Those are the ones who dispersed their definition of wisdom. Those who followed were members of the elite group of the religious clan and modified the definition of wisdom as time needed and was appropriate to fit the time. The elite also wrote their own opinions and ideas into the history books and religious books, which all their subjects followed, both present and future. New humans gave birth to thinkers, inventors, intellectuals, sages, gurus, Rishis, and prophets, who became the symbols of wisdom. Their words were the law of the time. Those who refuted the authorities were punished to extremes, even killed or crucified. For examples, please refer to the history of Sikh gurus and Jesus Christ. I presume the prophets did not declare other prophets, for some reason, because most of them were declared by new humans as prophets after their death. I have not heard of a new prophet from the last five hundred years or more for the reason that modern humans were born. They have a different outlook on wisdom and religion. My view about wisdom is that every living soul has some degree, strength, and power of it, and if measured in inches and pounds, we may find variation in the quantity and quality of wisdom. We can learn something from a homeless man who knows much more about the streets than we do. Doesn't he have more wisdom about the streets then we do? Though I call myself and others call me a wise man, I learned a lot from an old wise man whom my father hired as a guard to watch the fruit orchards behind our house to protect them from thieves who would steal them when they were ripe.

One day, I came home and was very angry because I had had a fight with another kid in the school. We called this man Mali Baba, which in Urdu means "holy guardian." I rushed to Mali Baba, who always waited for me, having saved a few sweet ripe apples. He looked at me and said, "You look mad. Why? What is wrong?" First, he offered me fruit and asked me to sit down in front of his little shack made out of straw.

I munched on the fruits while he waited for me to say something. I finally blurted out, "I am going to beat the hell out that kid!" I told him the true story of the fight.

He listened carefully, and I felt he was very concerned about me, which was very reassuring. I gave a sigh of relief. After I was finished with my tale, he replied to me, "No, you do not have to fight or beat him. You should kill him with your kindness." He explained this me with a simple statement. "If you can kill someone with sweet sugar, why use poison? Be kind to him. It is fine to say sorry. It is great to admit your fault. It is wonderful to acknowledge his mistakes and yours too. It is awesome to forgive and move on with love and friendship." He added, "You will find yourself that he will apologize to you too. If someone makes himself your enemy, go on trying to be kind to him. Be friendly from your heart, and do something by which he will know you want to be friendly. If that doesn't work, just silently give him your love. He will change. Love is a powerful magnetic force, which will give him your good vibrations. He will receive it in his soul. It is wrong if your motive is to control him. Never misuse the power of love but continuously increase it to help others after you learn from this experience."

Sure enough, I did all that Mali Baba had told me to do. It happened the next day as he described. The other kid apologized to me, and we were everlasting friends, classmates, and competitors. We fought a war over who was going to be number one in the class until tenth grade. This makes me to believe that you do not need a PhD, MD, or law degree to be a wise man. Mali Baba was an uneducated man who had the knowledge of any educated man and at times much more than anyone I knew. His depth and knowledge was far more than any educated man. His experience was written all over his face, and his wisdom oozed out of the pores of his body. With his disheveled face covered with a beard, his fluffy hair not made up that day, his gleaming eyes, his dusty clothes, his old rotten chair with one arm missing, his torn shoes, his little hut with a straw roof, and beautiful trees full of unripe and ripe shinning apples, the fragrance of fruits and birds flying around to take bites of the fruits, his alertness to keep the birds away, and his demeanor—all were shining with the glow of wisdom. Those who wanted it always got it since there was no dearth of it.

It is just like an ocean. Even if you take a dip in it, it won't dry up; you will feel cooler and may even feel pleasant. It may change your views, your perspective, your thinking, and sometimes your life. Who is there to tell me that wisdom needs a college degree or education? I do believe in education and gaining knowledge, which will enhance your cognition and outlook on life. It may lead you to the path of wisdom.

I was learning how to use computers and was not going anywhere. I asked my younger son to teach me how to use computers. He tried his level best, but I was not going anywhere. I pushed and pulled him. One day, he refused to do so and advised me that the only way to learn computers was get lost anywhere you wanted to by a click of a button. If you fail to reach where you want to go or want to find, all you have to do is click on the close sign (X). After that, you just have to keep trying. One day, you will be confident and your desire to explore more will grow. There is infinite information, more than you will ever need or you will ever know. It is your fear that is holding you back, or you are not spending enough time.

I did not buy that. I figured out I had to offer him money for each lesson to motivate him. He accepted the offer. After half an hour, he told me, "Dad, I will be a billionaire by the time you learn computers."

I asked him how.

He replied politely, "Dad, you will never learn, and I will keep collecting money forever. That is how I will be a billionaire."

I laughed then and laugh about that statement still today while I am writing this book. I asked myself a question: Didn't that kid have wisdom to figure about my shortfalls? Yes, we all have some knowledge, but we all have some degree of wisdom regardless of who we are. I think my son had accumulated some form of wisdom in some area of interest and shared it honestly with me. Some will call it learning, retaining gained knowledge and using that appropriately at the required time and on demand to build the seedling blocks of wisdom.

I will agree with that and postulate that learning is an essential ingredient of wisdom regardless of age, caste, creed, or color. I think my son saw beyond the veil of my ignorance, fear of the unknown, lack of experience, and exceptional lack of understanding of ordinary experiences and made a statement honestly in the form of a joke, since he knew I didn't have billions. He not only provoked my thoughts but also created curiosity to explore more beyond the unknown. What is there behind the veil, hidden and waiting to be explored? Wasn't it a smooth and balanced dialogue between him and me? He being a teacher, and I being the student? His statement included spending time, being afraid, failure, clicking the button, and he would be a billionaire. All of these tell me that time is the backbone of wisdom; it took decades or years for Guru Nank, Baba Fareed, Kabir, Aristotle, Jesus Christ, Prophet Mohammad, Buddha, the wise men of the Hindus, and all wise people of the world to gain wisdom. Some believe that some were born with wisdom blessed upon them by God. To them, I say, even if they were blessed with wisdom, it took decades to share and teach humans about their attained wisdom by whatever means they attained the ultimate wisdom in their lives. So my first lesson was take your time to learn and experience the learned art, assimilate the true art, and discard the errors made during this process.

Failures is the true teacher for us humans, teaching us to appreciate the successes. No failure exists without success, and no success exists without failure. These are the two sides of a coin. Don't look at the engraved side of the coin. Do look at the other side of the coin, which may not be engraved and be just plain. This makes this coin useless. It may not have the value that we perceive it to have. It will not be accepted by anyone. In that case, our own perception and value of truth will be useless, not only to our consciousness, but to others too. In that case, the truth shall be insulted and covered by a sheath of falsehood. If this goes on for an extended period of time, the falsehood has to keep covering it with more sheaths of lies until it bursts with the external pressure of the truth or it remains hidden in its own sheath of lies never to be found.

Time is just like a breeze that keeps passing by. All we get is few breaths; then a new breeze comes and passes away never to be found. Our time comes and passes away never to be found. Those of us who get hold of time and make use of it will gain wisdom. Those of us who let it pass by without even taking few breaths will lose it forever, never to be found. All those people will have is regrets, unpleasant memories, fake beliefs, and shadows of darkness. Those are the ones I call ignorant of the time. Their guilt shall haunt them for not holding on to time and making use of it to the maximum potential and create everlasting memories of our lifetime or experiences gained, good or bad. The good makes us to excel, and the bad makes us to learn about the future to use time for our pleasures, to gain our knowledge and experiences, to test our hypothesis that we created for ourselves and others, to find the right and the wrong, the good and the bad, the up and the down, the pain and the pleasure, the falsehood and the truth, the haves and the have-not's, the give and the take, the care and the share, and rest of the ingredients of a beautiful life, just merely to become a wise person.

With calmness, tranquility, patience, and acknowledgement of its value, time shall give you what you invested in, back with multiple gifts you never expected. Some of us hold on to time with a negative frame of thinking, not accepted in our social norms, like seeking pleasure at the cost others (please refer to personality disorders). Some in this modern world may not have enough time to achieve wisdom, and some may even question whether we even need wisdom in this hi-tech world. They argue that wisdom is a barrier to progress in this modern world, particularly when their focus is on new consumer markets, unbridled profits, nuclear weapons, human cloning, satellites, polluting factories, and corruptions. The simple answer to that is the wisdom of the modern human created all this for the convenience of modern humans, who learned from new humans, who learned from cavepeople. Wisdom and knowledge have been gained over millions of years. We modern people have changed the landscape of the world and have emerging technology every day. I would be willing to stick my neck out and take the blame for complimenting the wisdom of modern humans to execute the knowledge into practicality to enhance the quality of human life. I do admit though that new humans have created good, bad, and ugly.

All I can suggest to modern humans is to keep the good going and do not ignore the bad and ugly. We have enough intelligence to make use of the bad and ugly to make good and use them to our advantage, which we have already done by using nuclear energy to create nuclear power stations to generate electric power to provide light to millions of people and factories, and so on and so forth. We the modern humans have already realized the urgent need to develop something different to enhance the wisdom to deal with the bad and ugly. There is a constant urge and debate to solve global warming to avoid doom and gloom to the human race and other living creatures. We are still struggling with solutions to solve territorial disputes, racial dissention, terrorism, economic disparity, and the arms race to be the world power. I am confident human wisdom will prevail to solve the problems in this phase of modern humans. We have enough human capital and an abundance of wise people who will tackle such problems with the passage of time. These are not natural disasters, which we do not have control over; these are man-made problems and humans and humans only can solve such problems.

I understood and accepted the advice given to me by my son about being afraid. A wise person always puts his or her best foot forward without any fear, without knowing the unknown, and without looking backward, because he or she is aware of what was in the past, what follows the present, and what is in the near future. Franklin D. Roosevelt, during the 1932 presidential election, said, "The only thing we have to fear is fear itself." Wise people are cognizant of that.

Zoroastrianism emphasized the experience of joy and pleasure. The question was raised, "Is living in fear and falsehood worse than death?"

Wisdom answered, "Yes, living in fear and agony is worse than death, because you live with it every day, and death abolishes it forever."

The wisdom of Zoroastrianism teaches us about the thought process of evolution, which is ongoing. It is within the cumulative power of humans to rid the world of disorder, poverty, misery, pain, suffering, and eventually death. Grief should be kept to a minimum, as tears for the dead are a hindrance to the progress and well-being of the soul. The role of humans in this world is to cooperate with nature on the neutral plane and to lead a virtuous life of good thoughts, good words, and good deeds on the moral plane. It teaches us the wisdom of duty, taking a wife and rearing one's children with care and love; one should take on the responsibility of making earth a fruitful, strong, and abundant place in order to resist the onslaught of the enemy, who is responsible for disease and death. On the nature of the plane, then, virtue is synonymous with fruitfulness and vice with sterility. Celibacy is unnatural and wicked. The human is not just a puppet or a pawn in the unfolding of this cosmic drama but is a most productive, purposeful creation of God. His or her task is to erase the lie in order to bring forth the creative evolution of the world. Unhampered by the shackles of predestination, the role of humans is to become the master of the future and make a wonderful world.

The wisdom of Zoastrianism is to educate the children and parents, who are responsible to teach them their religion without distortion and recognize their free will. They should accept their physicality of life and needs. This will teach them about the biological self, social self, and private self, and it is assumed that the perception of threatening stimuli creates fear arousal. The state of fear is believed to be an unpleasant emotional state that involves physiological arousal that motivates cognitive, affective, and behavioral responses directed toward alleviating the threat or reducing the fear. A perceived threat is thought to be an important factor in the process of fear. It consists of the perceived severity of the threat and the perceived susceptibility to it. In day-to-day threats and perceived fear, the amygdala and hippocampus are the parts of the brain involved in perceiving and reacting to the threats, producing responses to them. A wise person has mastered through these parts of the brain the ability to abate the fear and any threat by analyzing them with an appropriate response, which is timely and avoids overreaction or underreaction. This is attained with experience and reserved knowledge to be used on demand.

Modern humans have begun to realize and understand that we need to start thinking again about how to create new thinking and wisdom frameworks if we are to work toward peaceful, just, and sustainable human-oriented development. We must acknowledge that there are different understandings of wisdom, which vary from culture to culture and country to country, but the word wisdom is universal. Harter and Andrew (361) elaborated on wisdom with following facets:

- Problem solving with self-knowledge and sustainable action
- Contextual, sincerity to the circumstances with knowledge of its negative and positive aspects
- Value-based consistent action with knowledge of diversity in ethical opinions

- Tolerance toward uncertainty in life with unconditional acceptance
- Empathy with oneself to understand one's own emotions and morals, as well as the feelings of others and of oneself

Wisdom is a magnetic force that tells us not to be a chatterbox—talk, talk, idle talk. It dissipates the magnetic energy of your soul. It is also dangerous, because those who talk too much end up always saying the wrong things. These little words that come out of a loud mouth can explode others' dignity. A person who talks too much is a shallow thinker. A wise person talks less and directly from deep thoughts of his or her soul. He or she listens to others just to learn what it is all about without any judgment.

When a wise man talks with truth and honesty, his words are just like pearls and are valuable. When you do talk, give your whole attention to the person you are talking to and make sense, which comes naturally from a wise soul. When you shake hands, do so consciously so that you can give the magnetic energy of sincerity and friendship and try to help that person. Be positive and develop your own spiritual magnetism, and you will have the power of changing others. Wisdom integrates one's own helplessness, despondency, and feelings of worthlessness by using his or her cognitive framework, which I call using self-experienced cognitive and behavioral modalities. This simply means a negative frame of thinking is reconstructed by reality-based positive thinking. As in depression, there is a distorted negative frame of thinking; therefore, everything appears in the form of doom and gloom without the existence of such events. Everything looks like a dark shadow with no beginning or end. To a wise person, everything shines without shining, everything is bright without brightness, everything is tasteful without having a taste, and everything is pleasurable without having pleasure. There is no rush for this or that. All is there within, known to him or her. Temptations are things of the past. The present is pleasant, and the future will be born to know, to give, and to receive. There is no rush to jump into the future. There is plenty of time to be there. The goal is to hold on to the present time to get the maximum out of it before it slips away, leaving wonderful memories never to be found again. Wise people make use of time to the best of their ability, since they know that time once gone never returns. New time brings new things to be dealt with by past experiences and knowledge accumulated over a period of time in life. The wise person treats time gently, tenderly, thoughtfully, and patiently, like a lover treats the beloved one, gently, honestly, and carefully.

A wise person does not gobble a hamburger, rushing to swallow as fast as he or she can while driving or walking and talking as if there are no more hamburgers left in the world; he or she takes a bite at a time to appreciate the taste and pleasure of eating to subdue the lust of hunger. He or she treats hunger as a blessing to provide nutrition to the body and soul. He or she does not treat hunger as an evil thrust upon him or her to fulfill it with anger and hatred by shoving a hamburger into his or her mouth. He or she knows there are plenty of them. If he or she does not get it first, he or she will get it at last. The wise person sees it first and then feels it; he or she admires its shape, size, and contents without rushing to swallow it. Dr. B. Legesse, a neuropsychiatrist, describes wisdom as a superior ability to predict behavior or events, which could be used for the benefits of self and others and for a large group of people to promote the survival, cohesion, and well-being of that group or other groups. He proposed the neuroanatomy of wisdom as processed by our brain using specific parts for development. They are the following:

- Frontosubcortical neural networks
- Limbic system
- Mirror neuron system

The working of these systems in concert weighs the benefits and risks of various mentally modeled courses of actions, which generate wisdom in human beings. In addition, recent studies have recorded this function of wisdom, empathy, interpersonal relationships, cooperation, valuing others, and copying and learning from others' actions and gestures as demonstrated in monkeys (refer to the chapter on the anatomy and physiology of the soul) (362).

I do agree with the anatomical sites mentioned by Dr. Legesse and Dr. Rmachandran, but there is much more that we need to know. My view is that wisdom is not localized action, behavior, attitude, and expression. Wisdom is global. It is the sum total of all the action, reaction, behaviors, and accumulated experiences with the time. I propose some of the processes involved in the evolutionary process of wisdom are the following:

- Accumulation of information
- Assimilation and processing of information
- Association of information
- Authorization of information to be dispersed
- Availability
- Addition

These six A's I call Amar's A's. Let me explain them briefly.

Accumulation—humans and animals use all the senses to accumulate exterior and interior information. For example, with our eyes, we see our surroundings, how they look, their shape, size, and the rest. We get all the information and send it to our occipital lobe, which in turn sends information received to the frontal lobe. Ears hear and send all the information to the temporal lobe, which sends and receives information from the frontal lobe. With our nose, we smell. The information is received by the olfactory lobe, which sends information to the frontal lobe. The skin on our body sends the information of touch, temperature, pain, and pressure to the parietal lobe, which sends information to the frontal lobe, through numerous connections and relay stations on the way to their final destination, such as the limbic system, the hypothalamus, the amygdala, and so and so forth. I really am trying to avoid complicated names, and I feel I am not doing justice to my readers who are not familiar with neuroanatomy. You can skip this part if it is boring. Let neuroscientists argue about it. Information from the internal organs is sent by the sympathetic and parasympathetic nervous system to their respective centers in the hypothalamus, limbic system, and other parts of the lower brain, finally to reach the frontal lobe through pathways. Our joints and muscles send information through the Golgi apparatus to the sensory and motor center in the parietal lobe. Sorry too much anatomy. To simplify this, all I have to say is the final destination is the frontal lobe for numerous connections and processes. Let us forget about them. Take a pause and just remember all the information is sent to your frontal lobe by hook or by crook. I am obligated to mention that our railroad track is the spinal cord; everything runs through the spinal cord except vision, hearing, smell, and taste.

Assimilation and processing of information—information received in the frontal lobe is processed, like what needs to be done, how to respond, for example fight or fight, move your hand when it is burning, remove the thorn from your foot, wipe your tears away, say what you have to say, do what you have to do, do nothing, or go to bathroom if needed. Appreciate the beauty or ignore the ugly. Some of these are stored as memory, which will be used in the future; some are not needed and are discarded. Wise people never grow old; they grow to be graceful, loving, and charming. They do not give up and change with time; they take care of themselves and always look bright. If they do not know, they go ahead and learn. They do not let their body decay with aging; they invent things to do to look young and healthy. Age for them is just a number added to the last year. They remain enthusiastic, ambitious, and psychologically fit to face the challenges of life.

Association of information—our frontal lobe compares this information with past registered information, like how we responded in the near past, which means our memory stores and associates and compares with the registered memory. Once the process is completed to its satisfaction, then the decision is made to take action. It is final—good, bad, or ugly, it does not matter.

Authorization to disperse the orders—decision is dispersed to the little guys, wherever this information came from, to execute the action. It's like a film director who shouts to actors, "Action!" Memories of such an action are registered, and the results are evaluated every time. Conclusions are drawn; good ones are registered in the brain of a wise person, like reward versus punishment, good, bad, and ugly. This story is repeated every second, every minute, every hour, and every day for the rest of our lives. Please imagine how often it takes place in your life. It occurs time and again. It is a never-ending song and dance. So what happens to those who retain and learn well is always good; they keep exploring well and enhance the processing system beyond the needs, greeds, wants, haves and have nots, desires, and much more. Some individuals who develop this system to extremes become wiser and wiser. Those who enjoy and get rewarded by the bad get stuck with bad, the evil with deviant activities. They do not analyze and expand on the analyzing system and become Bernie Madoffs forever. Antisocial personality is one of the examples of someone who has no remorse or guilt for his or her criminal activities. As a matter of fact, they get a thrill out of criminal activities. Most jailbirds have a lack of development and do not process information. They are unable to integrate into socially acceptable behavior and tend to be maladapted. Their behavior is unacceptable by the norms of social fabric. Sooner or later, they get in trouble with the law. A wise person keeps on working to accumulate as much knowledge as he or she can process. He or she never quits until the end of his or her life. This concept is supported by studying Alzheimer's patients, head trauma, multi-infarct dementia, and many other neurological diseases in which wisdom is lost due to a loss of cognitive functions.

Availability—availability is a fairly new concept I developed after a vast experience of practicing psychiatry. There has to be storage of years of information in the brain or somewhere else in the form of energy, readily available on demand for a wise person and for the rest us. My view is as scientific as it can be; for example, after reading what I wrote, the question arises of what happens? All the information sent to our frontal lobe is transmitted through electric current (proven fact in neuroscientific studies). The light we see, the sound we hear, our senses of smell and taste, and all other sensations are changed into electric current by transduction, which passes through all relaying stations to coordinate the multitask function or functions (described in the chapter on the anatomy and physiology of the soul). This current from multiple sources and parts of the body generates an enormous amount of magnetic field around our brain and the rest of the nervous system and the body. Each part of the brain is represented in the magnetic field generated by the regions of the brain; for example, the sensory system generates a magnetic field. It will represent sensations. The magnetic field generated by the motor will be represented in the motor part of the motor magnetic field. The same holds true for functional components, including cognitive and memory centers. This magnetic field is backup storage for our brain, just like the cloud computation systems of computers, where data is stored for billions of documents. I presume computers were developed by humans based on human neuroanatomy and neurophysiology. Like computers, we have software and hardware. On a small scale, our computers can store information in chips with memory, but without software, the functionality of the computer is limited, so we have software for anything we want our computer to do. Different software increases the functionality of the computer.

In the same way, our nervous system gets programmed by sensory input and other processes described, which go on for our lifetime to honor humans who have struggled to find answers about the soul. I call this cloud computation our soul. It is with us as long as we are alive, so don't look for your soul in Wyoming while you live in Virginia Beach. Your soul is part of your body. Hold on to it. In a wise person, the continuous search for ingredients that make him or her wise with time is stored in the cloud computation. Some neuroscientists will be ticked off if they ever read this, especially if I add that the binding process of the brain is done by the magnetic soul, which means coordinating all the bits and pieces of information from our senses. It is all put together to produce results. For example, you hear, you see, you smell, you touch. To put all this together, we need coordination to respond. You have to talk back or decide to smile. This process is called binding theory. It sounds so simple. In fact, it gets more complicated. Let's leave the rest for those who want to explore and educate us with new, wonderful ideas, inventions, and discoveries.

Addition—this is achieved by a wise person after mastering the five Ds. A wise person adds to the information available and needed at the time, in the circumstances, and at the phase of the human evolutionary process. For example, we started as cavemen and then moved to a phase of new humans. Finally, we are at a stage of a modern man. Each phase had its needs, requirements, changing demands, circumstances of the time, and the evolution of the external environment. What wisdom was to a caveman changed for new humans. What wisdom was for new humans is different for modern people. This makes me believe that the timely change of wisdom has taken place with the change of the times. As mentioned earlier, that wisdom is dynamic, not static. Cavemen had the wisdom to survive, protect himself from predators, reproduce, and carry on the species. New humans used that wisdom and added to the past wisdom to explore and invent to enhance the quality of life with culture, social norms, law and order, and many more aspects. Modern humans expanded on the previous wisdom to the extremes of their capabilities to reach the sky. Future humans will expand wisdom with artificial intelligence beyond the skies. Futuristic humans will expand to the galaxies. This will go on beyond my imagination. This makes me believe that wisdom is a continuous process with no limits. It goes to infinity. I do predict that it won't come easy or free. Humans will pay a price for that. It makes me believe that wisdom has never been free and will never be free. It is preceded by foolishness, errors, and mistakes. Wisdom is a refined product of foolishness, errors, and mistakes, which not only give birth to wisdom but also validate its existence.

Foolishness has produced weapons of mass destruction for humans. We nuked Japan in World War II, which gave us insight what that does to the human race. Humans will continue doing foolish things, which will give rise to new wisdom needed for their time. I learned during my research about wisdom that there are countless definitions of wisdom written by countless authors. They were consistent with the needs of time. Some believe that wisdom is like truth, which never changes. To me, the truth of yesterday may be false today, so it is a relative belief, not a concrete one. Most of the authors describe the development of wisdom as an integration or merging of opposite aspects of a personality, the cognitive and emotional aspects of humans. Wisdom brings together previously separated processes of logical knowledge with uncertainty, volition, willingness, and motivation to act. Some humans have the desire to identify the wise people to learn and seek advice from. Wise people exists regardless of recognition. They speak out. "You want to learn about wisdom? Come to me. I will give it to you. If you don't want it, don't come to me. My wisdom will be everlasting. It will be found when the time needs it."

To a wise person, creation is freedom from old, unfounded myths. It is boundless, infinite, without limits, so the wise person lives in the prison of creation. It is for us, and it is ours. Nature had and has its own creation, but what we create moves with us when our turn comes. A great wise man of India, Robindernath Tagore, wrote, "Construction is for a purpose, it expresses our wants; but creation is for itself, it expresses our very being." To him, creativity was a deep soul process through which we strive to relate our souls to the wholeness of life, to different cultures, to nature, and to the divine. Robindernath Tagore was a Nobel Prize laureate in literature in 1913. He gave us great insight into wisdom, which did not come easy to him. Eighty years of his life was the quest to achieve wisdom. He lived through British rule in India. His wisdom forced him to urge the masses to avoid victimization and instead seek self-help and education. He saw the presence of the British administration as a "political symptoms of the social disease." His view was to knock at heaven's door of wisdom was to be creative. According to him, an attitude of freedom and emotional sensitivity are central to creativity. He writes, "We must free ourselves to go beyond the constraints of the world presented to us to try to discover ourselves, only then we are able to create new realities and we must allow space for the expression of our feelings and senses in order to give 'intimate' life to the world around us.(384).

After his words of wisdom, the era of wisdom started to achieve freedom. Brutal times gave birth to wise people in the world like Gandhi, Nelson Mandela, Reverend Martin Luther King Jr., and many more who sacrificed their lives. Their goals were the same: to free us from the shackles of slavery. This makes me believe that brutality plays an important role in the creation of wisdom. All these known leaders had a common belief in "nonviolence" and freedom from any racial, cultural, or political dominance. Most of the wise people were born to curb the tyranny of barbarism and cruelty of rulers.

There is a good example from the birth of Sikhism in India. The first guru was Guru Nanak. The tenth guru was Gobind Singhji. Muslim rulers were ruling the in North India, called the Mogul Raj; all the gurus went through man-made torture where humanity did not exist. All the gurus were tortured and tormented, and some were killed. Hindu temples were dismantled and were forced to convert to Islam. I really do not have the exact number of Hindus killed or converted to Islam, but there is mounting evidence of that in literature. Both the ninth and the tenth guru, along with his four sons, were brutally murdered. These were saints, wise men of the time who believed in peace, love, and charity and refuted tyranny and cruelty. They may be gone, but their wisdom and legacy will remain everlasting. This makes me believe that brutality gives rise to wisdom, and wisdom with time will eradicate brutality forever until new events take place in the history of humankind and life goes on.

This gives us another clue that wisdom could be timely with the situation and conditions prevailing at the time, so it is fair for me to say that wisdom leaves its footing and changes with the passage time. It gives rise to persistence or persistence gives rise to wisdom and vise. I leave that for you to decide. This reminds me of Eric H. Erickson, an analyst who described wisdom as an "inner strength of human beings." He added that wisdom was detachment with life itself in the face of death itself. He believed that each generation owes the next generation the gift of wisdom, to learn it and use it as a guide for them and find for itself the wisdom of ages in the form of its own wisdom. The process of inheriting and refining wisdom has gone on from generation to generation; this is how common or practical wisdom has evolved in human society through the ages, which leads me to believe in my theory of the basic science of cloud computation mentioned earlier.

One evening, I invited a few friends over. One of them was an atheist who would argue and feel angry (mildly) every time God was mentioned by some. He refused to accept the concept of the soul as well. I asked him, "Why is it that you feel so upset about God and the soul?"

His answer was "This is all nonsense created by man to displace his action, his good and bad, right and wrongdoing to God so he does not get punished by his own guilt, so it is God's doing what I am doing, and the soul is part of all these myths, mysteries, and creations."

I paused and told him that the soul and nature existed way before religion was created by humans, and wisdom was created by humans through learning, experience, and the growth of the human brain. "So you don't have to believe in religion, but you have to acknowledge the existence of the soul and wisdom." I asked, "What is the symbol of God in your belief system?"

His answer was "The sun and the moon."

"All right," I answered, "so you call them the sun and the moon. Some call them God. Then what is the difference or dispute? You gained wisdom the same way a religious man gained wisdom. What is the difference?"

He refused to accept the whole argument and ended up with a statement: "This is all nonsense. I do not want to discuss it."

And we ended the discussion. The point I am trying to make is humans have developed their own rigid paths in life, but all of us walk on the same earth with different paths. In the end, there is the same end for all of us, regardless which path we traveled through or what color, creed, or race we belong to. The path of wisdom is the same for all of us no matter which country, culture, religion, or color we belong to. This inspires me to make a statement that wisdom has a universal, fundamental origin and development in all humans. Some could argue that a superior race has superior wisdom. Intelligent humans have superior wisdom. They can argue that a hungry man has no time to think about wisdom; all he can think about is how to quench his hunger day after day. His thinking is governed by food and food only. They are right to think that way since it is true even in the modern age that there are millions and millions of people who go hungry every day, and those who have abundance waste more than they can eat. This creates a hot debate among us and other selves. Who is right, and who wrong? The wisdom of cultures and societies does exhort us to share with the poor and needy. Even cave people did that. Those who are greedy glut themselves and overdose on food. They die of diseases caused by overeating. There is a difference between the two. The hungry man has developed wisdom to survive first, so he can continue the species. If he did not pay attention to survival, he would not be wise but ignorant. This probably happened to many species that went extinct. This forces me to make a statement that need is the mother of invention for the birth of wisdom.

I learned from a commercial on TV that a double hamburger is on sale and a Big Gulp is double in size. Coke is available, all you can drink. Both of my sons pushed me to take them to eat and drink that. To my surprise, they were not able to finish the food. I asked, "Do you want more?"

"No, Dad."

They never asked for that food again. This experience laid the foundation for early emergence of primitive wisdom. This event gave me insight to believe that wisdom must have stages of development, which I presume could be the following:

- Early onset—this stage has potential, and that potential is recognized and reinforced by subsequent experiences and cognitive functions.
- Late early onset—the experiences and learned behaviors are integrated into the self and soul. The self-identification and others are well understood and accepted. Altruism starts emerging. Good, bad, right, wrong, and other experiences are identified and differentiated at this phase of life reality. Reaction, response, and resolution are key ingredients leading to and strengthening wisdom.
- Middle stage onset—social, cultural, legal norms of society are well integrated in the self and academic knowledge is put to work. Self-reliance, independence, and the sense of duty to fulfill responsibilities are fully developed, for example raising a family and fulfilling responsibility to its full potential.
- Late middle stage onset—wisdom has emerged to a stage where the future and its planning dominate thinking and behaviors, like saving wealth for the future and planning for the well-being of the family and others around.
- Late onset—death is accepted as a truth of life. The desire to share, care, and give acquired knowledge of life to others becomes a dominant factor in this stage of wisdom. The resources, reasoning, responses, reality, results, reactions, and resolutions (7 Rs) are the hallmarks of wisdom of this stage of life. Resources are used appropriately without pollution or abuse. Reasoning is the yardstick by which to draw conclusions without the foul smell of unreasoning. Responses are weighed and calculated with the shining bright glory of reality. Results remain results to be resolved with time and conditions prevailing in the environment. Reactions are balanced with kindness and the patience of a wise person.

- Final stage onset—this is the concrete stage of wisdom. It is open to all and to self and others as well. Those who want it will ask for it and will get the benefit of the wisdom. Needs, greed, and desires are under control. Acceptance of death and others dying is a reality. Peace and love are the food for the soul. Mortality and death become the best and the last friend to make love to. The definition of wisdom does not matter to these people. Whether it is recognized by others or not makes no difference to them. Contentment and self-satisfaction become the breath of the soul. Beliefs of the past become the passion of the future, for example religion and its beliefs. For some, it is nature and serving humans and other nonhuman living souls, dedication to altruism, humbleness, or peace. Love is unconditional. Rewards, names, fames, and claims are things of the past. Detachment from possessions and achievements becomes the pleasure of the soul of a wise person. Pretentions, myths, falsehoods, control, power, and lust for sex and money are dissolved like a teaspoonful of salt in water, never to be seen again.
- Spirituality is the final stage of wisdom. Since wisdom is infinite, there is no control of humans. It will remain infinite as long as humans exist, and it will become finite upon the extinction of humans. It will then be taken over by an unknown species of humans or nonhumans never to be known.

John Uebersax, PhD, describes wisdom as having two different definitions: a practical knowledge gained by experiences associated with age, by which he means it comes with age; and a transcendent quality in the sense that it may be like a stepping outside of mental processes. He proposed extensive definitions of wisdom, some of which I am delighted to write about because without his definitions, wisdom would remain incompletely defined.

- Wisdom is discernment and judgment; transcendent knowledge; spiritual knowledge; mental skill, agility, and subtlety; discretion; mental dexterity; and knowledge of the best ends and means.
- Acuity (mental) is mental sharpness, the ability to resolve fine detail, quick and penetrating intelligence, and mental acuteness, sharpness, and keenness.

- Consciousness is knowledge of one's own thoughts or actions; the faculty, the power, or the inward principle that generally decides as to the character of one's own actions or specifically warning against and condemning that which is wrong and approving and prompting that which is right; and discernment of one's motives.
- Contemplation is the act of the mind in considering with attention or meditation on or mental communion with divinity.
- Discernment is the power or faculty of the mind by which it distinguishes one thing from another; the power of viewing differences in objects and their relations and tendencies; and penetrative and discriminative mental vision; acuteness; sagacity; or insight.
- Discrimination is distinguishing or noting and making differences; acute discernment.
- Foresight is the act or the power of anticipation; prudence; wise forethought.
- Illumination or enlightenment make clear to the intellect or conscience; shedding the light of truth and knowledge upon; spiritual insight.
- Insight is a sight or view of inside of the mind; a deep inspection or view; introspection, mental revelation.
- Intellect or intelligence is the part or the faculty of the human soul by which it knows; the capacity of higher forms of knowledge.
- Introspection is the act or process of self-examination or inspection of one's own thoughts and feelings; the cognition which the mind has of its own acts and states; self-consciousness; and reflection.
- Intuition is direct apprehension or cognition; immediate knowledge, as in perception or consciousness; quick or ready insight or apprehension.
- Judgment is the operation of the mind, involving comparison and discrimination, by which knowledge of the values and relations of things, whether of moral qualities, intellectual concepts, logical propositions, or material facts, is obtained.
- Prudence is sagacious, good mental judgment in adapting means to ends; circumspection, or determining any line of conduct; wise forethought (364).

I do not think he has left anything to be added, though I do believe that wisdom is a gift from wise people to nature and to the rest of the universe.

I would like to give credit for the contribution of the concept of wisdom to religions, which made people wise, though humans created God, which I presume has given us the power of the creation of wisdom. Which came first? I leave that for readers to decide. Hope and belief by themselves are a strong force to motivate us to look for the best rather than being hopeless, which itself is a negative and discouraging force. It suppresses initiative to even start taking action. Religion is a strong cohesive force to give support and strength to initiate and continue actions with the hope that God will take care of everything, even if things go bad. It is still a defense mechanism to say "It is all in God's hands, good or bad." When something bad happens, we say, "Well, it is due to his wishes, whatever happens," which gives us peace of mind to ride through believing that God will come to our rescue.

The word wisdom was derived from the Latin word sapient. The name Homo sapiens was given to humans by Carl Linnaeus (365). This gives me the freedom to write this poem.

O Wisdom! You are the flower of flowers, the color of colors, the shine of the shiner, the nectar for your bees who when they drink it are intoxicated by your fragrance and taste. They are addicted to your offer and addicted to your nectar. Once they have their fill, they remain intoxicated until the end. New ones look for you until they can haunt you and find you. There is no end to your intoxicating nectar. Those who like to find you will find you. Those who remain ignorant of your existence live as ignorants. You are deeper than deep oceans, wider than galaxies. You are a song for the singers. You are a musical instrument for artists.

O Wisdom! You are the dance to a dancer. You are the eyes to the blind. You are sound to the deaf. You are food for the hungry and water for the thirsty. Those who are blessed by your grace never go hungry or thirsty.

O Wisdom! Their hunger and thirst is gone forever.

O Wisdom! You are ointment for the pain. Those who use the ointment never have pain.

O Wisdom! You are the friend of friends, love to your enemies, peace to the angry.

O Wisdom! You are life to the living. You are feelings for a feeler.
O Wisdom! You are advice to an advisor. You have your own eyes, ears, smell, taste, pleasures, and pain.
O Wisdom! Teach my soul how you use them. I have used them but all in vain. I am blind to what you see. I am deaf to what you can hear. I feel the pain, which to you is pleasure. What you taste is delicious; to me, that is bitter. I surrender to you my belief, faith, religion, wealth, knowledge, needs, and greed. Just embrace me like a lover embraces a loved one, like a mother embraces her child, holding it in her lap never to let it go. So hold me in your lap and don't let me go.
O Wisdom! You be my king, and as my master, I will remain your slave. You be my teacher. I will remain your student. Hold my hand and walk me through the path of my life.
O Wisdom! I beg you, urge you, please don't abandon me. I want to live and die with your grace and your blessings.

This poem is my credo and vision on wisdom and how I view and value life.This I share with you.
—Amir J. Singh

Religious Definitions and Descriptions

Buddhists have expanded on wisdom, which is the fundamental principle for attaining wisdom that is very meaningful to their beliefs. A wise person is blessed with good physical, verbal, and mental conduct. A wise person conducts him- or herself pleasantly. They describe wisdom as an antidote for the self-chosen poison of ignorance, as described in book of Buddhist Dhammapada (366).

- A wise man is the one who discriminates right from wrong.
- A wise man leads others without violence and respects their rights and dignity.
- A wise man is fearless without hate and has a calm demeanor.

- A wise man discards the evil vengeance and understands good and evil.
- A wise man turns greed into generosity, anger into kindness, and ignorance into wisdom by the power of meditation.

Buddha emphasized that the mind without dispute is self-natured discipline, the mind without disturbance is self-natured meditation, and the mind without ignorance is self-natured wisdom (366).

Islam described wisdom to be greatest gift humans could ever have. According to the Koran, wisdom is provided to a person by God. It is given to whom he wishes. This is the best gift ever given to a person. The pilgrimage to Mecca (al-Hajj) itself reminds Muslims about wisdom through their seeing and hearing about the land.

Judaism regards wisdom as the highest virtue, along with kindness and justice. Some have said the word wisdom appears almost 222 times. Fear of YHWH created wisdom in humans. There are some references to wisdom being personified in a female form that calls aloud in the streets. She raises her voice in the marketplace. Wisdom in Judaism began with God and was given to humans to foresee the consequences of their choices for the future and so they could learn from the past.

Christians believe that Jesus represents the wisdom of God. Hindus believe that wisdom is a state of mind and soul in which a person achieves liberation (moksha). A Hindu believes wisdom is knowing oneself as the truth and basis for the entire creation in all its facets and forms and for having a true relationship with paramatma (God).

Confucianism teaches that wisdom can be attained by reflection, imitation, and experience. A wise person never tells his or her wisdom unless asked. The love of learning is related to wisdom.

Taoism relates wisdom to charity, simplicity, and humility. Knowing others is intelligence; knowing yourself is true wisdom. Mastering others is strength; mastering yourself is true power.

Sikhism teaches us to work, worship, and give to charity. Honest living, peace, and love come from wisdom. Our soul is part of Waheguru (God).

Going back to my son's advice (I will be a billionaire) makes me think hard about what he meant by that. It explains to me how a modern person thinks and will continue thinking. Humans have reached the climax of intelligence. Modern humans are disrupters of the past. We may call Warren Buffet and Bill Gates rich men, but I call them wise men of the present. You may call Google, Amazon, and Facebook a monopoly. I call them the wisdom of the present and of the future. With a few clicks of the computer, I can have anything I want. I used to cram with books in the medical school, but now, with a few clicks, I can have any information I need. We may not need as many doctors as we have now. Computers have already started diagnosing patients and spit out the treatment protocol. Our information is in our pockets or in our hands, held in devices which we call smartphones. Artificial intelligence of the present times will be called real intelligence and will control our lives. Modern wisdom will replace our old wisdom.

CHAPTER 7

SPIRITUALITY AND THE SOUL

S pirituality has been described by humans as the time and needs of the time evolved. From cave people to new humans to modern humans, we have always had the curiosity and desire to describe spirituality. The definition was dominated by the new humans in terms of religion, when it was invented by humans. The word *spirituality* is an English word originally developed mainly by believers of Christianity, referring to a life pointed toward the Holy Spirits (288). During late medieval times, the meaning was broadened to include the mental aspect of life; then it spread to other religious traditions and broadened to refer to a wider range of experiences. As a matter of fact, Hindus had developed their own explanations of spirituality in their own Sanskrit language, which the West translated after the English invaded India. In between, whoever learned and wanted to experience it and explain it did their best with the advent of knowledge and experience, either by good deeds or wrongdoings.

Traditionally, spirituality refers to the religious process of reformation, which aims to recover the original shape of humans, oriented at the image of God as exemplified by the founders and sacred texts of the religions of the world. Wise people have always existed, even when evil acts were at their worst because of the power and greed of certain people in human history, which exists even today. Hindus originally described spirituality in Sanskrit with the word kaistrajna. It defines spiritual practice as one's journey toward moksha (freedom from death and birth), awareness of self, the discovery of higher truth, and a consciousness that is liberated and content. Hindus describe four paths to attain spirituality.

- Jana marga is a path often assisted by a teacher (guru) in one's spiritual practice.
- Bhakti marga is a path of faith and devotion to a deity or deities; the spiritual practice often involves chanting or kirtan and music.
- Karma marga is the path of one's work and honest living; the honest practice of work itself is a spiritual practice in daily life, regardless of its rewards.
- Raj marga is the path of cultivating necessary virtues, like self-discipline, meditation, contemplation, and self-reflection, sometimes with isolation and renunciation of the world (391).

Buddhism has a deep-rooted philosophy about spirituality. It is unique in its own way compared to other religions. Some assert that it is not a religion but a way of life we want to lead regardless of any affiliation to any religion. Buddhists believe that there is no god, and Buddha himself was purely a human. Anyone can follow his path, and our enlightenment will be exactly the same as his. Ultimately, we are no different from him. It is all about your goodness as an individual. Buddhism is not about salvation or about sin. It is not about becoming somebody different. We all live in this world with its goodness and badness, ups and downs. We do not have to struggle against our world. We are basically good as well as confused, and we all have different minds, needs, and greed. Suffering is the starting place and inspiration of the spiritual path. The question is what is the cause of suffering? We are caught in a dream of "me and them," which we have created. The noble truth is cessation of the suffering, which could be attained by discipline, effort, meditation, and wisdom. The mind is the source of our suffering and joy. Meditation is the antidote for our wild mind, through which we develop a passion for ourselves and for others. Those who suffer our insight will encourage us to help others. We all have to do for ourselves because we have to face reality alone. There is no refuge, and not seeking protection is the only real protection. As humans, we are intelligent, strong, and creative, with loving hearts and proven, effective methods. Therefore, we can rouse our confidence and renounce our agony and pain. In Buddhism, there is a spiritual and nonmaterial reality. It is rational and scientific, helping us to lead better and more caring lives in this modern time without any restrictions.

Spirituality is in and from the human mind, not from God, since the mind has matter behind it with feelings and emotions. It undergoes constant growth and change. In Buddhism, nothing is accepted purely on the basis of somebody else's spiritual authority. The Dalai Lama has said that Buddhism must give up any belief that modern science disproves, which speaks for itself. In my research, this is the only religion that has adopted the modern scientific views with flexibility to prove them on your own, because spirituality is your own; you cannot borrow it or buy it. We should be willing to seek guidance when needed to walk us through the path of spirituality. For millennia, it could be the best tool in people's lives to attain spirituality and wisdom by making it a way of life (392). It is most important to develop spirituality and to realize that our soul is the seat of spirituality.

Zoroastrianism is based on an innovative and realistic approach to life; they emphasize the innate reasoning of humans. In their view, spirituality is not gained through blind faith and belief, but by using the mind and intellect, which allows a man to reason and thereby understand the purpose of life. Innate reason gives a person the power to think, infer, and comprehend in an orderly and rational way. It is the faculty of clear vision through which the person gains insight into the workings of nature and of the physical, psychological, and spiritual worlds. Reason in spirituality may be recognized as the super rational, which is often allied to the intellectual intuitions, a domain in which the human begins to understand the eternal and immutable principles of life. Innate reason is one of the components of the mind that has to be trained in order that humans may generate fewer wrong thoughts, words, and deeds. Reason on the psychological level is the power to arrive at the right decision and conclusion, while the source of orderly conduct is the manifestation of reason in the physical world. Reason is said to sustain will and impel it to perform certain actions Thus, in Zoroastrianism, humanity is encouraged to develop the faculty of reason in order that through controlled will, an individual may choose to generate the right words and deeds (416). The spiritual system involves the use of all the tools including reasoning and intellect for the progress of the person and the acceptance of many facets of human nature, like acknowledgment of the emotions of love and joy.

I describe spirituality as selflessness, one concerned more with needs and wishes of others than his or her own. These people are altruistic. They have little or no concern for themselves, especially with regard to fame, position, money, and so on, and they are unselfish. It sounds like a very harsh word, but it is important to understand that you do not lose yourself; rather you are willing to do something for others when needed. A soldier on a battlefield would do anything for his comrades, even sacrifice his life. We must have come across events where a police officer was killed while trying to save his comrade's life. Alvi Feldman put it right for us to understand what it meant. He wrote,

> Being selfless is a mind-set. On a simple level, it's about putting someone else before you. It's about doing somebody a favor even when it hurts a little. It's about realizing that life isn't just about your own needs and preferences, but rather looking out for another's as well.

Feldman wrote an interesting story about how, when we reach a certain point in life, we realize that a selfish life is a meaningless one. A wealthy man prepared two wills. The instructions were clear. The first was to be opened immediately after his death and the second one only a month later. A sad day came when he passed away. Upon opening the first will, his children were shocked. It read, "Bury me with my socks." That was the entire message. Obviously, even after many negotiations with the burial society, the children were unable to fulfill their father's last request.

A month passed, and the time came to read second will. Nervously, the eldest child opened it.

"My dear children," it read, "You are all undoubtedly still confused about my first will. It is an important lesson that I wanted to teach you: no matter how much wealth you accumulate, you won't even be able to take your socks along with you to the grave. Most of us are selfless when it comes to our relationships with our children or our wives and loved ones. We are willing to do anything for our children, like feeding them, schooling them, and much more. Selfless families are very healthily in their relationships and raise happy and healthy people. Some studies show that adults keep grudges and children don't, because adults want to be right over happy, while children choose to be happy over being right" (410).

- Poise-Balanced, gracious, tact in coping or handling.

These qualities are pleasant and result in tranquil interactions with others. Dignified and self-confident people who attains the wisdom and are poised have reached the stage of poisedom. This is my original thinking. I do not know that there is any word called poisedom. These are the processes of development of spirituality through wisdom. Poised individuals are balanced, like equal weight distributed into two pans of an old weighing machine, which is a symbol of justice and law. Some equate it to the hovering and gliding of a bird in the air. The bird remains evenly balanced. My feelings about being poised are expressed in the following poem.

> Oh, poisedom removes the veil of guilt and shame, which covers me both outside and inside.
> Dear poisedom, I confess to you about my ignorance, anger, and vengeance.
> I do not know where it came from or where it is going to take me.
> If only I knew, I would not ask you but would enjoy the glory.
> So do not let me down. It is not my fault, I tell you now.
> I was born and raised with that and am leading my life with that.
> My awareness is bothering me now, so I beg you,
> by your power, remove the veil of guilt and shame.

- Inspiring

These individuals are very encouraging to others and make others feel confident. They are also eager to learn. A spiritual relationship is a pure form of relationship. Both can express their feelings and thoughts openly and fearlessly. Interaction is expressed and acknowledged at an equal level. Expressions and even grievances are accepted without any anger. One has to learn to express feelings without blaming defenselessly. There are no hidden meanings or agendas. The joy of such a relationship is seamless and vibrational. Both operate at the level of equal vibration of the magnetic field of their souls.

- Rational

They are encouraging and cause people to want to do or create something. Sometimes, they give ideas to others to do something creative. These individuals are very animated and provide help to be confident to everyone they know or come in contact with.

- Intuitive

These wise people have the ability to know or understand things without proof or evidence, having intuitions based on or agreeing with what is known or understood.

- Thoughtful

These individuals are very thoughtful of others and are deep in their thoughts. They not only think before they speak but also understand how others think and act. They are reflective, introspective, meditative, cognitive, and thoughtfully expressive. They show consideration for the needs of other people and are attentive, helpful, kind, understanding, concerned, compassionate, and unselfish.

- Unconditional

Unconditional love is affection without any limitations. Sometimes, we call it altruism. It is not subject to any conditions. It is finite, wholehearted, unreserved, unlimited, unrestricted, unmitigated, and unquestioned.

- Authentic

Authentic is being genuine, not copied or false. Its origins are supported by unquestionable evidence. It is of undisputed origin.

- Loyal

Loyalty is giving or showing firm and constant support or allegiance to a person or institution. It is being faithful, true, and devoted. It is staunch, reliable, and trusted. It is trustworthy, dutiful, and dedicated.

- Informative

An informative source provides useful and interesting information. It is always instructive, illuminating, enlightening, revealing, and explanatory. It always serves to inform and provide disclosures.

- Trusting

Trusting people show sincerity, not suspicion. Trusting is a reliance on the integrity, strength, ability, and surety of a person or a thing. It is a firm belief in the character strength of someone or something It is a belief in some else's honesty.

- Yearning

Yearning is a feeling of intense longing for something. It is a longing, craving, desire, want, wish, hankering, urge, hunger, or passion. It is a powerful desire for something.

- Spirituality

Spirituality is the awakening of inner feelings about oneself and the higher consciousness. Spiritual humans acknowledge their present, past, and future state of reality, which caused and will cause suffering. They can overcome the suffering through discipline and by use of highly evolved cognition. Spirituality takes us beyond dogmatism, fundamentalism, and obscurantism, which are responsible for divisions and disunity between nations and people. Every discipline has tried to explain spirituality, depending upon their thought and the principles of the belief system they follow, including all the religions of the world. Harleah G. Buck says that most humans have a supreme being, which may or may not involve religious structures or traditions. Elkin expanded the definition of spirituality using both religious and nonreligious beliefs and expressions, which are (394):

o Transcendent dimensions—belief in more than that which is seen, which may or may not be belief in God, and belief that personal power is drawn through harmonious contact with these dimensions o Meaning and purpose in life—deep confidence that one's life has purpose, emerging from a quest for meaning

o Mission in life—sense of responsibility to life, knowing that in losing one's life, one finds it

o Sacredness of life—belief that life is holy

o Material value—realization that ultimate satisfaction is from spiritual, not material things

o Altruism—belief in social justice and awareness that "no man is an island"

o Idealism—commitment to the actualization of positive potential in all aspects of one's life

o Awareness of tragedy—deep awareness of human pain, suffering, and death and that life has value

o Fruits of spirituality—benefits of spirituality realized in relationship with the self, nature, and what one perceives as the ultimate

Roger in 1970 summarized his views as (395)

o Feeling confident that life is meaningful, which includes having a sense of mission in life

o Having a commitment to the actualization of positive potential in all aspects of life, which includes realizing that spiritual values offer more satisfaction than material ones and that spirituality is integral to one's relationship with self and all else

o Being aware of the interconnectedness of life, which includes being conscious of tragedy and being touched by the pain of others

o Believing that contact with a transcendent dimension is beneficial, which includes feeling that all of a life is sacred

These definitions are mostly generalized, because it is difficult to apply to all of us, since we are all wired differently biologically and genetically. We come from different cultures and religions or are nonbelievers in God, which includes atheists. The basic commonality among us humans is cognitive functioning, which raises many questions. Are we all cognitively functioning at the same level? Human development is a lifelong process, characterized by both predictable patterns and individual variations in multiple aspects and domains of life. Cognitive development does contribute to spirituality regardless of education level. I want to be very

184

clear about the educational levels of spiritual human beings. I have met the most uneducated people who were highly spiritual. So it is clear there is a distinction between the two. One example was already given in the story about the wisdom of my Mali Baba, who was not only a wise man but a highly spiritual man without any formal education. I have met the most intelligent doctors and lawyers with the least amount of spirituality. This makes me believe and think that there must be some other element involved in the development of spirituality. Some humans have very little experience with certain information. They usually demonstrate an earlier level of thought before exhibiting more cognitive processes. Some relate cognitive development to spirituality by ego development, autonomy, and self-awareness, as they affect and are affected by relationships to others along with the development of moral understanding and consequent behavior toward others. In the event of faith development, one has to understand his or her own life and the lives of others with whom he or she interacts. Conn (1993) suggested that a mature spirituality involves a kind of self-transcendence in which individuals develop the ability to go beyond themselves in truthful knowledge, free commitment, and loving relationship to others both human and divine. She added that transcendence of the self may be the means by which spiritual development is achieved (396). When individuals move into the formal operational level of reasoning, according to Piaget, they are finally capable of reasoning logically about abstract notions. At this level of spiritual development, individuals should consider abstract principles, like benevolence and love for humanity.

Spirituality is an individual realm of inner life, purity, affection, intentions, and perception. How one integrates them into one's soul is all dependent on the individual's preferences and needs. Some may claim that it is collective spirituality; if they are right, then it has to start within an individual. It is not a belief or collective thought which one can borrow, which makes it different than religious practices. You can be spiritual and not religious. An atheist can be a spiritual man or woman. It is not a transcendental idea, in my view. It is a learned process with time and age and experience. My definition of spirituality is that it is the final stage of wisdom as described in the chapter on wisdom and the soul. It emphasizes moral character and qualities, like love, compassion, patience, tolerance, forgiveness, contentment, responsibility, harmony, and concern for others. You do not have to be a wandering sadhu of the East or a saint to be spiritual. Some may argue that one does not have to be a wise person to be spiritual. I disagree with that. Wisdom is based on the magnetic soul energy of our body. It is based on the pure science of our neuronal functions.

Science and spirituality have to reconcile in a proper perspective. Science without a moral backbone will degenerate spirituality with harmful results. In fact science and spirituality are inseparable in the interest of the full development of humankind and our outer world. Science could be natural science and man-made inventions. We humans have done wonders by using science and will continue doing so. Though science has remained silent in the areas of religion, by having spiritual power, humans have achieved their scientific goals beyond our imaginations. There can be invention without spirituality. In a laboratory, a scientist performing experiments seeks truth and honesty and is guided by reason and proof—reason implying the ability of a human to reach agreement and results by discussions and thoughts. Religion is a way of life one decides to live. One abides by the principles laid down and adopted by him or her to lead to a path of life. So a religious man can be a scientist or a scientist can live his life without religious beliefs. Science is an action and reaction with proof and replication of the proof again and until the final invention is put into action. Science created everything we have in this modern world through failures, disappointments, and successes, through wisdom and spirituality. Years and years of dedication, patience, and learning have resulted in saving lives, flying to the moon, and getting information in seconds, for example. Spirituality is just like a flight from New York to London. Just think for a moment how much it involves. It includes an airplane without any defects or malfunctions, which represents our body. It needs energy, which represents our soul's magnetic energy. It needs the wisdom of pilots to have a smooth flight, facing all the turbulence and difficulties. Spirituality is the accomplishment of our goal.

In brief, spirituality needs a sound and healthy body, the wisdom of our soul, and the energy of our soul to achieve the final stage. Missing any one of the components will result in failure to attain spirituality, which is diverse. Humans develop this in the vast arena of human life. A scientist is spiritual in scientific fields, and others are in their fields—a doctor, a nurse, a leader, an artist, and a musician, for example. They all are spiritual. Each human has the potential to be spiritual. Those who seek the path in their lives through meditation, self-actualization, cognition, and attainment of wisdom will enjoy the sweet fragrance of spirituality. The achievements of science may be described as discoveries and inventions as the use of our discoveries, new or old. They are brought about by technology to change the existing environment. Scientific and technological development dominate our present life and will dominate our future lives. That leave us no choice but to evolve as humans to develop scientific spirituality and hijack it to use it to the fullest potential by understanding it and accepting the fact that science itself is a form of spirituality. For a modern person, scientific and technological development dominate every aspect of our lives, our intellect, our imagination, and the prosperity of millions and billions of men and women; thus, it has become a powerful force controlling our activities. The world has become smaller, and there is great interdependence of one part of the world on others. A great spiritual swami Vivekananda came to America to teach the spirituality of Hinduism and wrote (397),

> One atom in the universe cannot move without dragging the whole world along with it. There cannot be any progress without the whole world following in the wake, and it is becoming every day clear that the solution of any problem can never be attained on racial or national, or narrow grounds. Every idea has to become broad till it covers the whole world, every aspiration must go on increasing till it has engulfed the whole humanity and the whole life, within its scope

One would think to ask our human counterparts that our present civilization, based on science and technology, would not meet the fate of older civilization. Some believe that technology, by fulfilling humanity's material desires, would make modern humans comfortable and able to enjoy the modern facilities provided by inventions. It would reduce human tensions and conflicts since poverty and economic suffering were the root causes of turmoil in old, impoverished economies. But that is not true. We have seen the devastations of nuclear explosions in Japan in World War II. We may have learned from that devastation of the human race, which may prevent future nuclear explosions. I am of the opinion that spirituality, wisdom, and human consciences interjected in the science may prevent such devastations in the future. It is essential that our leaders with nuclear weapons should have mandatory spiritual knowledge and wisdom to qualify to lead such nations. We should use science and technology to solve these conflicts, which may be due to political racial, religious, economic, cultural, territorial, and other reasons. It is quite clear that we humans have made both beneficial and harmful progress in science and technology but are lacking emphasis on spirituality, which may save humankind from extinction. Spirituality has no religion, caste, creed, or color. It has no boundaries or territories. Advisors to the world leaders are wise enough to understand that spirituality is the ultimate stage of wisdom, so making spirituality part of their day-to-day functions is the solution to prevent any future destruction.

Disputes and wars have been part of the human race since the inception, so nothing is new for modern humans. The goal of the future is, if you believe in any religion, stick to that for your journey of life with introjections of elements of spirituality, which help us to realize that we are part of the world and of humanity. In scientific and technologically developed economies, money and materials are integral parts of modern humans. Without them, survival is impossible and unsatisfactory. Prosperity is essential for all of us; we all want to live a decent life. Nothing is wrong with that. The old thinking of the East about materialism is a thing of the past. It is simple; if you have it, then you have it, and if you don't, then you don't. Modern humans have to define the existing facts and figures to live a happy and prosperous life. Materialism has nothing to do with spiritual living. As a matter of fact, it is an asset and a superior way of living when spirituality is attained. Joglekar wrote about wisdom and spirituality. He says,

It is hardly possible for states to make progress without accepting religious toleration as a maxim for government. One of the greatest things our Constitution has done is to treat our country as a secular state. This idea of tolerance has to go hand in hand with the idea of unity. Freedom of thought, speech, and writing are necessary for the continuation of any intellectual progress, the basis for the progress in other aspects of life to make it worth living. In democratic institutions and states, it is necessary to choose wise people enlightened by spirituality to run the institutions or states (398).

The term spirituality is now frequently used in a context in which the term religious was used. We in the modern age have changed the use of such terms; currently, contemporary spirituality is also called posttraditional spirituality and New Age spirituality (399). Those who differentiate themselves from a religious aspect believe in finding one's own path of spirituality. According to one poll in 2005, about 24 percent of the US population identifies as spiritual but not religious (400). It emphasizes an inner path, enabling a person to discover the essence of his or her being and humanistic ideas on moral characteristics (401) like love, compassion, patience, tolerance, forgiveness, contentment, responsibility, harmony, concern for others, understanding reality, living with nature in harmony, being thoughtful and truthful to self and others, and the list goes on.

Stages of spirituality develop as we grow and attain wisdom. If we fail to mature or become sick (mentally) or injured or have brain trauma, our ability to grow is impaired, which gives us the insight that spirituality is purely a brain-functioning process. It is possible to become more focused, patient, and compassionate than one naturally tends to be, and there are many things to learn about how to be happy in this world. These are truths that Western psychologists and scientists are beginning to understand. It is human nature to brood about the past and worry about the future. This is stressful. Spiritual life is an ongoing process that will gradually unravel our confusion and bring this stress to an end through our attained willpower and wisdom.

Sam Harris describes enlightenment as an ultimate goal of meditation. It is generally described as being omniscient (knowing everything, having ultimate knowledge, perceiving all things). Does that mean we know everything? Can anybody know everything? Some may answer yes and some no. Well then, what is the answer? I think if we focus on what we want, we can become well informed in the area of our interest. As we go to school, we develop interests to be the one we want to be. This is the early attainment of spirituality in the area of our interest and development of specialty in the same area. For example, some of us become doctors, scientists, engineers, teachers, and so on. We attain the basic principles of spirituality. I am of the opinion that all human brains have the potential to develop spirituality in our respective areas.

Then comes the question of day-to-day life. We all have to live our lives and have families and responsibilities. Spirituality could be developed in all areas of our lives besides our specialty or areas of interests. No one can attain complete and ultimate enlightenment in life, even Buddha. Some could be far more enlightened than you or I. It is fair to say that spirituality is relative, not absolute. There are truths about our minds that we are better off knowing. We need to become happier and make the world a better place. No one can hesitate to admit that talent and training in the context of physical and intellectual pursuits need commitment, rigor, honest hard work, and spirituality to a certain extent, which makes us stronger, more athletic, or more learned than others.

A healthy spiritual life can begin only once our physical, mental, social, and ethical lives have sufficiently matured. We must learn to use language before we can work with it creatively or understand its limits, and the conventional self must form before we can investigate it and understand that it is not what it appears to be (403). Enlightenment is not permanent. With the change in our life events, there needs to be more attention and willingness to adjust with our own self and others in our life. So it is fair for me to say that spirituality changes and grows with changes and growth in lives. Enlightenment is the stage of life when the unconscious is brought into consciousness through any means, which I presume include the following.

- Meditation is well documented and has been tried for centuries with neuroscientific evidence that it can enhance neuroplasticity and neurogenesis and helps us to unravel the unconscious conflicts to our conscious level, which increases our capacity to deal with compassion and reality, as discussed in the chapter on meditation and the soul.
- Self-realization is fulfillment by oneself of the possibilities of one's character or "personality."
- Self-actualization is the realization or fulfillment of one's talent and potentialities, especially considering it is a drive or need present in everyone.
- Cognitive behavioral therapy is a key mode of restructuring the negative frame of thinking to a positive and appropriate way of thinking and behaving (while in a state of distorted thinking and behaving).

- Cognitive restructuring is accomplished either by learning by oneself or from others, like parents, teachers, peers, and gurus.
- Behavioral modification is learned from boot camps, professional treatment centers for eating disorders, or any other related gatherings, like churches, temples, and monasteries. Most important, in this era of epidemic drug and alcohol abuse, programs like AA and NA are essential in promoting spirituality.

Self-reflection is the capacity of humans to exercise introspection and the willingness to learn more about their fundamental nature, purpose, and essence. Some define it as careful thoughts about your own behavior and beliefs. A very impressive article written by Kevin Daum has left nothing to say about (from "The Power of Self-Reflection") (404)

Kevin has not only described a path to spirituality but has added the way to attain wisdom, which is a functional unit of our soul. My view is that Spirituality is a self-attained final stage of wisdom, which is ongoing process of journey of our life. As we all know, life is what we make it. Our attitude, emotions, feelings, reality, and actions have the power to change our DNA. It is only through the power of choice, the power we have in our free will. Carl Jung put it the right way as he said, "He who looks outside, dreams, one who looks inside, awakes." Sure enough, it is true. The internal exists first and then the exterior is perceived after we are born and grown. What do I mean by that? If you are never born, the exterior never exists for you. The exterior has existed way beyond our imagination and will exist for infinity. We can argue spirituality existed way before life was ever born in this universe. No wonder wise people flocked to caves in search of spirituality thousands of years ago. To a modern person spirituality is now and here. It is enlightenment for different people to have different concepts about spirituality. Modern spirituality is centered on the deepest value and meaning by which people live. It envisions an inner path enabling a person to discover the essence of his or her being (405). Some human experiences go beyond a purely materialistic view of the world without necessarily accepting belief in a supernatural reality or divine being. Anything and everything that is good and virtuous is spiritual. Aristotle was one of earlier Western thinkers who emphasized that morality, virtue, and goodness can be derived without appealing to supernatural forces. I believe it is fair to say that both material and nonmaterial aspects of our modern life could lead us to spirituality.

Let's look around for some of the rich and poor people. Bill Gates, Warren Buffet, and many rich people are spiritual by virtue of donating large sums of money to charity for the good of the human race. Their approach to life is not living lavishly but humbleness, wisdom, lack of arrogance, compassion, and love for what they do. They derive happiness from giving, helping the needy, and employing millions of people. Money, fame, name, and poverty have nothing to do with spirituality. Anyone who gains wisdom can attain spirituality, regardless of who they are. Spirituality is colorless, fameless, and shameless. It has no barriers, has no boundaries, and is limitless. Everyone and anyone can own it. Nobody can buy it because it is priceless. Some Eastern and Western wise people describe it as a variety of religious experiences and the holy. Some believe it to be personal experience. Some have popularized the idea of enlightenment as insight into timeless, transcendent reality. In my view, spirituality is so big and vast that it accommodates everyone without any discrimination. Spiritual experiences can include being connected to a large reality, yielding a more comprehensive self, or joining with other individuals, the human community, nature, the cosmos, or the divine realm (406).

Gabriel Cousens, MD, has written about the subtle body systems, which have seven anatomies: etheric, emotional, mental, astral, spiritual, causal, and soul. According to him, as the refined energy condenses from its cosmic or virtual state, it is stepped down via seven subtle anatomies, which personalize it and densify it to a level at which our physical body can incorporate it. It is the author's clinical experience that energy does not flow in one direction from the cosmos into the body; it can also flow in the opposite direction. For example, when someone's physical energy increases, a corresponding increase in psychological energy can often be seen; by implication, some of the increased physical energy has been converted to psychological energy. The soul is a magnetic energy generated by our body, and the brain has the capability to absorb cosmic energy and interact with that energy. We call it electromagnetic energy. It communicates with all our cells and with the external world. Electromagnetic fields (EMFs) generated by our body are the final links between the etheric and physical bodies.

Work done by Jose Delgado, an internationally known Spanish neuroscientist, gives indirect evidence of the effect of EMFs can have on our biological system. Delgado used EMFs that are one-fiftieth the strength of the earth's own magnetic field. These fields could be of the same nature as those transduced by our brain and the body, which have been shown to alter the mental functioning of a variety of animals and other body system activities. For example, by exposing monkeys to different types of EMFs, Delgado could make some to go to sleep and some became irritable. Researchers have detected EMFs in the brains and the bodies of humans, which gives us a clue that there could be an astral aspect of spirituality development or enhancement as well (407).

In this modern age, we are in a stage of collective enlightenment on this planet. With modern technology and by means of communication, we can share our spirituality with each other much more easily than before. There are organizations, like Rhadaswami Satsang in India and all over the world, where spirituality is shared with attendees by the transfer of magnetic energy; I was amazed to have such an experience where the collective sharing of spirituality just takes place by being among other spiritual people. I was attracted to others naturally after a session of meditation. Sitting in silence to reflect on yourself has a great effect on others sitting nearby you, and then it is amplified by sharing food together where all are equal without any discrimination, full of love and humility. It is a wonder of oneness and awareness. Satsang is the energy of truth in the presence of a liberated or awakened spiritual teacher. Satsang gives meaning, value, heart, and energy to spiritual wisdom teachings and spiritual life energies. Sangha is spending time with spiritual people or community, thus expanding and refining the mind with spiritual wisdom and teachings. In this world full of hostility and territorial wars, it has become impossible to develop a collective spirituality. The only answer is peace and becoming more rooted in the truth. Yoga is the science by which the soul gains mastery over our body and brain and uses them to attain self-realization. It reawakens the consciousness from unconsciousness. As an individualized self, the soul identifies the limitations of the body and sense of consciousness. Self remains throughout the body and works under the guidance of our higher functioning soul. Self is a reflection of our soul. Yoga is a complete science, encompassing the spiritualization of each aspect of mind, body, and soul.

The human organism is a gross condensation of subtle spiritual forces under the control of the soul and has a body, a life, and a consciousness within it. It is through the efferent and afferent nerves that our electric current flows, generating magnetic fields of the soul's communication with the matter (body) and spiritualizing this communication. Our soul expresses the highest potential. Our spiritualized soul has the highest energy to dim the strength of all our senses, like sight, hearing, touch, taste, and smell, whenever needed to avoid any disturbances, like desires, wishes, needs, greed, and much more. A spiritualized human can control it and can enter it at will, in the waking state or in the dream state, in deep sleep state and in a conscious state.

A highly spiritualized yogi or any human master of the art of control of the brain functions through the magnetic soul. He or she can shut off mental restlessness and the imagination and avoid absentmindedness by practicing the following (90):

- Passivity or even-mindedness under all conditions
- Positive concentration (keeping the mind on one particular thought at a time)
- Negative concentration (using discrimination and will to eliminate unwanted thoughts)
- Transferring consciousness from feelings to will or ideas
- Transferring consciousness from emotions, such as love or hatred, to self-control, creative thinking, or pure feelings
- Holding the thought to one sensation at a time (sight, sound, smell, taste, or touch)
- Visualization of mental images and creating and dissolving dreams at will
- Mental anesthesia (receiving the sensation of pain as an informative report rather than experience of suffering
- Postponement of instant gratification
- Anticipation—sometimes it is as you think and sometimes it is not the way you think, but working through the issue or a problem is the least distressing path and the outcome could be fruitful
- Weighing failures and successes equally—when failure occurs, reinventing is the key (Don't take success for granted; enjoy the results of it.)
- Expression of contentment and conscience

To attain all this, numerous physiological processes in our brain and our body are activated. A spiritualized soul has control over self-regulating mechanisms, through neurotransmitters, neurochemicals, and magnetic forces to create such results, some of which are

- Outward relaxation and removal of physical restlessness, anxiety, sadness, agitation, and verbal confrontation
- Relaxation of involuntary organs, such as the heart and lungs and other organ functions
- Use of appropriate nutrition and use of the energy of our body
- Learning to sleep and wake at will

This is all easy to say, but the reality of life is we have to make a living. That does not mean we can't be spiritual. First and foremost, we should remind ourselves that we have the right to a livelihood, which is extremely important in our lives. Our highest function is to rest totally in the awareness of our transcendent reality as our primary awareness. Eventually, we reach the stage in which it makes a difference to our spiritual state how much time and energy we put into our worldly work. However, for all but those in the most advanced stages of spiritual evolution, too much time and energy spent in work may dull our growing experience of the truth. We may find ourselves becoming self-willed doers rather than being in the state grace. As doers, we become attached to the reward of our work, and in that attachment, the ecstatic experience of our transcendent boringness is lost. By working too many hours, we can become depleted of mental and physical energy. In this depleted state, it is hard to remain awake. A balanced approach to this state is essential. Too much of too much is too much. Loving what you do and what kind of profession you have itself is spiritual attainment. Those who hate what they do and work do need to pay attention to self-awareness and self-reflection for change in their course of life.

Change seems very uncertain, unpredictable, insecure, and at times, scary. Courage itself is a form of spirituality. Once you have it, you can choose to do anything, which is joyful and gratifying financially, psychologically, and physiologically. What more do you need? Contentment, happiness, and gratification are attained by mere courage.

A true love between man and woman, wife and husband, parents and children, relatives and friends, and you and all around you is a spiritual essence. Eckhart Tolle (408) emphasizes the here and now form of love. He perceives that unless and until you access the consciousness frequency of presence, all relationships, particularly intimate relationships, are deeply flawed and ultimately dysfunctional. They may seem perfect for a while, such as when you are in love, but invariably that apparent perfection gets disrupted as arguments, conflicts, dissatisfaction, and emotional or even physical violence occurs with increasing frequency. Then it becomes a love-hate relationship. This may oscillate for a while and may fade away with time. A romantic love relationship is intense and a universally sought-after experience; it is a state of fear, need, lack, and incompleteness that is part of the human condition in its unredeemed and unenlightened state. There are both physical and psychological components to this state. On the physical level, you are obviously not whole, nor will you ever be. You are either man or woman, which means one half of the whole. On this level, the longing for the wholeness and return to oneness manifests as a male-female attraction. It is an almost irresistible urge to union with the opposite energy polarity. The root of this physical urge is a spiritual one. Sexual union is the closest relationship on a physical level. This the most satisfying experience the physical realm can offer, but it is a short-lived, fleeting experience. A consensual sexual relationship in which psychological barriers are compromised and well accepted by a male and a female is the ultimate spiritual experience for both male and female. It has both a physiological and an emotional relationship to our magnetic energy of the soul. As love and only as love can we live in right relationship with our mate, children, and all around us.

Unrelenting and unconditional love is the sole building block of the spiritual world. In building a right relationship, it is also necessary to organize our time, space, and energy intelligently so there is enough for individuals, couples, family, and societal expression of this love. People often think about communication problems when we think of right relationships. Communication is the source of our spiritual awareness.

Part of our spiritual world of experiences is already waiting for us to notice. It is in the natural laws of the universe and in nature for us to learn about it. Those of us who learn about it live a healthy and spiritual life. Going to the beach on a nice, beautiful sunny day to watch the beautiful waves of the ocean by itself is a spiritual feeling. Getting plenty of vitamin D freely and healing psoriasis and other ailments are highly spiritual feelings. I have the most spiritual feeling while I plant a kitchen garden in my backyard, starting from small seedlings to full, mature, fruit-bearing plants. I learned how to freeze tomatoes for the whole year after I shared with my neighbors and dear ones. I have a routine with my wife. In the morning, I, with a cup of coffee in my hand, and she, with a cup of warm, minty tea in her hand, walk outside to see our plants in the kitchen garden. We talk and share our thoughts for the day, enjoying the fresh fruits and vegetables. This is the best spiritual feeling we have for the whole summer.

Another spiritual experience I had was when a fox had given birth to five small kits under the shed in my backyard. I was surprised to see the beautiful babies wandering with their mom. My neighbors learned about that and suggested I call animal control to remove them and the mom as well. I refused to do so and enjoyed watching the litter grow. It was a wonderful spiritual experience to share my backyard with nature's gift.

A healthy body is essential for spiritual growth; therefore, a balanced diet is very essential. Overindulgence and underindulgence are unhealthy for spiritual growth. A lot literature is available about food products. I would like to mention one of the spiritual metals, which is mostly ignored. Cousens (407) has written extensively about it. There are numerous metals and rare earth elements, some of which are still unknown to us. As our body and soul keep evolving, there will be changes in diet and needs for our body. Phosphrous is an essential mineral for our spiritual growth. It has to do with psychic perceptions, idealistic tendencies, humanitarianism, and philanthropy. It has to do with the subjective functions of the brain and the sensory systems, like taste, touch, and smell. Phosphorus also has much to do with intelligence. Throughout history, phosphorus has been synonymous with intelligence and has been seen as the mineral that helps link the soul with matter. It is absolutely essential for spiritual life. The phosphorus for the brain needs to be absorbed from the environment in the form of lecithin; this is different than phosphorus needed for bone building. Phosphorus and lecithin are in vegetarian foods, including soybeans and bee pollen, which has 15 to 20 percent lecithin.

According to scientific studies, the actual process of thinking burns up phosphorus, so those who are doing a lot of thinking or meditation need much higher phosphorus input. It seems to be used in study, memorizing, reading, intellectual functioning, visualizing, and comprehension. With each thought we think, we use up phosphorus. So those who are intellectual need to eat a lot of lecithin, because the activity of all the neurons requires phosphorus. The principles of mineral use in the human body are not fully understood. The same holds true for some vitamins. For example, in the case of severe stress, vitamin B-12 is used in large amounts. Vitamin C is used more in minor infections. Thiamine is depleted in chronic alcoholics.

In cases of excessive activity of our brain, phosphorus and magnesium are needed more than in normal activity of the brain. There are some claims that phosphorus is used in excess in case of dreams, mental disorders that cause obsession, delusions, and hallucinations. Phosphorus is needed in bone and semen formation in the form of calcium phosphate. Adenosine triphosphate (ATP) is a major way energy is stored at the molecular level in the body. Phosphorus is needed for DNA and RNA production, white blood cell production, and numerous other metabolic productions. It is an illumination mineral. Phosphorus in Greek means "light-bearer." Therefore, there is a correlation with the glow of the aura around our body, which may explain the magnification of our glowing soul.

Phosphorus is found in excess in people who drink excessive cola and soft drinks, which is very unhealthy and can cause defective spirituality by effecting our behavior. Their minds work excessively and are affected by autosuggestion. They tend to be impulsive and to spend more money than needed. They have a decreased quality of decision making. They have a lack of practical judgment, concentration, and willpower.

Lack of phosphorus can cause numerous illnesses, too many to mention in this book. A few of them are feeling like fainting, poor sexual energy, low appetite, intense nerve pain, general weakness, and craving for cold drinks. Some of us with deficiencies feel anxiety, paranoia, lack of confidence, helplessness, and mild depression through the central nervous system functions.

Some of the foods rich in phosphorus are almonds, lentils, carrots, cashews, corn, olives, oats, sunflower seeds, walnuts, wheat bran, and honey, which is rich in lecithin (15 to 20 percent). There are countless minerals needed for bodily functions and survival. There is no life without the transfer of electrical energy through our body and soul. Minerals are the source of generation and transfer of such electric current for our survival, as discussed in the previous chapters.

We presume spirituality to be the sum total outcome of our full being, but the fact is spirituality is the fictional outcome of our neurons and cells in our body. It starts from cellular memory and the harmony of each cell working wisely to give birth to our spirituality. Our cell memory is the complete file of our biocomputers. In our cells, we find the information of genetic coding, which tells us about the past, present, and future. These cells in the body store memory from the inception of life to tell the story of who we are and will be by the data collected throughout our history of life. Some of this history remains hidden in the unconscious, and some is open in our conscious, which we exhibit in the form of emotions, feelings, actions, thoughts, reactions, and much more.

Any good event or trauma in our lives is stored in these cells, like in cloud computation, and could be released unconsciously or at will. Every traumatic experience is conserved in each cell responsible to do that. By external or internal stimulus, such traumatic experiences could be created and experienced. This is how our somatic system works. Our fear, sadness, anger, or happiness is expressed as a reflection or reaction of our various body parts in physical symptoms, like pain and other manifestations. Deepak Chopra stole the show in explaining the entire meaning of our cells and spirituality (409). Every cell in your body agrees to work for the welfare of the whole; its individual life comes second. If necessary, it will die to protect the body and often does. The lifetime of a cell is a fraction of our lifetime. Skin cells perish by the thousands every hour, as do immune cells fighting off invading microbes. Selfishness is not an option, even when it comes to a cell's own survival. A cell keeps in touch with every cell. Messenger molecules race everywhere to notify the body's farthest outposts of desires or intentions, however minor. Withdrawing or refusing to communicate is not an option. Cells adapt from moment to moment. They remain flexible in order to respond to immediate situations. Getting caught up in rigid habits is not an option. Cells recognize each other as equally important. Every function in the body is interdependent with each other. Going it alone is not an option.

Although every cell has a set of unique functions (liver cells, for example, can perform fifty separate tasks), these combine in creative ways. A person can digest food never eaten before, think thoughts never thought before, dance in a way never seen before. Clinging to old behavior is not an option. The cell obeys the universal cycle of the rest of the activity. Although this cycle expresses itself in many ways, such as fluctuating hormone levels, blood pressure, and digestive rhythms, the most obvious expression is sleep. Why we need to sleep remains a medical mystery, yet complete dysfunction develops if we don't enjoy its benefits. In the silence of inactivity, the future of the body is incubating. Being obsessively active or aggressive is not an option. Cells function with the smallest possible expenditure of energy; typically, a cell stores three seconds of food and oxygen inside of its cell wall. It trusts totally on the body to provide for it.

Excessive consumption of food, air, or water is not possible. Because of their common genetic inheritance, cells know they are fundamentally the same. The fact is that liver cells are different from heart cells, and muscle cells are different than brain cells. It does not negate their common identity, which is unchanging. In the laboratory, a muscle cell can be genetically transformed into a heart cell by going back to the source. Healthy cells remain tied to their source, no matter how many times they divide. For them, being an outcast is not acceptable. The primary activity of the cell is giving, which maintains receiving automatically. There is no hoarding. Cells reproduce in order to pass their knowledge, experience, and talent, withholding nothing from their offspring. This is a kind of immortality, submitting to death on the physical plane to defeat it on the nonphysical. There are no generation gaps. After all this, Chopra concludes that what my cells have agreed to is a spiritual pact in every sense of the word and at the broader level of the world.

I cannot ignore this truth, which our cells teach us to be. These are the words of wisdom written by Chopra, who raises many questions that need to be answered, like there is no option for selfishness, refusing to communicate, living like an outcast, overconsumption, obsessive activity, and aggression. It makes me think that everyone has the potential to be spiritual, because every cell in your body is functioning every second on the principles of purity, sincerity, loyalty, and harmony. When a newborn comes into this world, he or she is pure and in a real sense, spiritual. So what happens to us? All I can blame is our rearing, our development, our conditions, our cultures, and our beliefs. In summary, the environments takes our cells of the body to adapt to external stimuli and the prevailing conditions for mere survival. If you are born in an impoverished and poor country or culture, there is a massive adaptation to be made by your cells. There is no food to feed them. How can they become obese? The basic neuronal formation and development of our brain cells depend on the nutrition we receive, and to survive, we have to do what we have to do. Begging, borrowing, or stealing becomes the norm to survive.

Spirituality cannot feed you. The brain cells (neurons) will invent means and ways to kill or rob anyone. Their need will lead to greed, aggression, and other malicious behavior for survival, which teaches our cells to act according to the needs of time.

I remember when I was a child, my mother died when I was around five and a half years old, and my father remarried. My stepmother would not feed us while we were growing up. Hunger was dominating my behavior. I used to go to my neighbors' orchards and steal fruits until my hunger was quashed. My father would sit with us and recite hymns from Guru Granth Shiab (a holy book of the Sikh religion) every day to give us insight into true living so we would develop some spirituality. He would teach us about God and his power. I question myself now, "What happened to my spirituality?"

To those who have nothing to feed on, hunger is an enemy of spirituality. Even a well-fed lion does not go after a kill. It watches the wildebeests while relaxing under the shade of a tree. I think the lion at that moment may have a spiritual feeling of letting the wildebeests graze in the green pastures.

In my school, I did not see a single obese kid, but they were still athletic. They probably had enough food to keep them healthy. I wonder what happens to growing young children who have minimal food and no role model to guide them through the growing period of their lives. Isn't it true that we have our jails full as a result? Because people do not have enough food, guidance, and education during the growing period of their lives? Then there are children who grow up in war zones and see their parents, families, and friends dying every day. All they hear is bomb blasts and gunfire from the ground and from the air. Some of them hide in the trenches, and some are buried in the rubble of their homes without food or water for days and months. Some leave their homes to escape the horror of the war and save their lives and the lives of their children and loved ones. We call them refugees, people without a home or land, without their countries, and pride of being a nation. I wonder what happens to their spirituality and how they feel about God or other human beings destroying their existence. I wonder what happens to the spirituality of those who kill them for power, money, and control. Some are left with the scars of post-traumatic stress syndrome, depression, anxiety, fear, shame, and hopelessness, without any assurance of survival.

I wonder what happens to the spirituality of those who are struck with famine and natural disasters, like hurricanes, flooding, earthquakes, tsunamis, and fire. I wonder about holocaust victims. I believe they put the mental aspects of life back together and carry on living their lives in a somewhat stable way, and those who fail to piece the mental processes together lead a miserable life, full of pain and misery. Those who are able to establish socioeconomic security may do well in their lives. Those who have a genetic predisposition to mental disorders remain wandering in this vast, diversified world with their mental disorders until their deaths. Some reach out for spirituality and keep chasing it, sometimes in vain.

There is a strong correlation between mental disorders and attainment of spirituality. Those individuals who suffer from personality disorders have difficulty attaining spirituality because of dysfunctional neurotransmitters and neuronal connections; in the event they develop some degree of spirituality, they have a chance of improving their behavior and functioning in society. This is especially true in antisocial personality, narcissistic personality, and other personality disorders discussed in the previous chapter. Spirituality has a two-prong approach and understanding. Those who have attained some insight and practice a spiritual life have fewer incidents of mental disorders because of the fact that their brain is well developed and has balanced neurotransmitters. There has to be normal development of the neuronal functions to attain wisdom and meditation, which enhances neurogenesis and neuroplasticity. This is the primary source of development of spirituality.

The second prong of spirituality is those who have underlying mental illness can benefit from spirituality either through their religious belief, which structures their lifestyle based on the teachings. It gives them social support. They can understand the mental illness and accept it as it is, which gives them insight to seek treatment and follow it as long as they need. The same holds true in recovery from drug and alcohol abuse through Alcoholics and Narcotics Anonymous (AA and NA). Based on spirituality, AA and NA have made a difference between misery and sobriety and often between life and death. Therefore, no society of men and woman ever had a more urgent need for continuous effectiveness and permanent unity. Alcoholics see that they must work together and hang together; otherwise, they will die alone. The most important twelve traditions need to be followed to attain sobriety and maintain that. As they say, it is easy to quit drinking or using drugs, but it is difficult to remain alcohol or drug free for the rest of their lives. The twelve AA traditions are important to attain spirituality and remain drug or alcohol free (411). I was a strong believer in Alcoholics Anonymous during my practice when I treated patients with addiction.

I learned that AA was very effective in breaking down the denial, which by itself is a cancer. When you go to an AA or NA meeting, the first thing you say is "I am so-and-so. I am an alcoholic or am addicted to such-and-such drug." What a great thing to happen! Your unconscious denial is becoming conscious. Over a certain period of time, denial is broken into pieces, which promotes acceptance of the treatment. They develop spirituality, as described by the philosophy of the twelve steps. Willingness, honesty, and open mindedness are essentials of recovery from any addiction. Spirituality has been shown to make a marked improvement in schizophrenia. According to Harding Zahniser (1994), more than 50 percent experienced significant improvement or recovery (413). Though there are numerous studies conducted on mental health issues and illnesses, Koening and his associates reviewed over a thousand studies and concluded that spirituality was associated with increased adaptation to bereavement, self-esteem, social support, life satisfaction, happiness, hope, and optimism. People find purpose and meaning in their lives. These benefits occur in conjunction with decreased levels of anxiety and loneliness and fewer suicides (414). Some define spirituality as an individual's existential relationship with God or perceived transience. While religion is defined as an institutionalized set of beliefs and practices that have been developed in the community by people who share similar experiences. This has created a debate over whether spirituality is part of religious belief or creates religious beliefs. I would suggest that nonreligious people can be spiritual and religious people can be nonspiritual, so we really do not have answers.

Kerove and his colleagues from the United Kingdom (415) do emphasize that their clients with mental illness (61 percent) used religion as a primary tool to heal their mental illnesses and used religious support in tough times. For example, their clients reported that looking to God for assistance or knowing that he cares for them helped them to cope or recover from their mental illness. Many other studies indicated that female and nonwhite patients had more belief in religion and responded well to treatment. My experience is any kind of support and empathetic care given to a patient, spiritual experiences, and being spiritual by itself are very helpful in the treatment of any kind of mental illness.

The Joint Commission on Accreditation of Healthcare Organizations (JCAHO), a major health-care agency in the United States of America, has assessed the implementation of spirituality in 2002. This has created a spiritual awareness in the care of patients. It is important for all the health-care providers to have knowledge of their own spiritual worldview and associated biases, an empathic understanding of patients' spiritual worldviews, and the ability to develop intervention strategies that are appropriate, relevant, and sensitive to the patients' spiritual worldview. Azhar and his associates have demonstrated the effectiveness of spirituality in modified cognitive-behavioral therapy. With this approach, traditional cognitive-behavioral therapy is modified with tenets derived from the patient's spiritual belief system. With Muslims, for example, cognitive-behavioral therapy is modified with beliefs drawn from the Koran. This has been found to be as effective as traditional forms of therapy for anxiety disorders, bereavement, and depression.

NOTES

1 Saraswati, Chandrasekharendra. The Vedas. Bombay: Bharatiya Vida Haven, Havana's Book University, 2014, 400–407.

2 Eknath, Easwaran, and Michael N. Nagler. The Upanishads. Petaluma, CA: Nilgiri Press, 1987. Introduced and translated by Blue Mountain Center of Meditation, 2007.

3 Eknath, Easwaran. The Bhagavad Gita. Petaluma, CA: Nilgiri Press. Introduced and translated by Blue Mountain Center of Meditation, 2007.

4 Https. /Wikipedia. Foundation.org/wiki/Resolution "Encyclopedia of Soul." Wikimedia Foundation. Accessed April 5, 2016.

5 http://www.yoga-philosophy.com/2003.

6 Chopra, Deepak. How to Know God: The Soul's Journey into the Mystery of Mysteries. New York: Crown, 2000, 275–288.

7 Susan D. Gillespie, PhD, RPA, professor of anthropology, University of Florida, Gainesville.

8 Utley, Robert M., and Ellen Nanney. The Story of the West: A History of the American West and Its People. London: DK Pub., 2003.

9 Carlson, Paul Howard. The Plains Indians. Library of Congress Cataloging Publication Data, 1940.

10 Carlson, Paul Howard. The Plains Indians. College Station: Texas A & M UP, 1998.

11 Villoldo, Alberto. One Spirit Medicine: Ancient Ways to Ultimate Wellness. Hay House, 2015, 122.

12 Esposito, John L. The Oxford History of Islam. New York, NY: Oxford UP, 1999.

13 Esposito, John L. Islam: The Straight Path. 3rd ed. New York: Oxford UP, 1998, print, 73, 74, 12.

14 "Soul in Islamic Philosophy." Soul in Islamic Philosophy. Web.

15 www.itonline.org/shen/chapl.htm.

16 Wong, Eva. *Taoism: An Essential Guide*. Boston: Shambhala, 2011, print.

17 Ingerman, Sandra, and Henry Barnard Wesselman. *Awakening to the Spirit World: The Shamanic Path of Direct Revelation*. Boulder, CO: Sounds True, 2010.

18 "Rev. Criss Ittermann, Life Facilitator / Liberated Life Coaching." Rev. Criss Ittermann, Life Facilitator / Liberated Life Coaching. Web.

19 Sethi, Atul. "Rise of the Shamans." *Times of India*. N.P. Aug. 21, 2011. Web.

20 Theo, Peter. "A Brief Guide to Shamanism." petertheoaeffcu.org.

21 Judith, Anodea. *Wheels of Life: A User's Guide to the Chakra System*. St. Paul, MN: Llewellyn Publications, 1987.

22 Zack, Naomi. *The Handy Philosophy Answer Book*. Detroit: Visible Ink, 2010.

23 Pickren, Wade E., and Philip G. Zimbardo. *The Psychology Book: From Shamanism to Cutting-edge Neuroscience: 250 Milestones in the History of Psychology*. New York, NY: Sterling, 2014, 28, 38, 42, 44, 54, 80.

24 Stroll, Avrum. *Did My Genes Make Me Do It? And Other Philosophical Dilemmas*. Oxford: One World, 2004, 41–79.

25 Percival, Harold W. Thinking and Destiny: Being the Science of Man. Library of Congress, 47–1811 with printing, 1981, 22.

26 Martin, Raymond, and John Barresi. *The Rise and Fall of Soul and Self: An Intellectual History of Personal Identity*. New York: Columbia UP, 2006.

27 Goetz, Stewart, and Charles Taliaferro. A *Brief History of the Soul*. Malden, MA: Wiley-Blackwell, 2011.

28 Cottingham, John. *Descartes*. New York: Routledge, 1999.

29 *Descartes: Selected Philosophical Writings*. New York, NY: Cambridge UP, 1988, 218–230.

30 Shorto, Russell. *Descartes' Bones: A Skeletal History of the Conflict between Faith and Reason*. New York, NY: Doubleday Group, 2008.

31 Shaddock, Benjamin J., Harold I. Kaplan, and Virginia A. Shaddock. *Kaplan and Shaddock's Synopsis of Psychiatry: Behavioral Sciences / Clinical Psychiatry*. 11th ed. Philadelphia: Wolter Kluwer / Lippincott Williams & Wilkins, 2007. Print, 535.

32 Stock, Brian. *Augustine the Reader*. N.P.: Harvard UP, 1998. Print, 10, 11, 15, 16.

33 Ley, D. Forbes. *The Best Seller*. Newport Beach, CA: Sales Success, 1990, 53.

34 Zukav, Gary, and Simon Schuster. *The Seat of the Soul*. N.P.: Fireside Book, 1990. Print, 30, 31.

35 Eagleman, David. *The Brain: The Story of You*. New York, NY: Pantheon Book, 2015.

36   Jeeves, Malcolm A. *From Cells to Souls, and Beyond: Changing Portraits of Human Nature*. Grand Rapids, MI: W. B. Erdmans, 2004. Print, 17.

37   Idris, Zamzuri, Mustapha Muzaimi, Rahman Izaini Ghani, Badrisyah Idris, Regunath Kandasamy, and Jafri M. Abdullah. "Principles, Anatomical Origin and Applications of Brainwaves: A Review, Our Experience and Hypothesis Related to Microgravity and the Question on Soul." *Journal of Biomedical Science and Engineering* 7 no. 8 (2014): 435–45.

38   Woods, Tiger. *How I Play Golf*. New York: Warner, 2001. Print.

39   Carpenter, R. H. S., and Benjamin Redid. *Neurophysiology: A Conceptual Approach*. London: Hodder Arnold, 2012. Print.

40   Waxman, Stephen G. *Clinical Neuroanatomy*. 27th ed. New York: Lange Medical / McGraw-Hill, Medical Pub. Division, 2013. Print.

41   Penfield, Wilder. *The Mystery of the Mind: A Critical Study of Consciousness and the Human Brain*. Princeton, NJ: Princeton UP, 1978. Print.

42   Eccles, John. *Brain, Speech and Consciousness: The Understanding of the Brain*. N.P.: McGraw Hill Book, 1973. Print, 189.

43   Jones, W. H. S., and E. Withington, Eds. *The Sacred Disease*. 4th ed. Vol. 2. N.P.: Loeb Classical Library. Cambridge: Harvard UP, n.d. Print, 127–185.

44   Jackson, J. H. *On the Anatomical, Physiological, and Pathological Investigation of Epilepsies*. Rep. N.3 p. 315 n. p. 339, 1873. West Lunatic Asylum Medical Report. Web.

45   Magoun, H. W. "An Ascending Reticular Activating System in the Brain Stem." A Res. Nervous and Mental Disease Proceeding 3 (1950): 480–92.

46   Moruzzi, Giuseppe, and Horace Winchell Magoun. "Brain Stem Reticular Formation and Activation of the EEG Electroenceph." *Clin. Neurophysiology*. S.l.: S.n., 1949. Print, 1: 455–473.

47   Pavlov, I. P. *An Investigation of the Physiological Activity of the Cerebral Cortex*. London: Oxford UP, 1960. Print.

48   Fleming, G. W. T. H. "Diencephalic Autonomic Epilepsy." *Arch. of Neur. and Psychiatric*. (August 1929). Penfield, W. *British Journal of Psychiatry* 76, no. 312 (1930): 358–74.

49   Jasper, H. H. *Epilepsy, Neurophysiology, and Some Brain Mechanisms*. 1969. Print.

50   Penfield, Wilder, and Joseph Evans. "The Frontal Lobe in Man: A Clinical Study of Maximum Removals." Brain 58.1 (1935): 115–38.

51   Sherrington, Charles Scott. "Man on His Nature." Cambridge U, 1940. The Gifford Lectures 1937–1938, 74.

52   E. Hamilton, and H. Cairns. Translated by W. K. C. Cuthrie Phaedo. Translated by H. Trednnick Phaedrus. Translated by Hackforth. Theatetus translated by F. M. Conford. Timaeus translated by B. Jowett. Princeton: Princeton University Press, 1961.

53 Brann, E., P. Kalkavage, and E. Salem. Translated. Plato: Phaedo. Newbury Port, MA: Focus, 1998.

54 Lawson, Hugh. *Aristotle De Anima*. Translated. New York, NY: Penguin, 1986.

55 G. Zilboorg, C. L. Temkin, G. Rosen, H. E. Sigerest. "Paracelsus—Diseases That Deprive Man of His Reason, 1567. Such as St. Vitus Dance, Falling Sickness; Melancholy and Insanity and Their Correct Treatment." Trans. Baltimore, MD: John Hopkins University Press, 1996.

56 Bruno, Giordano, and Arthur D. Imerti. "The Expulsion of the Triumphant Beast, New Brunswick." New Jersey: Rutgers UP, 1964. Print.

57 Edited and Translated by Curley, Edwin. "The Collected Works of Spinoza." Volume I. Benedictus De Spinoza. First ed. Vol. 1. New Jersey: Princeton UP, 1985. Print.

58 Dennett, D. C. "Kinds of Minds: Toward an Understanding of Consciousness." New York, NY: Basic, 2006. Print.

59 MacDonald, Patrick E., and Patrik Rorsman. "Oscillations, Intercellular Coupling, and Insulin Secretion in Pancreatic β Cells." Plops Biology. Plops Boil, 49th ser. 4.2 (February 2006). Web.

60 St. Augustine. "The City of God." Translated by Marcus Dods. New York: Modern Library, 1993. Print.

61 St. Augustine. "The Trinity." Translated by Edmund Hill. Hyde Park, NY: New City, 1991.

62 St. Augustine. "On Genesis." Translated by Edmund Hill. Hyde Park, NY: New City, 2002.

63 Barnett, M. W., and P. M. Larkman. "The Action Potential." 192-7 7.3 (June 2007).

64 Junge, Douglas. "Nerve and Muscle Excitation." 2nd ed. Sunderland, MA: Sinauer Associates, 1981, 115–132.

65 Bullock, Theodore Holmes, Richard Orkand, and Alan Grinnell. "Introduction to Nervous Systems." San Francisco: W. H. Freeman, 1977. Print, 478–480.

66 Bullock, Theodore Holmes, and G. Adrian Horridge. "Structure and Function in the Nervous Systems of Invertebrates." San Francisco: W. H. Freeman, 1965. A Ser. of Books in Biology.

67 Martin, Raymond, and John Barresi. "Hazlitt on the Future of the Self." *Journal of the History of Ideas* 56 no. 3 (1995): 463–81.

68 Reid, Thomas, James Walker, and William Hamilton. *Essays on the Intellectual Power of Man*, 1785. Philadelphia: Butler, 1895, 1: 213–508.

69 Clarke, Samuel, and Anthony Collins. "A Letter to Mr. Dodwall and Etc.—In the work of Samual Clark." 1 vol. 1738 no. 3: 720–913. Reprint. New York: Garland, 1978.

70 Hume, David, L. A. Selby-Bigge, and P. H. Nidditch. *A Treatise of Human Nature*. Oxford: Clarendon, 1988. Print.

71 Hazlitt, William. "An Essay on the Principles of Human Action, and Some Remarks on the Systems of Hartley and Helvetius." Gainesville, FL: Scholars' Facsimiles and Reprints, 1969. Print.

72 Coleridge, Samuel Taylor. *Coleridge*. New York, NY: Dell Pub., 1772–1834. Print, 183–184.

73 Fichte, Johann Gottlieb, and Daniel Breazeale. *Foundations of Transcendental Philosophy: (Wissenschaftslehre) Nova Methodo (1798–99)*. London: Cornell UP, 1992. Print.

74 http://www.ecomaill.com/greenshopping/otusa.htm 11/26/2015 3.26p (1–5).

75 Dr. Pawluk. "About Dr. Pawluk–Dr. Pawluk." Web. www.drpawluk.com/education/about dr_pawluk.

76 McFadden, Johnjoe. "Conscious Electromagnetic (CEMI) Field Theory." *Neuro Quant Logy* 5 no. 3 (September 2007): 262–70.

77 Hegel, Georg Wilhelm Friedrich, Arnold V. Miller, and J. N. Findlay. *Phenomenology of Spirit*. Oxford: Clarendon, 1977. Print.

78 Pierre, Cabins, and Jean Georges. "The Relationship of the Physical and the Moral in Man." 1802. Ed.George Mora. Marggaret Duggan Saidi; Baltimore Md, John Hopkins University Press 1981.

79 Marx,Karl and Friedrich Eagles.Capital:A Critique of Political Economy. New York International.1975.

80 Mill, James, A. Findlater, and G. Grote. *Analysis of the Phenomena of the Human Mind*. Vol. 2. London: Longman's Green Reader and Dyer, 1869.

81 Stronk, G. "Principles of Magnetism." In Williamson, Samuel J., *Advances in Biomagnetism*. New York: Plenum, 1999, 47–57.

82 Schwartz, G. E. "Energy Cardiology: A Dynamical Energy Systems Approach for Integrating Conventional and Alternative Medicine." *Advances in Mind-Body Medicine* 12 no. 4 (1996): 4–24.

83 Kleiner, R., D. Koelle, F. Ludwig, and J. Clarke. "Superconducting Quantum Interference Devices: State of the Art and Applications." *Proceedings of the IEEE*. Proc. IEEE 92 no. 10 (2004): 1534–548. Web.

84 Isselbacher, Kurt J., Eugene Braunwald, Jean D. Wilson, Joseph B. Martin, Anthony S. Fauci, and Dennis L. Kasper. *Harrison's Principles of Internal Medicine*. 13th ed. New York: McGraw-Hill, 1994. Print.

85 Sherwood, Laura Lee. *Human Physiology: From Cells to Systems*. Australia: Thomson/Brooks/Cole, 2007. Accessed from Cengage Learning, 2008.

86 Rosch, Paul J. *Bioelectromagnetic and Subtle Energy Medicine*. 2nd ed. New York: CRC Taylor and Francis Group, 2015.

87 "Your Heart's Electrical System." National Heart, Lung, and Blood Institute, NIH. Web. Updated November 17, 2011.

88 Rama, Rudolph Ballentine, and Alan Hymes. *Science of Breath: A Practical Guide.* Honesdale, PA: Himalayan International Institute of Yoga Science and Philosophy, 1979. p59

89 Chardin, Pierre Teilhard De. *Let Me Explain.* New York: Harper and Row, 1972. Print, 66.

90 Yogananda, Paramahansa. *The Divine Romance.* Los Angeles, CA: Self-Realization Fellowship, 1986.

91 Prescott, James W., PhD. "The Origins of Human Love and Violence." *Pre and Perinatal Psychology Journal* 10 no.3 (Spring 1996). Web.

92 Rabbin, Robert. *Igniting the Soul at Work: A Mandate for Mystics.* Charlottesville, VA: Hampton Roads Pub., 2002. Print.

93 Sternberg, Robert, J. "Triangulating Love." In Oord, T. J. *Altruism Reader's Selection from Writings on Love, Religion, and Science.* West Conshohoken: Templeton Foundation, 332.

94 Acker, M., and M. H. Davis. "Intimacy, Passion, and Commitment in Adult Romantic Relationships: A Test of the Triangular Theory of Love." *Journal of Social and Personal Relationships* 9 no. 1 (1992): 21–50. Web.

95 Prescott, J. W. "Somatosensory Deprivation and Its Relationship to the Blind." In *The Effects of Blindness and Other Impairments on Early Development,* edited by Z. S. Jastrembke. New York: American Foundation for the Blind (1976), 65–121.

96 Prescott, J.W. "Early Somatosensory Deprivation as an Ontogenetic Process in the Abnormal Development of the Brain and Behavior." In *Medical Primatology* 1970, edited by I. E. Goldsmith and J. Moor-Jankowski. New York: S. Karger, Basel, 1971.

97 Prescott, J.W. "Sensory Deprivation Versus Sensory Stimulation during Early Development: A Comment on Berkowitz's Study." *Journal of Psychology* 77 (1971): 189–191.

98 Meissuer, W. W. "Theories of Personality in Psychotherapy." In Kaplan and Shaddocks Comprehensive Textbook of Psychiatry. 9th ed. Vol. I. edited by B. J. Saddock and V. A. Shaddock. Philadelphia: Lippincott Williams and Wilkins, 2009, 788.

99 Thompson, Richard F., and Michael M. Patterson. *Bioelectric Recording Techniques: Receptor and Effecter Processes.* New York: Academic, 1973. Print.

100 Brodal, Alf. *Neurological Anatomy.* New York: Oxford UP, 1998. Print.

101 Kenshalo, D. R. "Correlates of Temperature Sensitivity in Man and Monkey: A First Approximation." In Sensory Functions of the Skin in Primates, edited by Y. Zotterman. Oxford: Oxford University Press, 1976.

102 Nolte, J. *The Human Brain.* St. Luis Mosby, 1999.

103 Penfield, Wilder, and Theodore Rasmussen. *The Cerebral Cortex of Man: A Clinical Study of Localization of Function.* New York: Macmillan, 1950. Print.

104 Baker, D. "The Innervations of the Muscle Spindle." *Quarterly Journal of Microscopic Science* 89, (1948): 143–186.

105 Dodson, R. S., and J. H. King. "A Determination of the Normal Threshold of Hearing and Its Relation to the Standardization of Audiometers." *Journal of Laryngology and Otology J. Laryngol. Otol.* 66 no. 8 (1952): 366–78. Web.

106 De Reuck, Anthony V.S., and Julie Knight. *Hearing Mechanisms in Vertebrates.* London: J. and A. Churchill, 1968. Print.

107 Békésy, Georg Von., and Ernest Glen Wever. *Experiments in Hearing.* New York: McGraw-Hill, 1960. Print.

108 Yasuji, Katsuki. "Neural Mechanism of Auditory Sensation in Cats." *Sensory Communication* (1961): 561–83. Web.

109 Carpenter, Malcolm B., and J. Sutin. *Human Neuroanatomy.* Baltimore: Williams & Wilkins, 1983. Print.

110 Aguilar, M., and W. S. Stiles. "Saturation of the Rod Mechanism of the Retina at High Levels of Stimulation." *Optica Acta: International Journal of Optics* 1 no. 1 (1954): 59–65. Web.

111 Moncrieff, R. W. *The Chemical Senses.* London: Hill, 1967. Print.

112 Firestein, S., and F. Warbling. "Ionic Mechanism Underlying the Olfactory Response." *Science* 244 (1989): 79–82.

113 Tanabe, T., M. Iino, and S. F. Takagi. "Discrimination of Odors in Olfactory Bulb, Pyriform-Amygdaloid Areas, and Orbitofrontal Cortex of the Monkey." *Journal of Neurophysiology* 38 no. 5 (September 1975): 1284–1296.

114 Amoore, J. E. "Stereochemical Theory of Olfaction." *Nature* 198 no. 4877 (1963): 271–72. Web.

115 Watkins, Herman A. "Perception of Body Position and of the Position of the Visual Field." Washington: American Psychological Association, 1949. Psychological Monographs 302 no. 3: 1–46.

116 Fitzgerald, M.J.T. *Neuroanatomy, Basic, and Applied.* London: Baillière Tindall, 1985. Print.

117 Llinas, R. R. "Bursting of Thalamic Neurons and States of Vigilance." *Journal of Neurophysiology* 95 no. 6 (2006): 3297–308. Web.

118 Steriade, Mircea, and Robert W. McCarley. *Brainstem Control of Wakefulness and Sleep.* New York: Plenum, 1990. Print.

119 Richter-Levin, Gal. "The Amygdala, the Hippocampus, and Emotional Modulation of Memory." *Neuroscientist* 10 no. 1 (2004): 31–39. Web.

120 O'Keefe, J.I. "The Hippocampus as a Cognitive Map." *Neuroscience* 4 no. 6 (1978): 863. Web.

121 Koenig, M., and J. Grafman. "Posttraumatic Stress Disorder: The Role of Medial Prefrontal Cortex and Amygdala." *Neuroscientist* 15 no. 5 (2009): 540–48. Web.

122 Bostock, Elizabeth, Robert U. Muller, and John L. Kubie. "Experience-Dependent Modifications of Hippocampal Place Cell Firing." *Hippocampus* 1 no. 2 (1991): 193–205. Web.

123 Warner-Schmidt, Jennifer L., and Ronald S. Duman. "Hippocampal Neurogenesis: Opposing Effects of Stress and Antidepressant Treatment." *Hippocampus* 16 no. 3 (2006): 239–49. Web.

124 Gibbins, Ian. "Peripheral Autonomic Pathways." *Human Nervous System* (2004): 134–89. Web.

125 Talman, W. T., and E. E. Benarroch. "Neural Control of Cardiac Functions." In *Peripheral Neuropathy*. 3rd ed., edited by P. J. Dyck, P. K. Thomas, J. W. Griffin, et al. WB Saunders, 1993.

126 Jänig, Wilfrid. *Integrative Action of the Autonomic Nervous System*. Cambridge University Press, 2006.

127 Goyal, R., and I. Hirano. "The Entire Nervous System." *N. Engl, J. Med* 334 (1994): 1106.

128 Renaud, Leo P., and Charles W. Bourquet. "Neurophysiology and Neuropharmacology of Hypothalamic Magnocellular Neurons Secreting Vasopressin and Oxytocin." *Progress in Neurobiology* 36 no. 2 (1991): 131–69. Web.

129 Steriade, Mircea, and Robert W. McCarley. *Brain Stem Control of Wakefulness and Sleep*. New York: Plenum, 1990. Print.

130 Marsden, C. D., P. A. Merton, and H. B. Morton. "Servo Action in Human Voluntary Movement." *Nature* 238 no. 5360 (1972): 140–43. Web.

131 Nolte, J. *The Human Brain*. St. Luis Mosby, 1999.

132 Ito, Masao. *Brain and Mind*. Elsevier, 1992. Print.

133 *Diagnostic and Statistical Manual of Mental Disorders*. 5th edition. American Psychiatric Association, 2013.

134 Bateman, A. Fonagy. "Eight-Year Follow-Up of the Patients Treated for Borderline Personality Disorder: Metallization-Based Treatment Versus Treatment as Usual." *Focus* 11 no. 2 (2013): 261–268.

135 Helgoland, M.I. "Kjelsberg Torgersen's Continuous between Emotional and Disruptive Behavior Disorder in Adolescence and Personality Disorder in Adulthood." *Am. J. Psychiatry* 162 (2005): 1926–1947.

136 Linechan, M.M., K. A. Comtois, A. M. Murry, M. Brown, R. J. Gallop, H. L. Heard, K. E. Korslund, D. A. Tutek, S. K. Reynolds, and V. Liridenbiom. "Two-Year Randomized Controlled Trial and Follow Up of Dialectical Behavior Therapy Versus Therapy by Experts for Suicide Behavior and Borderline Disorder. *Arch. Gen. Psychiatry* 63 no. 7 (2006): 757–766.

137 Ozkan, M., and A. Altindag. "A Co-Morbid Personality Disorder in Subjects with Panic Disorder: Do Personality Disorders Increase Severity?" *Comp. Psychiatry* 46 (2005): 20–26.

[138] Schwarze, C., A. Mobascher, B. Pallasch, et al. "Parental Adversity: A Risk Factor in Borderline Personality." *Psychol. Med.* 43 no. 6 (2013): 1279–1291.

[139] Svrakic, D.M., and C. R. Cloninger. "Personality Disorder." In *Kaplan and Sadock's Comprehensive Textbook of Psychiatry*, edited by B. J. Sadock and V. A. Sadock. 8th ed. Vol. 2. Philadelphia: Lippincott Williams and Wilkins, 205, 206.

[140] Kenneth, R., and M. D. Silk. "Personality Disorder, Part I." *Psychiatric Times* 33 no. 2 (February 2016): 10–15.

[141] Zimmerman, M.I., Rothschild, and I. Chelminski. "The Prevalence of DSM IV Personality Disorder in Psychiatric Outpatient." *Am. J. Psychiatry* 162 (2005): 1911–1918.

[142] Pincus, A.L., and M. H. Lukowltsky. "Pathological Narcissism and Narcissistic Personality Disorder." *Ann. Rev. Clin. Psychol.* 6 (2010): 421–446.

[143] Buscaglia, Leo. *Loving Each Other.* New Jersey: Slack Incorporated, 1984.

[144] Buscaglia, Leo F., PhD. *Living, Loving, and Learning.* First Ballantine Book Trade Edition, 1983.

[145] Buscaglia, Leo F., PhD. A Fawcett Book, the Ballantine Publishing Group, 1972.

[146] Hanson, J. S., and R. W. McCollum. "The Diagnosis and Management of Nausea and Vomiting." *Am. J Gastroenterology* 80 no. 210 (1985).

[147] Mitchelson, F. "Pharmacologic Agents Affecting Emesis: Review (Part I)." *Drugs* 43 (1992), 295.

[148] Millward, Sadler G.H. et al. *Wrightos Liver and Billiary Disease.* 3rd ed. London: Saunders, 1992.

[149] Sherlock, S., and J. Doodley. *Diseases of the Liver and Billiary System.* 9th ed. Oxford: Blackwell, 1993.

[150] Beaumont, J.G. *Introduction to Neuropsychology.* Guildford, NY, 2008.

[151] Carlson, N. R. *Physiology of Behavior.* Boston: Ally and Bacon, 1999.

[152] Okeefe, J., and L. Nadal. *The Hippocampus as a Cognitive Map.* Oxford, 1978.

[153] Clarendon, Lopes, F. M. de Silva, and D. E. Arnold. "A Physiology of the Hippocampus and Related Structures." *Annual Review of Physiology* 40 (1978): 185–216.

[154] Libet, Benjamin. "Unconscious Cerebral Initiative and the Role of Conscious Will in Voluntary Actions." *Behavioral and Brain Science* 8 (1985): 529–566.

[155] Libet B., E. W. Wright, and Gleason. "Readiness Potentials Preceding Unrestricted Spontaneous Preplanned Voluntary Acts." *Electroencephalographic and Clinical Neurophysiology* 54 (1983): 322–325.

[156] Libet, Benjamin. *Mind Time: The Temporal Factor in Consciousness.* Harvard University Press, 2004.

157 www.mpg.de/rearch/unconscious-decision-in-the brain Dr-John-Dylan Haynes, Accessed April 14, 2008.

158 www.skillsyoungneed.com/ps/selfmotivation html.

159 Blair, C., and C. C. Raver. "Child Development in the Context of Adversity: Experiential Canalization of Brain and Behavior." *Am. Psychol.* 67 (2012): 309–318.

160 Rizolatti, Giacomo, and Laila Craighero. "The Mirror Neuron System." *Annual Review of Neuroscience* 27 no. 1 (2004): 169–192.

161 Keysers, Christian. "Mirror Neurons." *Current Biology* 19 no. 21 (2010): 97–973.

162 Keysers, Christian. 1-06-23 *The Empathic Brain.* Kindle June 2011 as a kindle E Book.

163 Theories of Emotions."Psychology about.com.Accessed September 13,2013

164 .

165 Boufon, M.E. "Learning Theory." In Kaplan and Sadock's *Comprehensive Textbook of Psychiatry.* 9th ed., edited by V. A. Sadock and P. Rulz. Philadelphia: Lippincott William and Wilkins 2009, 647.

166 Whitbourne, S.K., and S. B. Whitbourne. *Plagetis Cognitive Development Theory in Adult Development and Aging.* Biopsychosocial Perspectives. 4th ed. Hoboken: John Wiley & Sons, Inc., 2011, 32.

167 Kolanowski, A.M., D. M. Fick, A. M. Yevechak, N. I. Hill, P. M. Muchall, and J. A. McDwell. "Pay Attention: The Critical Importance of Assessing Attention in Old Adults with Dementia." *J. Gerontol Nurs.* 38 no. 11 (2012), 23.

168 Fox 2008, 16–17.

169 Scherer, K. K. "What Are Emotions? And How Can They Be Measured?" *Social Science Information* 44 (2005):693–727.

170 Dyer, Wayne W. *The Shift.* California: Hay House Inc., 2010.

171 Dyer, Wayne. *Ten Secrets for Success and Inner Peace.* Hay House Inc., 2001.

172 Ramachandran, V. S. *The Tell-Tale Brain.* W.W. Norton and Company, Inc., 2012.

173 Blom, R.M., C. Hagestein-de Bruijic, R. de Graaf. M. Ten Have, and D. A. Denys. "Obsessions in Normality and Psychopathology." *Depression Anxiety* 28 no. 10 (2011).

174 Macaskill, A. "Differentiating Dispositional Self Forgiveness from other Forgiveness: Associations with Mental Health and Life Satisfaction." *J.SOC. Clin. Psychol.* 31, no. 28 (2012).

175 Sajobitt, T.T., L. M. Lix, I. Clara, J. Walker, L. A. Graff, P. Rawsthorne, N. Millee, L. Rogala, R. Carr, and C. N. Berrstein. "Measures of Relative Importance for Health-Related Quality of Life." *Res.* 21 no. 1 (2012).

176 Vaillant, G.E. "Positive Mental Health: Is There a Cross-Cultural Definition?" *World Psychiatry* 11 no. 93 (2012).

[177] Vaillant, G.E. "Spiritual Evolution: A Scientific Defense of Faith." New York Doubleday Broadway, 2008.

[178] Lovheim, H. "A New Three-Dimensional Model for Emotions and Monoamine Neurotransmitters." *Med Hypothesis* 78 (2011): 341–8. doi:10 1016/J.Mehy2011.

[179] Harmon-Jones, E., K. Vaughn-Scott, S. Mohr, J. Sigelma, and C. Harmon Jones. "The Effect of Manipulated Sympathy and Anger on Left and Right Frontal Lobe Activity." *Emotion* 4 (2004): 95–101. doi.10.1017.

[180] Kanner, Leo. (1943) Autistic Disturbances of Affective contact (PDF) Nervous child (1943).

[181] Olds, J., and P. Milner. "Positive Reinforcement Produced by Electrical Stimulation of Septal Area and Other Regions of the Rat Brain." *J. Comp. Physiol. Psychol.* 47 (1954): 419–27.

[182] Olds, J. "Reward from Brain Stimulation in the Rats." *Science* 122: 878.

[183] Draghi-Lorenz, R. "Five-Month-Old Infants Can Be Jealous: Against Cognitive Solipsism." Paper presented, inc.

[184] "Symposium Convened for the Biennial International Conference on Infant Studies" (ICIS) 16–19. Brighton, UK, 2000.

[185] Hart, S. "Jealousy in Six-Month-Old Infants." *Infancy* 3 (2002): 395–402.

[186] Hart, S. "When Infants Lose Exclusive Maternal Attention: It Is Jealousy?" *Infancy* 6 (2004):57–78.

[187] Parrott, W. G. "The Emotional Experience of Envy and Jealousy." In *The Psychology of Envy*, edited by P. Salovey. New York: The Guilford press, 1992, 3–29.

[188] Parrott, W.G., and R. H. Smith. "Distinguishing the Experiences of Envy and Jealousy." *Journal of Personality and Social Psychology* 64 (1993): 906–920.

[189] Darwin, C. *Expression of Emotions in Man and Animals.*

[190] Claton, G., and L. Smith. *Jealousy.* New Jersey: Prentice-Hall Inc., 1977.

[191] Buunk, B. "Jealousy as Related to Attributions for the Partner's Behavior." *Social Psychology Quarterly* 47 (1984): 107–112.

[192] Dehaene-Lambertz. "Ongoing Research at Nicoglab, Neurospin Center." Gif-sur-Yvette, France.

[193] Dehaene, Stanislas. *Consciousness and the Brain.* New York: Penguin Group, 2014.

[194] Lagercraritz and Changeux, 2009.

[195] www.youtube.com, Animal Odd Couple Series.

[196] Kovaes, Vogels, and Orban, 1995; Meknik and Haglund, 1999.

[197] Locktefeld, James. *Brahman: The Illustrated Encyclopedia of Hinduism* Vol 1. A-M Rosen Publishing.

[198] Brodd, Jeffery. *World Religions: A Voyage of Discovery.* Saint Mary's Press, 2009.

199 Bailey, Alice. *The Soul and the Mechanism*, 1973, 82-89 199,*Chattej J.C. The Wisdom of the Vedas.* Quest Books, Theosophical Publishing House, 2012, 56.

200 *Merriam-Webster*, s.v., "consciousness."

201 Van Gulick, Robert. "Consciousness." *Stanford Encyclopedia of Philosophy*, 2004.

202 Farthing, G. *The Psychology of Consciousness.* Prentice Hall, 1992.

203 Popper, Karl R., and John C. Eccles. *The Self and Its Brain.* New York: Springer Verlag, Inc., 1977.

204 Blakeslee, Sandra. "How the Brain Might Work: A New Theory of Consciousness." *New York Times*, March 21, 1995.

205 Andreass, J. L. *Psychophysiology: Human Behavior and Physiological Response.* 5th ed. New Jersey: Lawrence Erlbaum Associates, 2007.

206 Chang, B.S., D. L. Shomer, and E. Niedermyer. "Normal EEG and Sleep Adult and Elderly." In *Electron Cephalography: Basic Principles, Clinical Application, and the Related Field*, edited by E. Neidermeyer. Philadelphia: Lippincott Williams, 2011, 183–214.

207 Barclay, N. L., and A. M. Gregory. "Quantitative Genetic Research on Sleep: A Review of Normal Sleep, Sleep Disturbances, and Associated Emotional, Behavioural, and Health-Related Difficulties." *Sleep Med. Rev.* 17 no. 1 (2013): 29–40.

208 Jenni, O.G. "How Much Sleep Is 'Normal' in Children and Adolescents? Normal Sleep Durations in Children and Adolescents." *JAMA Pediatr.* 167 no. 1 (2013): 91–92.

209 Krieger, M., H. Roth, and T. Dement. *Principles and Practice of Sleep Medicine.* 4th ed. Philadelphia: Saunders, 2005.

210 Haydon, M.M., C. F. Reynolds III, and Y. Dauvilliers. "Excessive Sleep Duration and Quality of Life." *Ann. Neurol.* 73 no. 6 (2013): 785–794.

211 Breger, L. *A Dream of Underlying Fame: How Freud Betrayed His Mentor and Invented Psychoanalysis.* New York: Basic Books, 2009.

212 Freud, S. *The Standard Edition of the Complete Psychological Works of Sigmund Freud.* 24 vols. London: Hogarth Press, 1953–1974.

213 Hess, E. H. "Dilated Eyes and Attractiveness: The Role of Pupil Size in communication," *Scientific American* 233: 110–12.

214 Scheele, D., A. Wille, K. M. Kendrick, B. Stoffel-Wagner, B. Becker, O. Gunturkum, and R. Hurl Mann. "Oxytocin Enhances Reward Responses in Men Viewing the Face of Their Female Partner." *Proceedings of the National Academy of Science* 110 no. 50 (2013) 110, 20308–20313.

215 Fingelkurt, Andrew A., Alexander A. Fingelkurts, and Carlos F. H. Neves. *Consciousness as a Phenomenon in Operational Architectonics of Brain Organization:* Chaos, Solitons and Fractals Press, 2013.V 55 p13-31

216

216   *Merriam-Webster Dictionary*, s.v., "consciousness."
217   Van-Gulick, Robert. *Consciousness*. Stanford Encyclopedia of Philosophy, 2004.
218   Farthing, G. *The Psychology of Consciousness*. Prentice Hall, 1992.
219   Sacraic, Weiskrantz Barbur, Simmons, William, and Brammer, 1997. See also Morris, Degelder, Weiskrantz, and Dolah, 2001.
220   Sackur, Naccache, Pradat Diehl, Azouvi, Mazevet, Katz Cohen, and Dehaene, 2008; Glinchey-Berroth, M. C., Milberg, Varfaellie, Alaxander, and Kilnduff, 1993.
221   Bahrami, Olsen, Latham, Roepstorff, Rees, and Frith, 210.
222   Marti, Sackur, Sigman, and Dahaene (2010).
223   Baars, Bernard. *A Cognitive Theory of Consciousness*. Cambridge University Press, 1993, 15–18.
224   Block, Ned. "On a Confusion about a Function of Consciousness." In *The Nature of Consciousness*, edited N. Block, O. Flanagan, and G. Guzeldere. Philosophical Debate. MIT Press, 1998, 375–415.
225   "Animal Consciousness Officially Recognized by Leading Panel of Neuroscientists," September 3, 2012 via YouTube.
226   Cambridge Declaration on Consciousness (http://femconference.org) img/ Cambridge Declaration on Consciousness.PDF.
227   Koch, *The Quest for Consciousness*, 105–116.
228   "Francis Crick and Christ of Koch: A Framework for Consciousness." (PDF) *Nature Neuroscience* 6 no. 2: 119–126.
229   Graziano, M.S.A., and S. Kastner. "Human Consciousness and Its Relationship to Social Neuroscience: A Novel Hypothesis." *Cog. Neuroscience*, 98-113.
230   Adenauer G. Casali, Olivia Grosseries, Marlo Rosanova, Melanie Boly, Simone Savasso, Karina R. Casali, Silivia Casarotto, Marie-Auelie Bruno, Steve Laureys, Giulio Tononi, and Marcello Massimini. "A Theoretically Based Index of Consciousness Independent of Sensory Processing and Behavior." *Science Translational Medicine* S. 198 (August 2013), 105.
231   Johanson, M., V. Alli, K. Revonsuo A, and J. Wedlund. "Content Analysis of Subjective Experiences in Partial Epileptic Seizures." *Epilepsy and Behavior* 12 (2008): 170–182.
232   Johanson, M., K. Valli, A. Revonsuo, et al. "Alteration in the Contents of Consciousness in Partial Epileptic Seizures." 13 (2008): 366–371.
233   Diefer, Vaitl et al. "Psychobiology of Altered States of Consciousness." *Psychological Bulletin* 131 no. 17 (2005): 98–12.
234   Murphy, M., S. Donovon, and E. Taylor. *The Physical and Psychological Effects of Meditation: A Review of Contemporary Research with a Comprehensive Bibliography, 1931–1996*. Institute of Noetic Science.

235 Blumenfeld, Hal. "The Neurological Examination of Consciousness." In *The Neurology of Consciousness: Cognitive Neuroscience and Neuropathology*, edited by Steven Laureys, Guiulio Tononi. Academic Press, 2009.

236 Bhattacharya, A. Sutapas. *The Brainstem Brain Wave of Atman Brahman.* New Delhi, India: Gyan Publishing House, 2015.

237 Ogawa, Lee, Kay, and Tank, 1990.

238 Amar, J. "Singh Blood Supply Increases Magnetic Energy of the 'Soul.'"

239 Baker, A.T., R. Jalinous, I. L. Freeston. "Noninvasive Magnetic Stimulation of the Human Motor Cortex. *Lancet* 1 (1985): 1106–7.

240 Roth, B.J., J. M. Saypo, M. Hallet, and L. G. Cohen. "A Theoretical Calculation of the Electric Field Induced in the Cortex during Magnetic Stimulation Electroencephalogram." *Clin. Neuro* 81 (1991): 47–56.

241 Faradar, M. "Effects on the Production of Electricity: Ferom Magnetism (1831)." In *Michael Faraday*, edited by L. P. Williams. New York: Basic Books, 1965, 531.

242 George, M., S. Lisanby, and H. A. Sakeim. "Transcranial Magnetic Stimulation: Application in Neuropsychiatry." *Arch Gen Psychiatry* 56 no. 4 (1999): 300–11.

243 Brake, A.T., I. L. Freeston, and J. A. Jarratt, and R. Jalinous. "Magnetic Stimulation of the Human Nervous System: An Introduction and Basic Principles." In *Magnetic Stimulation in Clinical Neurophysiology*, edited by S. Chokroverty. Boston: Butterworth, S., 1989, 55–72.

244 Hanlon, C.A., M. Canterberry, J. J. Taylor. W. Devries, X. Li. T. R. Brown, et al. "Naloxone Reversible Modulation of Pain Circuitry by Left Prefrontal r TMS." *Neuropsychopharmacology* 38 no. 7 (2013): 1189–97.

245 Wu T., M. Somme, F. Tergau, and W. Paulus. "Lasting Influence of Repetitive Transcranial Magnetic Stimulation on Intracortical Excitability in Human Subjects." *Neuroscience* Let 287 (2000): 37–40.

246 Teneback, C., C. Nahasz, A. M. Speer, M. Molly, L. E. Stallings, K. M. Spicer, et al. "Two Weeks of Daily Left Prefrontal rTMs Changes Prefrontal Cortex and Paralimbic Activity in Depression." *J Neuropsychiatry Clin. Neurosci.* 11 (1999): 426–35.

247 Nahas, Z., M. Lomarev, D. R. Robers, A. Shastri, J. P. Lorberbaum, T. Teneback, et al. "Unilateral Left Prefrontal Transcranial Magnetic Stimulation (TMS) Produces Intensity Dependent Bilateral Effects as Measured by Interleaved BOLD FMRT." *Biol. Psychiatry* 50 no. 9 (2001): 712–20.

248 Paus, T., M. A. Castro-Alamancos, and M. Petrides. "Cortico-Cortical Connectivity of Human Middorsolateral Frontal Cortex and Its Modulation by Repetitive Transcranial Magnetic Stimulation." *Eur. J. Neuroscience* 14 (2001): 1405–11.

249 Lan and Passingham, 2006.

250 Desmurget Reilly, Richard,Szathmari, Mottolese, and Sirigo, 2009.

251 Tenebaek, C.C., Z. Naha, A. M. Speer, M. Molly, L. E. Stallings, K. M. Spicer, et al. "Two Weeks of Daily Left Prefrontal rTMS Changes Prefrontal Cortex and Paralimbic Activity in Depression." *Neuropsychiatry Clin. Neurosci.* 11 (1999): 426–35.

252 Shajahan, P.M., M. F. Glabus, J. D. Steel, A. B. Doris, K. Anderson, J. A. Jenkins, et al. "Left Dorsolateral Repetitive Transcranial Magnetic Stimulation Affects Cortical Excitability and Functional Connectivity but Does Not Impair Cognition in Major Depression. *Prog. Neuropsychopharmacol Biol. Psychiatry* 36 no. 5 (2002): 945–54.

253 Phelp, James, MD. "Cranial Electrotherapy Stimulation for Bipolar Depression." *Psychiatric Times* (December 2015): P 20, E 20 F.

254 Goodman, Wayne K. "Deep Brain Stimulation Yields Positive Results in Patients with Obsessive Compulsive Disorder." Department of Psychiatry, Mount Sinai Hospital. Winter 2016 Chair's Report, 1–2.

255 Alberstone, C.D., S. L. Skirboll, J. A. Sandra, B. L. Hart, N. G. Baldwin, et al. "Magnetic Source Imaging and Brain Surgery: Presurgical and Intraoperative Planning in 26 Patients." *Journal of Neurosurgery* 92 (2000): 79–90.

256 Smith, S.D., B. R. McLeod, A. R. Liboff, and K. Cooksey. "Calcium Cyclotron Resonance and Diatom Motility." *Bioelectromagnetics* 8 (1987): 215–27.

257 Liboff, A.R. "Electric Field Ion Cyclotron Resonance." *Bioelectromagnetics* 181 no. 1 (1997): 85–7.

258 Perlmutter, J.S., and J. W. Mink. "Deep Brain Stimulation." *Ann Rey Neurosci.* 29 (2006): 230–57.

259 Hynynen, K., and N. McDannold. "MRI-Guided and Monitored Focus Ultrasound Thermal Ablation Method: A Review of Progress." *Int. J. Hyperth.* 20 (2004): 725–37.

260 Mishelevich, D., T. Sato, W. Tyler, and D. Wetmore. "Ultrasound Neuromodulation Treatment of Depression and Bipolar Disorder." US patent No. (20, 120, 283, 50). Washington, DC. US Patent and Trademark Office.

261 www.heartmath.org/reasearch/global-coherencel.

262 McCraty, R., and D. Childre. "Coherence Bridging Personal, Social and Global Health." *Alternat therap. Health Med* 16 no. 4 (2010): 10–24.

263 McCraty, R., M. Afkinson, D. Tomasino, and R. T. Bradly. "The Coherent Heart Brain Interaction: Psychophysiological Coherence and the Emergence of the System-Code Order." *Integr RV* 5 no. 2 (2009): 10–115.

264 Doronin, V.N., V. A. Parfentev, S. Z. Tleulin, R. A. Namvar, V. M. Somsikov, V. I. Drobzhev, et al. "Effects of Variation of the Geomagnetic Field and Solar Activity on Human Physiological Indicators." *Bio Fizka* 43 no. 4 (1998): 647–53.

265 Mikulecky, M. "Solar Activity Revolution and Cultural Prime in the History of Mankind." *Neuroendocrinol Let* 28 no. 6 (2007): 749–56.

266 Burch, J.B., J. S. Reif, and M. G. Yost. "Geomagnetic Disturbances Are Associated with Reduced Nocturnal Excretion of Melatonin Metabolites in Humans." *Neurosci. Let* 266 (1999): 209–12.

267 Cernousss, Vinogradov A., and E. Vlassova. "Geophysical Hazard for Human Health in Circumpolar Auroral Belt: Evidence of Relationship and Electromagnetic Disturbances." *Nat. Hazards* 23 (2001): 121–35.

268 Villoresi, G., N. G. Ptitsyna, M. I. Tiasto, N. Lucci. "Myocardial Infarction and Geomagnetic Disturbances: Analysis of Data on Morbidity and Mortality" [in Russian]. *Biofizika* 43 no. 4 (1998): 623–32.

269 Gorden, C., and M. Berk. "The Effect of Geomagnetic Storms on Suicide." *South African Psychiatric Rev.* 6 (2003): 24–7.

270 Subramanyam, S., P. Narayan, and T. Sirinivasan. "Effect of Magnetic Microstimulations on the Biological Systems—A Bioenvironmental Study." *Int. J. Biomeorol.* 29 no. 3 (1985): 293–305.

271 McCranty, R. "The Energetic Heart Bioelectromagnetic Communication within and between the People." In *EDS Bioelectromagnetic Medicine*, edited by P. J. Rosh, and M. S. Markov. New York: Marcel Dekker, 2004, 541–62.

272 Kemper, K.J., and H. A. Shaltout. "Nonverbal Communication of Compassion: Measuring Psychophysiological Effects." *BMC Compl. Alternat Med* 11 (2011): 132.

273 Persinger, M. "On the Possible Representation of the Electromagnetic Equivalents of All Human Memory within the Earth's Magnetic Field: Implications of Theoretical Biology." *Theor. Biol. Insights* 1 (2008): 3–11.

274 Montagnier, L., J. Aissa, E. Del Guidice, C. Lavelle, A. Tedeschi, and G. Vitiello. "DNA Waves and Water." *J. Phys. Conf. Ser.* 306 (2011): 1–10.

275 Kirsch, D.L., and M. Gilulu. "Cranial Electrotherapy Stimulation in the Treatment of Depression." *Practical Pain Manage.* 7 no. 47 (2007): 33–41.

276 Skou, J.C., and M. Esmann. "The Na, K-ATPase." *J. Bioenerg. Biomember.* 24 (1992): 249–261.

277 Sodi Pllares, D., G. Melrano, A. Bisteni, and J. J. Ponce de Leon. "Deductive and Polyparametric Electrocardiography." Mexico D. F. Inst. National de Cardiol., 1970.

278 www.gavcamera.com.

279 http://www.dictionary.com.

280 Horney, K., MD. Self-Analysis. W. W. Norton & Company, Inc., 1942.

281 Jung, C. G. Ther. Archetypes and the Collective Unconscious. Translated by R. F. C. Hull. Princeton University Press, 190.

282 Adams, M. B. "Evolution of Theodosius Dobzhansky: Essay on His Life and Thought in Russia and America." Princeton University Press, 2014.

283 Kanagawa, C., S. Cross, and H. R. Markins. *Who Am I? The Cultural Psychology of the Conceptual Self.* Sage Publication. Personality and Social Psychology, 2001.

284 Somerville, L.H., R. M. Jones, E. J. Ruberry, J. P. Dykes, G. Glover, and B. Casey. "The Medical Prefrontal Cortex and the Emergence of Self-Conscious Emotion in Adolescence." *Psychology Science* 24 no. 8 (2013): 1554–62.

285 Blackmore, S.J. "Development of Social Brain in Adolescents." *JR Soc. Med.* 105 (2012): 111–116.

286 Farina, B., and G. Liotti. "Does a Dissociative Psychopathological Dimension Exist? A Review on Dissociative Processes and Symptoms in Development Trauma Spectrum Disorders." *Clin Neuropsychiatry* 10 no. 1 (2013): 11–18.

287 Markowitsch, H.J. "Psychogenic Amnesia." *Neurogenimage* 20 (2003): s132–s138.

288 Martinex-Taboas, A., M. Dorahy, V. Sar, W. Middleton, and C. Krngar. "Growing Not Dwindling: International Research on the World Wide Phenomenon of Dissociative Disorders." *J. Nerv. Ment. Dis.* 201 no. 4 (2013): 253–354.

289 Thompson, Richard F. *The Brain: A Neuroscience Primer.* 2nd ed. W. H. Freeman and Company, 1993, 6.

290 Kluget et al. "Is God in Our Genes?"

291 Fang, A., and S. G. Hofmann. "Relationship between Social Anxiety Disorder and Body Dysmorphic Disorder." *Clin. Psychol. Rev.* 30 (2010): 1040.

292 Philipp, K.A., A. Pinto, A. S. Hart, M. E. Coles, J. L. Eisen, W. Menard, and S. A. Rasmussen. "A Comparison of Insight in Body Dysmorphic Disorder and Obsessive Compulsive Disorder." *J. Psych. Res.* 46 (2012): 1293.

293 Frost, R.O., D. F. Tolin, G. Stette, K. E. Fitch, and A. Selbo-Bruns. "Excessive Acquisition in Hoarding." *J. Anxiety Disorder* 23 (2009): 632.

294 Grisham, J.R., M. M. Norberg, A. D. William, S. P. Certoma, and R. Kadib. "Categorization and Cognitive Deficits in Compulsive Hoarding." *Behave Res Ther.* 48 (2010): 886.

295 Lervolino, A.C., N. Perrond, M. A. Fullana, M. Gulpponi, L. Cherkas, D. A. Collier, and D. Matrix-cols. "The Prevalence and Heritability of Compulsive Hoarding: A Twin Study." *Am. J. Psychiatry* 116 (2009): 1156.

296 Ronald, W., and M. D. Pres. "Depression: A Five-Minute Seminar for Patients." *Psychiatric Times* 32 no. 3 (March 2016): 28A–28E.

297 Lebano, Lauren. "Novel Therapeutics for Major Depression." *Psych. Congress* 1 no. 2 (Fall/Winter 2015), 40.

298 Tomolo, J. "New Connection Gluctamate and Psychiatry." *Psych congress.* Summer 2016, 32.

299 Seley, Hans. *The Stress of Life.* Rev. ed. New York: McGraw Hizz, 1978.

[300] Corr, C.A., and D. M. Corr. *Death and Dying, Life and Living.* 7th ed. Belmont, CA: Wadsworth, 2013.

[301] Learning, M.R., and G. E. Dickinson. *Understanding Death, Dying, and Bereavement.* 7th ed. Stamford, CT: Cengage Learning, 210.

[302] Brunk, D. "Earlier Intervention Urged in Prodromal Depression." *Clinical Psychiatry News* (April 2016): 35.

[303] Miller, B., MD, PhD, MPH. "Adjunctive Monoclonal Antibody Immunotherapy in Schizophrenia." *Psychiatric Times* (February 2016), 28E.

[304] Lonveau, A., I. Smirnov, T. Keyes, et al. "Structural and Functional Features of Central Nervous System Lymphatic Vessels." *Nature* 523 (2015): 337–341.

[305] Aspelund, A., S. Antila, S. T. Proulx, et al. "A Dura Lymphatic Vascular System that Drains Brain Interstitial Fluid and Macromolecules." *J. Exp. Med.* 212 (2015): 991–999.

[306] Palta, P., J. Samheli, E. R. Miller, et al. "Depression and Oxidative Stress: Results from a Meta-Analysis of Observational Studies." *Psycho Son Med.* 76 no. 1 (2014): 12–19.

[307] Ferrari, A.J., F.J. Charlson, R. E. Norman, et al. "Burden of Depressive Disorder by Country, Sex, Age, and Year: Finding from the Global Burden of Disease Study 2010." *Plos Med.* 10 no. 1 (2013): e1001547.

[308] Maes, M., P. Galecki, Y. S. Chang, et al. "A Review on the Oxidative and Nitro Stative Stress (OXNS): Pathways in Major Depression and Their Possible Contribution to (Neuro) Degenerative Process in the Illness. *Prog. Neuropsychiopharmacol. Biolpsychiatry* 35 no. 3 (2011): 676–692.

[309] Dodd, S., M. Maes, G. Anderson, et al. "Putative Neuro Protective Agents in Neuropsychiatric Disorders." *Prog. Neuropsychopharmacol. Biol. Psychiatry* 42 (2013): 135–145.

[310] Jimenz-Fernandez, S., MD, M. Gurpegui, MD, F. Diaz Atienz, MD, L. Perez Costilla, MD, M. Gerstenberg, MD, and C. U. Correll, MD. "Oxidative Stress and Antioxidant Parameters in Patients with Major Depressive Disorder Compared to Healthy Controls before and after Antidepressant Treatment." *J. Clin. Psychiatry* 76 (12 December 2015): 1658–1659.

[311] Monn, M. A. "Residents, Interns Report Depression Rate of 28.8%." *J. Clinical Psychiatric News.* (Jan. Nov. 2015).

[312] American Foundation for Suicide Prevention: Facts about Physician Depression and Suicide. Updated February 2015.

[313] Brower, K.J., MD. "Avoid Burnout with Self-Cave and Wellness Strategies." *Psychiatric Times* 33 no. 4 (April 2016): 9–11.

[314] Maslach, C., S. E. Jackson, and M. P. Later. *MBI: The Maslach Burnout Inventory Manual.* Palo Alto: Consulting Psychologists Press, 1996.

[315] Kraft, U. "Burn out." *Scientific American Mind* (June/July 2006), 28–33.

[316] Thurschwell, P. *Sigmund Freud.* 2nd ed. New York: Routledge, 2009.

[317] Freud, S. *The Standard Edition of the Complete Psychological Works of Sigmund Freud*, 24 vols. London: Hogarth Press, 1953–1974.

[318] Massey, C. *American Constitutional Law: Power and Liberties*. 2nd ed. Aspen Publishers, 2005, 40.

[319] Vaishnavi, S. MD, PhD. "Neural Circuits Approach Could Change Psychiatry for Better." *Clinical Psychiatric News* (May 2016), 23.

[320] Mclean, C.P., A. Asnaani, B. T. Litz, and S. G. Hofmann. "Gender Differences in Anxiety Disorder, Prevalence, Course of Illness, Comorbidity, and Burden of Illness." *Psychiatry Res*. 45 (2011): 1027.

[321] Stahs, S. *Anxiolytics and Sedatives-Hypnotics, Inc. Essential Psychopharmacology: Neuroscientific Basis and Practical Applications*. Cambridge University Press, 1996, 167–215.

[322] McKay, D., and E. A. Storch, eds. *Handbook of Treating Variants and Complications in Anxiety Disorders*. New York: Springer Science and Business Media, 2013.

[323] Kalat, J.E. *Biological Psychology*. 2013, 381.

[324] *Psychiatr. clin. North Am*. 21 (2001): 75–97.

[325] Noel, J.M., and J. L. Gurtis. "The Pharmacological Management of Stress Reaction." In *A Clinical Guide to the Treatment of the Human Stress Response*, edited by G. S. Everly Jr. and J. M. Lating. New York: Springer Science and Business Media, 2013, 2017.

[326] Pena, G., S. Dacco, R. Menoth, and D. Caldero. "Antianxiety Medication for the Treatment of Complex Agoraphobia: The Pharmacological Intervention for Behavioral Conditions." *Neuropsychiar Dis. Treat*. 7 (2011): 621.

[327] Coelho, C.M., and H. Purkis. "The Origin of Specific Phobia: Influential Theories and Current Perspective." *Rev. Gen. Psychology* 13 (2009): 335.

[328] Potina, I.T., E. H. W. Kosteb, P. Philoppote, V. Dethiere, and David Do. "Optimal Attention Focus during Exposure in Specific Phobias: A Meta-Analysis." *Clin Psychol Rev*. 33 (2013), 1172.

[329] Karas, P.J. et al. "Deep Brain Stimulus: A Mechanism and Clinical Update." *Neuro Surgery Focus* 35 no. 5 (2013), E1.

[330] Benabid A.L., A. Benazzous, and P. Pollack. "Mechanism of Deep Brain Stimulation." *Mov. Disorder* 17 (suppl. 3) (2002): S 73–4.

[331] Taghva, A.S. "Deep Brain Stimulation for Treatment Resistant Depression." *World Neurosurg* 80 no.3 (2013): S 27.e 17-s27. E 24.

[332] Heller, L., and D. B. Van Hulsteyn. "Brain Stimulation Using Electromagnetic Sources: Theoretical Aspects." *Biophys J* 63 (1992): 129–38.

[333] Roth, Y., A. Amir, Y. Levokovitz, and A. Zengen. "Three-Dimensional Distribution of Electric Field Induced in the Brain by Transcranial Magnetic Stimulation Using Figure-8 and Deep H-Coil. *J. Clin. Neurophysiology* (2007): 31–8.

334 Roth Y., A. Zangen, M. Hallet. "Transcranial Magnetic Stimulation of Deep Brain Regions." *Clin. Neurophysiology* (19) 2002: 361–70.

335 Goodman, Wayne, K., Chair, Report, Department of Psychiatry Mount Sinai Hospital. *New York Deep Brain Stimulus Yields Positive Results in Patients with Obsessive-Compulsive Disorder* (16 Winter), 111.

336 Gersper, R., E. Toth, I. Lesserless, and A. Zangen, "Site Specific Antidepressant Effects of Repeated Subcortical Stimulation: Potential Role of Brain-Derived Neurotrophic Factors." *Biol. Psychiatry* 67 (2010): 125–32.

337 Phelps, J., MD. "Cranial Electrotherapy Stimulation and Bipolar Depression: New Data." *Psychiatric Times* (December 2015): 20 E.

338 Tatum, W.O. IV, J. A. Ferreira, S. R. Benbadis, et al. "Vagus Nerve Stimulation for Pharmaco. Resistant Epilepsy. Clinical symptoms with End of Service." *Epilepsy Behav.* 5 (2004): 128–32.

339 Zaba, J. "Controlling Seizures by Changing GABA Receptors Sensitivity." *Epileplesia* 28 (1987), 604.

340 Bassett, C.A. "Becker Regeneration of Electric Potential in Born in Response to Mechanical Stress." *Science* 137 (1962): 1063–4.

341 Chaudhary, S.S., R. K. Mishra, A. Sware, and J. M. Thomas. "Dielectric Properties of Normal and Malignant Human Breast Tissue at Radio Wave Frequencies." *Indian J Biochem. Biophys.* 21 (1984): 76–9.

342 Neuman, E., M. Shaefer-Ridder, Y. Wang, and P. H. Hofschneider. "Gene Transfer in to Mouse Lymphoma Cell by Electroporation in High Electric Field." *EMBO.J* 7 (1982): 841–5.

343 Boggio, P.S., S. P. Rigonatti, R. B. Ribeiro, M. L. Myezknowski, M. A. Nitsche. "A Randomized, Double Blind Clinical Trial on the Efficacy of Cortical Direct Current Stimulation for the Treatment of Major Depression." *Int. J. Neuropharmacol.* 11 no. 2 (2008): 249.

344 Korotkov, K. Ed. *Measuring Energy Field: State of the Art.* Fairlawn: Backbone Publishing, 2004, 1–270.

345 Schroeder, L., Ostranders. *Psychic Discoveries behind the Iron Curtain.* Surrey: Conoda Hancock Books (1977), 124–9.

346 Zhandin, M.N., V. V. Novikov, F. S. Barnes, and N. F. Pegola. "Combined Action of Static and Alternating Magnetic Field on Ionic Current in Aqueous Glutamic Acid Solution." *Bioelectromagnetics* 10 (1998): 41–5.

347 Jhon, Kabata-zinn. *Full Catastrophe Living.* Bantam Books, 2013, 45.

348 Schwitzgebel, Eric. "Belief in Zalta Edward." *Stanford Encyclopedia of Philosophy.* Stanford, CA: The Metaphysics Research Lab, 2006.

349 http://www.religioustolerance.org/Buddhism.htm.

350 http://www.Islam-guide.com/ch3-2 htm.

351 http://www.cofchurist.org/basic belief. Community of Christ.

352   http://www.chabad.org/library/article codo/aid/332555/Jewish/maimonides-13-principlesoffaith.htm.
353   http:/www orthodox-jews.com/Judaism-beliefs-htm#ax224VarchAwl.
354   Taube, Karl, "Ritual Humor in Classic Maya Religion." In *Word and Image in Maya Culture*, edited by William F. Hank and Don S. Rice. Salt Lake City: University of Utah Press, 1989.
355   Vogt, Evan Z. *Tortillas for the Gods: A Symbolic Analysis of Zinacanteco Rituals*. Cambridge: Harvard University Press, 1976.
356   https://Stephenpirie.com/faq/what-is-a-belief-system, 2016.
357   Laugdon, Roben, and Emily Connaughton. *The Neural Basis of Human Belief System*. New York: Psychology Press, Tylor and Francis Group, 2013, 20.
358   Dictionary.com, s.v., "wisdom."
359   *Wisdom*. Oxford University Press.
360   "Character Education: Our Shared Responsibility," Ed, gov.31, May.
361   Harter, Andrew. "C 8." In *Character Strengths and Virtues: A Handbook and Classification*, edited by Christopher Peterson and Martin E. P. Seligman. Oxford University Press, 2004, 181–196.
362   Largesse, B., B. H. Price, and E. D. Murry. "Brain Behavior Relation." *Encyclopedia of Human Behavior*. 2nd ed., edited by V. S. Ramachandran, MD, PhD. Academic Press, 2012.
363   Shiksha, Vimkut. "Understanding Wisdom." Issue Z (February 1999). http://www Swaraj.org/Shikshant.wmkut.02.html.
364   Ubersax, John S. "Wisdom Lexicon Project: Steps towards the Scientific Study of Sapiens." Online article. 2007. http/John-ubersax.com/Plato/Lexicon.Htm.
365   Lewis, C.T., and C. Short. *Latin Dictionary*, Oxford University Press, 1963.
366   Dhammapada, V., 256, 268–9.
367   Begley, Sharon. "Train Your Mind Change Your Brain." New York: Ballantine Books, 2007.
368   Kabat-Zinn, Jon. *Full Catastrophe*. Living Bantam Books Trade, 2013.
369   Brown, Richard, P., MD, and Patricia L. Gerberg, MD. *The Healing Power of the Breath*. Boston: Shambhala, 2012.
370   Luders, Eileen, Florian Kuth, Emeran A. Mayer, Arthur W. Toga, Katherine L. Narr, and Christian Gaser. "The Unique Brain Anatomy of Meditation Practitioners: Alteration in Cortical Gyrification." *Frontiers in Human Neuroscience* 6 no. 34 (2012).
371   Critchley, H. D., S. Weins, P. Rotshtein, A. Ohman, and R. J. Dolan. "System Supporting Introspective Awareness." *Nat. Neurosci*. 7 (2004), 189–195. 10-1038/nn1176 [Pub. Med].

372 Hoffman, S.G., P. Grossman, and D. E. Hinton. "Loving-Kindness and Compassion Meditation: Potential for Psychological Intervention." *Clin Psychol* Rev. (2011): 1126–1132. 10.1016/J.Cpr. 2011.07.003 [pub med].
373 Bartley, A.J., D. W. Jones, and D. R. Weinburger. "Genetic Variability of Human Brain Size and Cortical Gyral Pattern." *Brain* 120 no. 2 (1997): 257–269. 10.1093/brain/120.2.257 (PubMed).
374 Kenneth, G. Walton, PhD, Robert H. Schneider, MD, and Sanford Nidich, EdD. "Review of Controlled Research on the Transcendental Meditation Program and Cardiovascular Diseases Risk Factors, Morbidity, and Mortality." *Cardio Rev.* 12 no. 50 (2004): 262–260. http://www.ncbi.nlm.nih.gov/mc/articles/PMC2211376 (HHS public access).
375 Sant Rajinder Singh Ji Maharaj. "Meditation Is Connecting with Our Soul." http/www.sos.org/Meditation connecting-with-our-soul.html.
376 Hozel, B.K., J. Carmody, M. Vangal, S. M. Yerramsetti, T. Gard, and S. W. Lazar. "Mindfulness Practice Leads to Increase in Regional Brain Grey Matter Density." *Psychiatry Research: Neuroimaging* (2010). dio.10 1016/J. Psych resns.2010.08.006. In *Full Catastrophe Living* (2013).
377 Fab, N.A.S., Z. A. Segal, H. Maberg, J. Bean, D. McKeon, Z. Fatima, and A. K. Anderson. "Attending to the Present: Mindfulness Meditation Reveals Disconnect Neural Modes of Self-Reference. *Social Cognitive and Affective Neuroscience* 2 (2007): 313–322.
378 Hozel, B.K., J. Carmody, K. C. Evans, E. A. Hoge, J. A. Dusek, L. Morgan, R. Pitman, and S. W. Lazar. "Stress Reduction Correlates with Structural Changes in the Amygdala." *Social Cognitive and Affective Neuroscience Advances* 5 no. 1 (2010): 11–17. In *Full Catastrophe Living* (2013).
379 David, R.J., J. Kabat-Zinn, J. Schumacher, M. A. Rosencrantz, D. Muller, S. F. Santoru, R. Urbanowski, A. Harrington, K. Bonus, and J. F. Sheridan. "Alteration in Brain and Immune Functions Produced by Mindfulness Meditation." *Psychosomatic Medicine* 65 (2002): 564–570.
380 Creswell, R., M. R. Irwin, L. J. Burklund, M. N. Lieberman, J. M. G. Arevalo, J. Ma, E. C. Breen, and S. W. Cole. "Mindfulness-Based Stress Reduction Training Reduces Loneliness and Pro-Inflammatory Gene Expression in Older Adults: A Small, Randomized Controlled Trial." *Brain, Behavior, and Immunity* 26 (2012):1095–1101.
381 Khurshid, A. Khurshid, MD, FAASM. "Neuromodulation in Neuropsychiatric Disorders." *Psychiatric Annals* 46, no. 11 (2016).
382 Moscrip, T.D., H. S. Terrance, H. A. Sackheim, and S. H. Lisanby. "Randomized Controlled Trial of the Cognitive Side Effects of Magnetic Seizure Therapy (MST) and Electroconvulsive Shock. *Int J Neuropsychopharmacol* 9 no. 1 (2006): 1–11.
383 http://Wikipedia.org/Wiki/Robindernath, Tagore.

384 http:/www.cnn.com/Interactive/2014/12/shared death, "Beyond Good-Bye," July 2014.

385 Carroll, Bret E. *Spiritualism in Antebellum America*. Religion in North America. Bloomington: Indiana University Press, 248.

386 Braude, Ann. "Radical Spirits: Spiritualism and Women's Rights in Nineteenth-Century America." 2nd Edition. Indiana University Press (2001), 296.

387 Wong, 2009. http://en Wikipedia.org/wiki/Spirituality.

388 *Gavin Flood Brill's Encyclopedia of Hinduism*, edited by Knut Jacobsen 11 (2011). See article on "Wisdom and Knowledge," 881–884.

389 https://www.lionesroar.com/Christof-Koch-unites-buddhism-neuroscience-nature-mind. Sam Uttleafair, January 8, 2017, 2.

390 King, Richard. *Indian Philosophy: An Introduction to Hindu and Buddhist Thoughts*. Edinburg University Press, 1999, 69–71.

391 Macleod, Melvin. "Are You Spiritual but Not Religious? Ten Reasons Why Buddhism Will Enrich Your Path." http://www.Lionsroar.com. Accessed January 25, 2017.

392 Buck, Harleah, G.MSN, RN. *Spirituality: Concept Analysis and Model Development*. Lippincott Williams & Wilkin Inc., 2006.

393 Elkin, D. N. *Spiritual Orientation Inventory*. 1988. Available from D. N. Elkin S., PhD, Pepperdine University Center. Published by Smith, Dorothy Woods. January 1, 1994.

394 Roger, M.E. *An Introduction to the Theoretical Basis of Nursing*. Philadelphia: F. A. Davis, 1997.

395 C. J. W. "Spirituality and Personal Maturity." In *Clinical Book of Pastoral Counseling*, edited by R. J. Wickers, R. D. Parson, and D. Capps. Volume 1. Expanded edition. 1993. Mahwah, NJ: Panlist Press, 1993, 37–57.

396 Swami Nityaswarupananda, Swami Vivekananda, School of World Civilization. New Delhi: Ramakrishna Mission, 1967, 25.

397 Joglekar, D.G. *Science and the Spirituality*. Global Religion Vision, Vol. 1 (2001), 111.

398 Otterloo, 2012, 23.

399 Heelas, Paul (ed). *Spirituality in the Modern World within Religious Traditions and Beyond*. Rutledge, 2012.

400 Dalai Lama. *Ethics for the New Millennium*. New York: River Head Books, 1999.

401 Khan, Moosa Murad. Understanding Suicide Bombing through Suicide Research: The Case of Pakistan. *Psychiatric Annals*, 47, no.3 (2017): 145–149.

402 Harris, Sam. *A Guide to Spirituality without Religion*. Simon & Schuster, 2014, 43–49.

403 Daum, Kevin. *The Power of Self-Reflection.* http:// www.Inc.com/Kevin-daum-/The-power-of-self-reflection.html. Accessed November 21, 2014.
404 Sheldrake, Philip. *A Brief History of Spirituality.* Wiley Blackwell, 2007, 1–2.
405 Burkhardt, Margaret A., and Mary Gail Negai-Jacobson. *Spirituality: Living Our Connectedness.* Delmar Cengage Learning, 14.
406 Cousens, Gabriel, M.D. *Spiritual Nutrition.* Berkeley, CA: North Atlantic Books, 2005, 124–125.
407 Tolle, Eckhart. *The Power of Now.* Namaste Publishing and New World Library, 1999, 147.
408 Chopra, Deepak. *Unlocking the Hidden Dimensions of Your Life.* New York: Three Rivers Press, 2004, 8–10.
409 Feldman, Avi. *The Value of Selflessness.* http://www.meaningfyllife.com/The value-of-selflessness/.
410 Alcoholics Anonymous, World Service Inc. New York, 1991, 564–570.
411 Nicoll, Maurice. *Psychological Commentaries on the Teaching of Gurdjieff at Ouspensky.* Boston and London: Shambla, 1985, p. 142–44.
412 Harding, C.M., and J. H. Zahniser. "Empirical Correction of Seven Myths about Schizophrenia with Medication for Treatment." *Acta Psychiatrica Scandinavica* 90 (1994): 146–149.
413 Koening, H. G., M. E. McCollough, and D. B. Larson. *Handbook of Religion and Health.* New York: Oxford University Press, 2001.
414 Krov, G., R. Kemp, K. Kirov, and A. S. David. "Religion Faith after Psychotic Illness. *Psychopathology* 31 (1998): 234–245.
415 Mistree, K.P. *Zoroastrianism: An Ethic Perspective.* Mumbai: Zoroastrian Studies, 1998.
416 Maqsood, P.W. *Living Islam.* India: Good Word Books, 1998.
417 Haneef, S. *What Everyone Should Know about Islam.* Delhi: Adam Publishing and Distributors, 1994.
418 Novroji, D.M. *The Moral and Ethical Teachings of Zarathustra.* The University of Bombay, 1928.
419 Singh, I.J. *Philosophy of Guru Nank: A Comparative Study.* New Delhi: Ranjit Publishing House, 1997.
420 James, W. *Principles of Psychology.* New York: Holt, 1890.
421 Dawkins, R. (1989) The selfish genes, Oxford: Oxford University Press, 1989.
422 Stuss, D.T. "Self-Awareness and the Frontal Lobe: A Neurophysiological Perspective." In *The Self-Interdisciplinary Approach,* edited by J. Strauss and G. R. Goethals. New York: W. W. Norton, 1991.
423 Damasio, A.R. *The Feelings of What Happens in the Making of the Consciousness.* New York: Harcourt Brace, 1999.

[424] Marwaha, B. Sonali. *Colors of Truth: Religion and Emotions.* New Delhi: Concept Publishing Company, 2006.

[425] Bach,George,andDeutch,Ronald,Pairing.New York;Avon Book,1970 in (Leo F. BuscagliaPh,D. Loving eachother.The challenge of Human Relationship,Fawacett Columbine New York 1984,p 196.

Printed in the United States
By Bookmasters